MULTINATIONAL INDUSTRIAL RELATIONS SERIES

No. 7. Multinational Union Studies
(7c—Ocean Transport)

THE INTERNATIONAL TRANSPORT WORKERS' FEDERATION AND FLAG OF CONVENIENCE SHIPPING

by

HERBERT R. NORTHRUP
Professor of Industry
Director, Industrial Research Unit

and

RICHARD L. ROWAN
Professor of Industry
Co-Director, Industrial Research Unit

INDUSTRIAL RESEARCH UNIT
The Wharton School, Vance Hall/CS
University of Pennsylvania
Philadelphia, Pennsylvania 19104
U.S.A.

Foreword

Since 1972, the Industrial Research Unit of The Wharton School at the University of Pennsylvania has been actively engaged in research pertaining to many facets of the field of multinational industrial relations. Studies that have been completed, or that are currently being undertaken, deal with areas such as profit sharing, employee stock ownership, savings, and asset formation plans; shift practices and hours of work on an annual basis; and layoffs and plant closings. This monograph is the third of several that will explore the history and current status of the international trade secretariats, which have been quite active in recent years in their objective of achieving direct contact, consultation, and negotiation with multinational firms in the hope of influencing conditions of employment on a worldwide basis. The monographs can be looked upon as companion pieces to our major study, *Multinational Collective Bargaining Attempts: The Record, the Cases, and the Prospects,* in which we attempt to explain the interaction between the secretariats and the multinational firms.

This monograph analyzes the International Transport Workers' Federation (ITF) and its activities involving so-called "flag-of-convenience" shipping. Similar in many aspects of its operation to other principal International Trade Union Secretariats (ITSs), the ITF has gone far beyond the traditional role of the trade union secretariats in boycotts, enrolling members directly, obtaining millions of dollars in payments from shippers for a "welfare fund" and in signing agreements both with shipowners and with an international federation of employers. It is thus both a traditional secretariat and a unique organization.

Originally we had hoped to include the ITF story in a larger book which would also contain studies of the various international air transport organizations including the International Federation of Air Line Pilots' Associations (IFALPA) and the International Federation of Air Traffic Controllers Associations (IFATCA). Since research on these organizations is still in process and interest in the ITF is so substantial, we decided to publish the ITF study separately.

We are indebted to many persons for assistance in this work. Over the years both ITF representatives and numerous shipping and labor organizations in the United States, Europe, and Asia have spent time with us, provided documents, and endeavored to be of assistance. Research assistance over the years has been provided by Dr. Kenneth J. Pitterle, Messrs. Andrew Schindler, Philip Miscimarra, and Craig Leman and Ms. Mary J. Immediata. Our librarian, Ms. Lynn A. Deglin, M.S., was an excellent document and source finder and fact-checked the manuscript. Our French and German translators and researchers, Dr. Betty J. Slowinski and Christian F. Schneider, M.A., made documents and information available to us from French and German sources.

The manuscript was edited by Mr. Robert L. Walker under the direction of Ms. Patricia Dornbusch, Chief Editor of the Industrial Research Unit. Mrs. Margaret E. Doyle handled the various administrative matters involved in the work, and Mrs. Cynthia K. Smith did the word processing. Initial financing of the research for the study was provided by the Wharton School's Labor Relations Council. Since 1975, the research has been underwritten principally by subscriptions to the Industrial Research Unit's Multinational Research Advisory Group Information Services and other such funds. These funds are unrestricted, although it is understood that they will be utilized for multinational industrial relations studies. The first of a series of five annual grants by the General Motors Corporation in support of multinational industrial relations research was also supportive of this work. For this we are very grateful to the corporation and particularly to Mr. Alfred S. Warren, Jr., Vice-President, Industrial Relations.

The authors are solely responsible for the study's content and for the research and views expressed, which should be attributed neither to the University of Pennsylvania nor to any of the grantors.

HERBERT R. NORTHRUP
Professor of Industry
Director, Industrial Research Unit
The Wharton School
University of Pennsylvania

Philadelphia
April 1983

TABLE OF CONTENTS

LIST OF TABLES

TABLE

LIST OF FIGURES

CHAPTER I

Introduction

The International Transport Workers' Federation (ITF) is unique among the International Trade Union Secretariats (ITSs)[1] in several ways. Unlike the others ITSs, the ITF directly represents employees, sometimes with their consent, and often without authorization; it signs agreements with individual companies; it has even negotiated an agreement with its counterpart, the International Shipping Federation; by virtue of the strategic location of many of its affiliates, it has been able to exert enormous economic power through boycotts in order to gain its objectives; and as a result of this power, it has accumulated considerable financial reserves.

Because the ITF's activities in ocean transport, and particularly its activities in regard to the so-called "flag-of-convenience" (FOC) ships are the principal reason for its unique and economically significant activities, a major portion of this monograph deals with this segment. To aid the reader in understanding how the ITF operates, we describe the history, organizational structure, membership, and finances in Chapter II. Chapter III, the main body of the work, deals with the FOC campaign; and Chapter IV with our conclusions. Appendix A reproduces an early Wharton study which examined ITF activity in Australia; Appendix B provides a summary by a British legal and marine expert of ITF action and legal provisions in major countries; Appendix C examines ITF use of international governmental organizations to further the FOC campaign; and Appendix D reviews ITF activities in air transport.

---

[1] For a general description of the international labor movement and of the activities of the international trade union secretariats, see Herbert R. Northrup and Richard L. Rowan, *Multinational Collective Bargaining Attempts*, Multinational Industrial Relations Series No. 6 (Philadelphia: Industrial Research Unit, The Wharton School, University of Pennsylvania, 1979), pp. 11-22.

1

CHAPTER II

ITF's History, Organization, Structure, and Government

The International Transport Workers' Federation (ITF) was established as the International Federation of Ship, Dock, and River Workers by dockers' and seamen's representatives attending the London congress of the Socialist International in July 1896. The following year the organization was expanded to include all transport workers and its name was changed accordingly. Representatives from Great Britain, Sweden, Germany, the Netherlands, Belgium, France and the United States were present at the first meeting.[1] The secretariat was dominated by maritime unions until 1904 when railway affiliates began to assume a significant role. Railwaymen and seafarers remain the largest industrial sections within the ITF.[2]

The Pre-World War II Years

Under British leadership, the newly organized ITF invested much of its time and limited resources in futile industrial disputes. Upon removal of the secretariat to Hamburg (1904) and later Berlin, leadership passed to the Germans. Under President Hermann Jochade the importance of organizing and strengthening new unions was recognized. Affiliated membership increased rapidly from less than 80,000 in 1904 to 1,000,000 ten years later.[3]

---

[1] K.A. Golding, "In the Forefront of Trade Union History, 1896-1971: Looking Back on 75 Years of the ITF," *ITF Journal*, Vol. 31, No. 2 (Summer 1971), pp. 31-33; ITF, *A Brief Survey of the History and Activities of the International Transport Workers' Federation* (Amsterdam: 1952), p. 5, hereafter cited as *ITF History*.

[2] Golding, p. 33; Charles Blyth, "Stockholm—a Significant City in the ITF's Life," *ITF Journal*, Vol. 34, No. 2 (Summer 1974), p. 1; interview with Harold Lewis, then Assistant General Secretary, ITF, September 3, 1973.

[3] Golding, pp. 33-38; *ITF History*, p. 6.

International trade union activity ceased during World War I, but the ITF was reestablished in Amsterdam in 1919 mainly through the efforts of British, Swedish and Dutch transport unions.[4] In order better to coordinate the activities of national unions in the respective transport industries, the ITF created separate industrial sections for seafarers, dockers, road transport workers and railwaymen. Those sections in turn formulated demands and resolutions for presentation at the newly created International Labour Organisation (ILO), an international body towards which the ITF directed a good deal of its attention at this time,[5] and which later became a most significant aspect of the ITF's successful efforts in the maritime field, as is discussed in Chapter III and Appendix C.

The ITF was weakened by the suppression of the trade union movement in Italy, Austria, Germany and Spain during the 1930s. Shortly before the outbreak of war in 1939, the ITF moved its headquarters to London, enabling the secretariat and several industrial sections to remain active. The organization encouraged the trade union resistance movement in occupied countries while the industrial sections managed to hold meetings and conferences throughout the war.[6]

The Seafarers' Section staged a joint wartime conference in July 1944 with the International Mercantile Marine Officers' Association, which it later merged into its organization. Those attending the conference demanded the fixing of minimum international standards for maritime nations and formulated an International Seafarers' Charter which was subsequently considered and adopted by a tripartite meeting of the Joint Maritime Commission of the ILO. The Railwaymen's Section, for its part, met in 1943 and issued a pledge of cooperation with the Technical Advisory Committee for Inland Transport (TACIT). The railwaymen asked for representation through the ITF at the peace and reconstruction conferences and proposed the formation of a committee to study the problems of post-war inland transport. The European Transport Committee, which was in fact then established, drew up a plan calling for the creation of a European Transport Authority to coordinate and integrate continental transport after the war.[7]

---

[4] *ITF History*, p. 6.

[5] Golding, p. 41; *ITF History*, pp. 8-12.

[6] Golding, pp. 41-48; *ITF History*, pp. 12-14.

[7] *ITF History*, pp. 14-18.

1946—Present

After World War II, the ITF gained many new affiliates in North America, Africa, Asia and Latin America. By 1953 it was the second largest international trade secretariat, claiming 5,000,000 members in over 40 countries.[8] The ITF's first post-war congresses, held in Zurich (1946) and Oslo (1948), recognized the need for reorganization along regional lines and so proposed the establishment of regional offices throughout the world. With the opening of a sub-secretariat in Havana in 1949 and the setting up of a regional information office in Bombay, the ITF formally committed itself to an increased role in the trade union affairs of developing countries.[9]

The industrial sections were active particularly in the late 1940s. It was at that time that new sections for fisheries and civil aviation were created. Encouraged by the adoption of the International Seafarers' Charter, the dockers', fishermen's and inland transport workers' sections of the ILO pressed for the adoption of their respective charters embodying recommendations and proposals for minimum wage levels, improved working conditions, safety standards and collective bargaining rights.

The ITF sought to influence other intergovernmental organizations as well. The Economic and Social Council (ECOSOC) of the United Nations (UN) granted the ITF consultative status enabling the secretariat to participate in conferences of its specialized agencies. ITF representatives presented recommendations and programs drawn up by the secretariat or its industrial sections to such organizations as the UN Transport and Communications Commission, the European Conference of Ministers of Transport (CEMT), the Inter-Governmental Maritime Consultative Organization (IMCO) now the International Maritime Organization (IMO) and the International Civil Aviation Organization (ICAO). Because of both the ITF's participation in these meetings and the pace of technological developments within the transport field in general, the secretariat has had to allocate considerably more time and money to research activities in the post-war period.

---

[8] *Ibid.*, p. 42; Lewis L. Lorwin, *The International Labor Movement: History, Policies, Outlook* (New York: Harper, 1953), p. 311.

[9] *ITF History*, pp. 20, 36-37, 42-44.

ORGANIZATIONAL STRUCTURE

The main organizational components of the ITF include the congress, general council, executive board, management committee, secretariat, and industrial sections. A general secretary, president and three vice-presidents make up the ITF's principal officers.

Congress

The congress, the "supreme authority" of the ITF,[10] is convened once every three years by the executive board in order to review the federation's activities, propose policy outlines for the future, examine financial statements and auditors' reports, adjust affiliation fees, consider proposed amendments to the constitution and other motions, elect the general secretary, president and vice-presidents and determine the membership of the general council and executive board. The size of an affiliated organization's delegation to congress is based on the number of members for which it pays dues. The ITF uses a formula for determining representation which favors smaller affiliates. Voting is generally by simple majority, but amendments to the ITF constitution require a two-thirds majority.[11]

General Council

The general council, which is intended to reflect both the geographical distribution and industrial activity of the ITF's membership, stands next in line of authority after the congress. It is made up of the general secretary and delegates elected at congress from among those persons nominated by individual affiliates and regional union groupings. The council meets immediately after each ordinary congress and at the discretion of the executive board. It offers instructions to the executive board, hears appeals from groups whose membership has been suspended and holds the power of expulsion. It is also the final arbiter when the general secretary or his assistants wish to appeal their own suspension. In addition to these duties, the congress can assign additional tasks of its choosing to the general council.[12]

---

[10] ITF, *Constitution of the International Transport Workers' Federation* (1974), p. 5.

[11] *Ibid.*, pp. 5-8, 10, 12-13, 18.

[12] *Ibid.*, pp. 4-5, 8-10, 14.

Executive Board

The executive board is made up of the general secretary and twenty-five other persons elected from among the members of the general council. No single ITF affiliate may contribute more than one member to the executive board, and those who do serve represent specific geographic constituencies. The board, which must meet at least twice a year, directs the affairs of the ITF between congress and general council meetings. It accepts or rejects new affiliates, decides in the first instance on the suspension of standing members, grants reductions in or exemptions from payment of affiliation fees, levies supplementary assessments, establishes regional offices and new industrial sections, sets conditions of employment and tenure for staff members, including the general secretary, and nominates from its own membership candidates to fill the ITF presidency and vice-presidency.[13]

The executive board's decisions concerning the organizational, administrative and financial operations of the ITF are subject to review by the general council. Because the executive board is usually comprised of the most powerful and influential ITF affiliate trade union leaders, however, its decisions are rarely overturned. Table II-1 lists the members of the executive board as constituted at the ITF's 1980 congress.

Executive Officers

The ITF president and three vice-presidents are elected by the congress, serve for three years and are eligible for reelection. The vice-presidents must come from different regions and at least one must be a Third World representative. Fritz Prechtl of the Gewerkschaft der Eisenbahner of Austria has been president of the ITF since 1971, when he replaced the retiring Hans Düby of the Schweizerischer Eisenbahnverband (Switzerland) (see Table II-2 for a complete listing of the ITF's presidents). At the ITF's congress in 1980, Theodore Gleason of the International Longshoremen's Association of the United States was confirmed in office as an ITF vice-president. At the same time, Siegfried Merten of the German Gewerkschaft Öffentliche Dienste, Transport und Verkehr and Eduardo Vanegas of the Unión de Marinos Mercantes de Colombia were chosen to fill the other two vice-presidential slots.[14]

---

13 *Ibid.*, pp. 4, 6, 10-15, 17.

14 ITF, *Report on Activities 1971-1973*, p. 11; *ITF Panorama*, Vol. 2, No. 2 (1980), pp. 7-8.

TABLE II-1
ITF Executive Board
(1980)

Region	Member	Union	Country
Europe/Middle East	F. Prechtl	Gewerkschaft der Eisenbahner	Austria
	S. Merten	Gewerkschaft Öffentliche Dienste, Transport und Verkehr	Germany
	E. Baudet	Belgische Transportarbeidersbond	Belgium
	Y. Lequoy	Fédération des Travaux Publics et des Transport F.O.	France
	H. Frieser	Gewerkschaft der Eisenbahner Deutschlands	Germany
	S. Weighell	National Union of Railwaymen	Great Britain
	A. M. Evans	Transport and General Workers' Union	Great Britain
	B. Kok	Vervoersbonden FNV	Netherlands
	H. Aasarod	Norsk Sjømannsforbund	Norway
	V. Sanchez	Federación de Trabajadores del Transporte, UGT	Spain
	B. Gustavsson	Svenska Transportarbetareförbundet	Sweden
	M. Beit-Dagan	Transport Workers' Union	Israel
Africa	D. Oyeyemi	Union of Railwaymen	Nigeria
	A. Mhungu	Railway Workers' Union	Zimbabwe
Asia/Australia	M. Morikage	National Railway Workers' Union	Japan
	C. H. Fitzgibbon	Waterside Workers' Federation	Australia
	K. P. Hong	Korean Seamen's Union	Korea
Latin America/Caribbean	M. Sant'anna	Brazilian Engineer Officers' Union	Brazil
	D. C. Fanuele	Unión Personal de Aeronavegación de Entes Privados	Argentina
	E. Vanegas	Unión de Marinos Mercantes de Colombia	Colombia
North America	W. C. Y. McGregor	Brotherhood of Railway, Airline and Steamship Clerks	Canada
	D. Nicholson	Brotherhood of Railway, Transport and General Workers	Canada
	T. W. Gleason	International Longshoremen's Association	United States
	J. F. Peterpaul	International Association of Machinists and Aerospace Workers	United States
	J. F. Otero	Brotherhood of Railway, Airline and Steamship Clerks	United States
	H. Lewis	ITF General Secretary	Great Britain

Sources: *ITF Newsletter*, No. 8 (August 1980), p. 70; *ITF Newsletter*, No. 3 (March 1981), p. 25; ITF, *Provisional Delegate List*, 33d Congress, Miami, July 17-25, 1980; *ITF Panorama*, Vol. 2 No. 2 (1980), pp. 7-8.

TABLE II-2
ITF Presidents

Name	Country	Period
Thomas Mann	Great Britain	1896-1901
Thomas Chambers	Great Britain	1901-1904
Ben Tillett	Great Britain	1904 [a]
Hermann Jochade	Germany	1904-1916
Robert Williams	Great Britain	1920-1925
Concemore Thomas Cramp	Great Britain	1925-1933
Charles Lindley	Sweden	1933-1946
John Benstead	Great Britain	1946-1947
Omer Becu	Belgium	1947-1950
Robert Bratschi	Switzerland	1950-1954
Arthur Deakin	Great Britain	1954-1955
Hans Jahn Acting	Germany	1955-1958 [b]
Frank Cousins	Great Britain	1958-1960
Roger Dekeyzer	Belgium	1960-1962
Frank Cousins	Great Britain	1962-1965
Hans Düby	Switzerland	1965-1971
Fritz Prechtl	Austria	1971-

Sources: *ITF Journal*, Vol. 31, No. 2 (Summer 1971), pp. 29- 56-57; *Report on Activities 1971-1973*, p. 11.
[a] temporary president
[b] acting president 1955-1956

Management Committee

The management committee is made up of the president, vice-presidents, general secretary, three designated members of the executive board and those other executive board members representing the country in which the ITF's headquarters are located. As of 1980, the management committee's members included Fritz Prechtl, Theodore Gleason, Siegfried Merten, Eduardo Vanegas, Harold Lewis, Henrik Aasard, Yves Lequoy, John Peterpaul, Sidney Weighell and Moss Evans. The committee exercises such authority and performs such functions as are delegated to it by the executive board. It serves as a standing orders committee for congress and general council meetings, negotiates with the staff's union representatives on salaries and conditions of employment and generally oversees the daily business of the secretariat. The management committee must meet at least once between executive board meetings, and members are reimbursed for the expenses they incur in attending.[15]

---

[15] *Constitution of the International Transport Workers' Federation* (1974), pp. 7, 10, 12, 14; *ITF Panorama*, Vol. 2, No. 2 (1980), p. 8.

General Secretary and Secretariat

The general secretary, who is elected by congress for a three-year, renewable term, is responsible for the general administration of the ITF and for implementing the policies and directives of the congress and the executive board. The general secretary is himself a member of the general council, the executive board and the management committee. He receives applications for membership in the international, circulates draft motions and constitutional amendments before congress sessions, collects and accounts for ITF revenues, helps settle disputes between affiliates, supervises the work of assistant and industrial section secretaries and appoints headquarters and regional and other office staff. The present general secretary, Harold Lewis, served for eleven years as assistant general secretary before being chosen to succeed retiring General Secretary Charles Blyth in 1977.[16]

The ITF secretariat offices are located in London. The secretariat staff has expanded gradually in recent years and now exceeds forty persons. As of the end of 1979, General Secretary Lewis was served by two assistant general secretaries, J. Hauf and Å. Selander, as well as three section secretaries, M.S. Hoda (Civil Aviation and Travel Bureau Staff), Brian Laughton (Special Seafarers) and Kenneth A. Golding (Research and Publications). Golding, his two research/editorial assistants and a librarian coordinate information and answer questions from affiliates, help industrial sections with the preparation of questionnaires and conference documentation, produce triennial congress and activities reports and edit and publish the *ITF Newsletter* and *ITF Panorama*. Because these last publications, together with many other ITF materials, appear in four languages, the secretariat maintains a permanent team of translators/interpreters. The remaining staff positions at the secretariat run the gamut from administrative secretary, lawyer and finance officer to clerks, typists and assistants.[17]   (See Figure II-1.)

Industrial Sections

The ITF has established eight sections grouping affiliates with similar interests. These represent trade unions from the railway, road transport, inland navigation, ports and docks, shipping, fishing, civil aviation and travel bureau industries. Any ITF affiliate

---

[16] *Constitution of the International Transport Workers' Federation* (1974), pp. 3, 7-11, 13-16; *ITF Newsletter*, No. 8 (August 1977), pp. 68-69.

[17] ITF, *Report on Activities 1977-1979*, pp. 13-16.

FIGURE II-1
Administrative Structure of the ITF

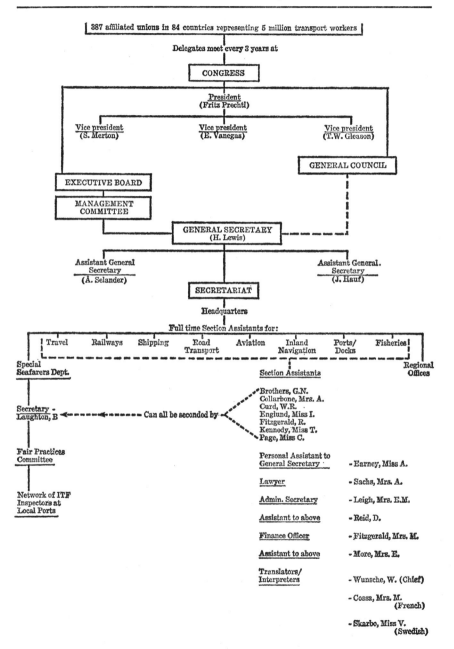

Source: B.L. Williamson, Esq., unpublished study of ITF, 1982.

paying dues for members in one of these areas of activity is eligible to participate in the work of the appropriate industrial section. Secretaries appointed by the executive board and working under the supervision of the general secretary oversee the administrative functioning of each section. At ordinary congresses, those taking part in the activities of a section meet both to elect a chairman, vice-chairman and other officers and to determine the section's program for the immediate future. Such programs, worked out in cooperation with the ITF secretariat, generally consist of international and regional conferences as well as specific, sector-related projects. Any decisions reached at sectional conferences that bear on other industrial sections or on the ITF as a whole must be approved by the executive board. The board also has the power to create new sections and determine their mandate.[18]

Prior to the ITF's 1980 congress in Miami, the Federation had for many years maintained a ninth industrial section known as the Special Seafarers' Section. The section had been established in connection with the ITF's campaign against flag-of-convenience (FOC) shippers which began in 1948 and the activities of which are discussed in detail in Chapter III. In 1980 this special section was transformed into a Special Seafarers' Department. Like its predecessor, the Special Seafarers' Department was created to help fight the FOC ships. The department does this by negotiating individual wage agreements with FOC shippers and by obtaining from such shippers special contributions to the Seafarers' International Assistance, Welfare and Protection Fund of the ITF. The fund itself is managed by the ITF's Fair Practices Committee, which is made up of representatives from ITF seafarers' and dockers' unions. The committee meets regularly to set the wage scales demanded for FOC crews and to oversee boycott activities against those shippers who refuse to sign ITF wage agreements. As a direct result of increasing challenges brought by shipowners in the courts to the ITF's flag-of-convenience campaign, the Federation was compelled at its Miami congress to draft new, more comprehensive rules governing the Special Seafarers' Department and the management of the Seafarers' International Assistance, Welfare and Protection Fund.[19]

---

[18] *Constitution of the International Transport Workers' Federation* (1974), pp. 1, 14-16.

[19] Golding, p. 50; *ITF Newsletter*, No. 8 (August 1980), p. 69; *ITF Newsletter*, No. 5 (May 1980), supplement; *ITF Panorama*, Vol. 2, No. 2 (1980), p. 2.

As noted, the FOC campaign, the Special Seafarers' Section and its finances will all be discussed at length in Chapters III and IV.

MEMBERSHIP

Although the ITF has experienced several periods of fast-paced growth, the organization finally saw its affiliated membership decline somewhat after the late 1950s before stabilizing at the present level. In the early years of the century, the Federation expanded rapidly. Membership increased from 150,000 in 1905 to approximately one million at the outbreak of World War I. In the immediate aftermath of the war, the ITF gained many new affiliates, boosting membership to around the three million mark by 1920. After suffering major setbacks in the years before World War II, the ITF went through a revitalization after the war. By the early 1950s, it could claim to speak for more than 4.5 million affiliated unionists worldwide. Membership continued to rise to a highpoint of 5.7 million in 1957. By 1970, however, the figure had fallen to 4.4 million and remained at about that level throughout the decade. As of the end of 1979, the ITF counted 4,390,992 affiliated members from 387 affiliates and 84 countries within its ranks.[20]

Both trade unions and trade union federations are eligible for membership in the ITF. Once accepted, such organizations are obliged to pay affiliation fees on a regular basis, furnish the ITF with their publications and other relevant documents, keep the international apprised of their activities, carry out the policies of the ITF's governing bodies and inform their own members and constituents of the actions of the ITF, if possible by means of national-level advisory committees made up of representatives from a country's various ITF-affiliated unions.[21]

In the majority of cases, affiliates which lose their membership in the ITF do so because they have failed to pay their dues. This is particularly true for affiliated unions from the Third World whose attachment to the ITF has often been shaky at best because of those unions' own organizational weaknesses and severely restricted financial bases. In other instances, however, disputes between the ITF and certain of its affiliates have led to suspen-

---

[20] Golding, pp. 37, 40; ITF, *Report on Activities 1968-1970*, p. 23; ITF *Report on Activities 1977-1979*, p. 23.

[21] *Constitution of the International Transport Workers' Federation* (1974), pp. 3-4.

sion or withdrawal from the international. In 1961, for example, the Seafarers' International Union of North America (SIU) was suspended for overstepping its jurisdictional bounds. This in turn led three other U.S. affiliates representing longshoremen, marine engineers and masters, mates and pilots to leave the ITF. All eventually returned to the federation's ranks. More recently, a major conflict developed between the ITF and the National Union of Seafarers of India (Bombay) (NUSI) because of the Indian union's reluctance to support the ITF's flag-of-convenience campaign. The executive board suspended the Indian union in October 1978, but the NUSI's membership was eventually reinstated in 1980.[22] (See Chapter III for details.)

One major reason for the recent decline in ITF membership is technological change and rationalization,[23] particularly in the labor-intensive railway industry. Because railway unions have traditionally formed the backbone of the ITF's membership, the resulting decrease in the number of railwaymen employed has been the largest single cause of the ITF's loss of members. The drop in affiliated membership from 5,043,104 at the end of 1961 to 4,991,543 at the end of 1964 was attributed by the ITF entirely to the decline in railway employment. Between 1970 and 1973, the ITF lost 60,000 members of its Mexican railway affiliate, 145,000 affiliated railway workers from Japan and 20,000 members of Britain's National Union of Railwaymen (NUR). Between 1973 and 1976, 100,000 railway workers from the United States and 93,000 members of the German railway union, the Gewerkschaft Eisenbahner Deutschlands, were dropped from ITF membership rolls. This trend continued in the 1977-1979 period when the ITF lost the 300,000 railway employees of its one-time affiliate, the National Federation of Indian Railwaymen.[24] Through 1979, railway unions still comprised one-half of the ITF's ten largest affiliates (see Table II-3), but were it not for the income from its FOC campaign the steady erosion of railway union membership would have presented a serious challenge to the ITF's financial health.

---

22 ITF, *Reports 1958-1959*, p. 57; ITF, *Reports 1960-1961*, p. 69; *Report on Activities 1977-1979*, p. 25; *ITF Newsletter*, No. 3 (March 1980), p. 28.

23 A good example is containerization in the shipping industry.

24 ITF, *Report on Activities 1962-1964*, p. 21; *Report on Activities 1968-1970*, pp. 8, 30-32; ITF, *Report on Activities 1974-1976*, pp. vi, xvi; *Report on Activities 1977-1979*, p. viii.

TABLE II-3
ITF's Ten Largest Affiliates
(December 1979)

Union	Country	Affiliated Membership
Transport and General Workers' Union	Great Britain	360,000
Gewerkschaft der Eisenbahner Deutschlands	Germany	262,332
International Association of Machinists and Aerospace Workers	United States	200,000
National Union of Railwaymen	Great Britain	180,000
Gewerkschaft öffentliche Dienste, Transport und Verkehr	Germany	163,000
United Transportation Union	United States	125,000
Brotherhood of Railway, Airline and Steamship Clerks	United States	123,600
National Railway Workers' Union (KOKORO)	Japan	120,000
Gewerkschaft der Eisenbahner	Austria	120,000
Korean Seamen's Union	Korea	102,952

Source: ITF, *Report on Activities 1977-1978-1979*, pp. i-xvi.

Table II-4 summarizes the most recent changes in the ITF's affiliated membership throughout the world. Although the ITF has expanded slightly the number of countries and unions represented in its ranks, the number of union workers it can claim to represent has actually fallen by a few thousand. The overall picture, however, is one of general stability. Like most international trade secretariats, the ITF originated with European trade unions and more than one-half of its membership is still found in Europe. The United States and Canada now provide the second largest contingent of ITF-affiliated workers. In Asia and Africa, the Federation has recently lost ground, but there has been some compensation for these losses through the addition of new affiliates from France, Portugal, and the Netherlands, further emphasizing the European predominance in the ITF. New affiliates from Europe, and from the developed countries generally, are especially important because such unions are able to contribute financially to the ITF's work. It is important to keep in mind—particularly in light of the ITF's efforts to enforce essentially European wage scales on shipowners worldwide—that a large percentage of the international's sizeable membership from the Third World actually pays dues either at a reduced rate or not at all.

TABLE II-4
ITF Affiliated Membership Distribution
(1976, 1979)

Region	12/31/76	12/31/79
	Number of Countries [a]	
Europe	20	21
Asia/Pacific	20	20
United States/Canada	2	2
Latin America/Caribbean	28	27
Africa	11	12
Total	81	82
	Number of Unions	
Europe	105	114
Asia/Pacific	78	86
United States/Canada	19	21
Latin America/Caribbean	133	136
Africa	41	28
Total	378 [b]	387 [b]
	Total Membership	
Europe	2,143,960	2,280,150
Asia/Pacific	1,000,082	821,955
United States/Canada	845,361	853,410
Latin America/Caribbean	302,192	329,894
Africa	116,106	105,260
Total	4,408,783 [b]	4,390,992 [b]

Sources: Calculated from figures appearing in: ITF, *Report on Activities 1974-1975-1976*, pp. i-xvi; ITF, *Report on Activities 1977-1978-1979*, pp. i-xvi.
[a] and dependencies
[b] including two unions-in-exile

FINANCES

The ITF's finances are divided into three accounts: a general fund, a special regional activities account, and the Seafarers' International Assistance, Welfare and Protection Fund. In 1974, an earlier solidarity and reserve fund was closed and its remaining assets (£ 12,867, then US $30,218) were assigned to the general fund.[25]

---

25 ITF, *Proceedings of the 32nd Congress* (1977), p. 93.

General Fund

The general fund is used to meet the headquarters and overall administrative expenses of the federation. It also covers the deficits and receives the surpluses of the regional activities accounts. Money from the general fund has traditionally paid about half the costs of holding the ITF's triennial congresses as well. Through 1980 the balance of the congress expenses were contributed by unions from the country hosting the congress meetings; but because this has limited congress locations to the developed countries, ITF delegates gathered in Miami in 1980 approved a dues increase sufficient to allow general fund revenues alone to meet the costs of staging future congresses.[26]

Until quite recently, affiliation fees represented the single largest source of general fund revenues (see Table II-5). By rule, 70 percent of such dues payments are allocated to the general fund while the remainder goes to pay for special organizing and educational programs in developing countries. Since 1977, 10 percent of the previous year's receipts to the ITF Seafarers' International Assistance, Welfare and Protection Fund have been transferred to the general fund. This transfer is viewed by the ITF as a reimbursement for the expenses incurred by the secretariat in managing the flag-of-convenience campaign. In 1979, this allocation from the welfare fund came to £325,418 (US $723,730), an amount considerably larger than the £292,405 (US $650,309) raised for the general fund from dues payments from affiliates. Unaudited accounts indicate the allocation from the welfare fund continues to rise. The ITF itself admits that the rising revenues from the welfare fund are to a large extent responsible for the general fund's recent surpluses.[27]

Nevertheless, the ITF compares quite favorably with other international trade secretariats when it comes to the collection of affiliation fees from member unions. Table II-6 offers a geographic breakdown of affiliates paying dues at reduced rates. As is the case with all ITSs, many unions from the Third World find it impossible to remit the standard assessment. The few European unions which fail to pay dues at the standard rate are located in France, Spain and Italy. On the whole, however, the most recent figures available reveal that almost 88 percent of the ITF's affiliates paid full dues.

---

[26] *ITF Newsletter*, No. 8 (August 1980), p. 69.

[27] ITF, *Financial Statements and Auditor's Reports 1977 to 1979*, presented to the 33d ITF congress, Miami, July 17-25, 1980, p. 1.

TABLE II-5
ITF General Fund
Income and Expenditure Accounts
(1977-1979—in pounds sterling, £)

	1977 [a]	1978 [b]	1979 [c]
Income			
70 Percent of Affiliation Fees	248,020	265,871	292,405
Bank and Loan Interest (Net)	8,633	6,824	12,467
Sales of Publications, etc.	58	13	60
Allocation from Seafarers' International Assistance, Welfare and Protection Fund	163,841	207,597	325,418
Total Income	420,552	480,305	630,350
Transfer from Regional Activities Fund [d]	+13,288	−1,605	−1,291
Adjusted Total Income	433,840	478,700	629,059
Expenditure			
Meetings, Conferences and Activities	26,703	60,433	72,889
Publications, Public Relations	12,509	12,520	24,028
Headquarters	240,318	343,221	424,304
Miscellaneous Costs	6,653	8,444	20,810
Congress 1977	32,243	—	—
Special Projects	15,878	1,252	—
Total Expenditure	334,304	425,870	542,031
Reserves/Depreciation			
Congress 1980	25,000	25,000	25,000
Headquarters Removal and Equipment	25,000	20,000	20,000
Pensions	—	5,000	5,000
Office Furniture and Equipment Written Off	18,753	—	—
Automobile Written Off	3,753	—	—
Total	72,506	50,000	50,000
Net Surplus	27,030	2,830	37,028

Source: ITF, *Financial Statements and Auditors' Reports 1977 to 1979*,
         presented to ITF 33d Congress, Miami, July 17-25, 1980, p. 5.
[a] £ = US$1.9060.
[b] £ = US$2.0345.
[c] £ = US$2.2240.
[d] unutilized allocation = +; excess expenditure = −.

Note: All currency conversions are given as of the current month and year.

TABLE II-6
*ITF Affiliated Membership Paying Affiliation
Fees at Reduced Rate
By Region, 1976, 1979*
(Percent)

Region	1976	1979
Europe	3.3	5.3
Asia/Pacific	53.0	25.3
United States/Canada	0.0	0.0
Latin America/Caribbean	39.3	50.4
Africa	47.2	36.8
TOTAL	17.6	12.1

Source: Calculated from figures appearing in: ITF, *Report on Activities 1974-1975-1976*, pp. i-xvi; ITF, *Report on Activities 1977-1978-1979*, pp. i-xvi.

Regional Activities Account

The regional activities account, also known as the Edo Fimmen Special Account in honor of a former general secretary responsible for ITF expansion outside Europe, receives 30 percent of all affiliation fees collected. In 1979, this amounted to £125,317 (US $278,705). Although generous compared to the funds available to some other international trade secretariats, regional fund revenues in the past proved insufficient for the ITF's work in the Third World. As a result, the fund was heavily dependent on voluntary contributions from affiliates to maintain the federation's regional activities. American and Swedish member unions were particularly forthcoming in this respect. In 1954, for example, affiliates from the United States contributed over one-half the fund's income. The following year contributions from two American unions alone nearly equalled the total contributions from all other affiliates combined. The account was also dependent for many years on grants from the International Confederation of Free Trade Unions' (ICFTU) International Solidarity Fund until the fund was liquidated in 1969. As Table II-7 indicates, revenues from sources other than affiliation fees have become negligible.[28]

---

[28] ITF, *Reports 1954-1955* and *Proceedings of Congress at Vienna (1956)*, p. 154; *Reports 1960-1961*, pp. 47, 135; *Report on Activities 1962-1964 and Proceedings of 28th Congress at Copenhagen (1965)*, pp. 208, 270.

Over the last few years, the ITF has devoted the largest share
of its regional activities resources to Latin America and the
Caribbean. In 1979, for example, almost half the money spent
went to that region. Africa and Asia have been the focus of
smaller expenditures. The regional activities fund has also helped
maintain an ITF office in Tokyo. Finally, the ITF secretariat
receives a payment from the fund for the regional activities duties
of its staff.

TABLE II-7
ITF Regional Activities Fund
(1977-1979—in pounds sterling, £)

	1977 a	1978 b	1979 c
Income			
30 Percent of Affiliation Fees	106,295	113,945	125,317
Special Contributions	265	405	216
Interest Receivable (Net)	5	3	3
Total Income	106,565	114,353	125,536
Expenditure			
Office Expenses (including Salaries), Educational/ Organizational Activities: Africa	22,698	32,483	32,734
Grants: Africa	—	5,244	—
Relocation of African Office	—	2,484	—
Office Expenses (including Salaries), Educational/ Organizational Activities: Asia	17,736	19,203	21,234
Office Expenses (including Salaries), Educational/ Organizational Activities: Japan (Net) d	4,662	5,493	4,598
Office Expenses (including Salaries), Educational/ Organizational Activities: Latin America/Carib.	42,251	51,395	62,645
Salary, Travel and Sundry Expenses of Regional Secretary (London)	5,665	5,550	5,616
Total Expenditure	93,012	121,852	126,827
Operating Surplus	13,553	—	—
Operating Deficit	—	7,499	1,291
Unutilized Special Contributions Brought Forward	5,629	5,894	—
Net Surplus (to General Fund)	19,182	—	—
Net Deficit (to General Fund)	—	1,605	1,291

Source: ITF, *Financial Statements and Auditors' Reports 1977 to 1979*, pre-
          sented to ITF 33d Congress, Miami, July 17-25, 1980, p. 6.
a £ = US$1.9060.
b £ = US$2.0345.
c £ = US$2.2240.
d i.e., after contributions by Japanese affiliates.

Seafarers' International Assistance, Welfare and Protection Fund and the Seafarers' Trust

The ITF Seafarers' International Assistance, Welfare and Protection Fund (the Fund) operates with money received from payments made by flag- or crew-of-convenience operators as a result of agreements connected with the FOC campaign. The Fund, which was separated from the general fund in 1965, was founded to make assistance and welfare payments, such as seamen's homes, on behalf of seafarers. Those attending the ITF's 1980 congress adopted an amendment to their organization's constitution specifically authorizing the international to provide help to individual transport workers, including seamen.[29] In addition to this, the ITF Seafarers' Trust (the Trust) was subsequently created with money from the Fund. The Trust serves as a disbursing account to which money from the Fund is transferred for disbursement to various projects. These clarifications obviously came in response to recent court action against the ITF by shippers opposed to the federation's drive to force contributions to the Fund. These important court challenges, as noted in Chapter III, have imposed increasing staff and legal costs upon the ITF. An examination of the Fund and the Trust is best postponed until after the FOC campaign has been examined in Chapter III, and is found in Chapter IV.

REGIONAL ACTIVITIES

The ITF encourages geographical and industrial cooperation among its affiliates. Of the two, cooperation among the ITF's industrial sections has become the more important. In fact, the sections have sponsored regional sectional conferences on their own initiative. First regional and then non-FOC sectional activities are discussed in the balance of this chapter.

Regional Activities—Historical Development

The ITF's interest in expanding its influence and membership in Latin American, Asian, and African regions stems from the mid-1950's when American unions were anxious to extend their influence, particularly in Latin America. In 1954, the ITF's affiliates donated monies earmarked for regional activities equal to one quarter of the ITF's total income; over one half of this amount was

---

[29] *ITF Newsletter*, No. 8 (August 1980), p. 69.

donated by U.S. unions, the Railway Labor Executives Association (RLEA) and Teamsters in particular. In 1955, RLEA specified that its contributions to regional activities be used only in Latin America. Speaking before the ITF's 1965 Congress, one RLEA spokesman explained his organization's reasons for promoting regional activities:

> I think it is in our selfish interest to do everything we can to encourage the peoples of these countries to develop their free trade union organizations, if we, in the more advanced countries, expect to continue the progress that we have made, not only in the economic field but in . . . the battle that is raging for the loyalties of the minds and hearts of the millions of the peoples on the one side of totalitarian philosophy and the other.[30]

The late Joseph Curran, then president of the U.S. National Maritime Workers' Union (NMU), was more blunt before the Copenhagen Congress in 1965: "If we fail in our task in the developing countries we would be defaulting to the Communists." [31] ITF regional activities throughout the 1960s were supported also by grants from the international solidarity fund of the International Confederation of Free Trade Unions (ICFTU). Since that time, the constriction of these sources of funding has necessitated a strict ordering of regional priorities. Consequently, the ITF has shifted the emphasis of its programs from material assistance to leadership training and trade union education. The ITF advises regional unions in technical matters, organizational problems and approaches to employers and government bodies, makes requests to government and management on affiliates' behalf, and on occasion has sent ITF representatives to assist unions negotiating contracts with employers. The ITF maintains two regional offices in Asia, one in Manila (formerly Kuala Lumpur), and one in Tokyo. Latin American offices are located in Lima, Peru. Since the closing of the Accara, Ghana, office in 1978, the ITF has maintained its African field representative in Nairobi, Kenya.[32] Yet there are strong regional identities among the ITF's industrial sections, and a considerable jockeying for power between the traditional European power base of the ITF and the emerging Third World takes place. These strains are particu-

---

[30] ITF, *Proceedings of the Vienna Congress* (1956), p. 318.

[31] ITF, *Proceedings of Copenhagen Congress* (1965), p. 271.

[32] ITF, *Report on Activities 1971-1973*, pp. 57-70; ITF, *Report on Activities 1974-1976*, pp. 35-66; ITF, *Report on Activities 1977-1979*, pp. 33-45.

larly apparent in the debates over the FOC campaign, but a brief discussion is presented below.

Africa

The ITF has had a long and serious involvement in Africa. Two members of the twenty-four member executive board are Africans, representing unions in Nigeria and Zimbabwe. Ben Udogwu, the African representative, spends the majority of his time on education and organization. Seminars on such topics as collective bargaining are aimed at trade unionists below the leadership level. While these seminars are often purely national in character, a number of sub-regional conferences have been held under ITF affiliate auspices.

The ITF is heavily involved in efforts to foster black trade unions in South Africa. This is especially difficult, as the apartheid laws prohibited recognition of black unions by employers until recently.

Efforts to assist union leadership in Tunisia following a 1978 general strike and resultant crackdown have also met with limited success, although a great deal of time has been devoted to helping the leaders concerned avoid prison sentences. Abderrazak Ayoub, First Assistant General Secretary of the Tunisian Railwaymen's Federation and a member of the ITF Executive Board was sentenced to five years hard labor, despite ITF protests.[33] He was, however, later released.

Asia

ITF's relations with its Asian affiliates are closely entwined with the flag-of-convenience campaign and are therefore best left to the following chapter. In addition, an incident involving the official airline of Malaysia brought the ITF in direct conflict with the authorities in this country. That story is found in Appendix D.

Latin America and the Caribbean

Although the ITF maintains a regional office in Lima, Peru, under the direction of the representative for Latin America and the Caribbean, the ITF's activities in Latin America are limited by the nature of the governments in the area (several governments there, however, have become more tolerant of union activi-

---

[33] ITF, *Report on Activities 1977-1979*, p. 36.

ties). As a result of this atmosphere, the most visible ITF involvement in Latin America is limited largely to statements of
support for unions in the area and cables of protest to governments when union leaders are jailed or unions are crushed.

In the Caribbean, the political environment has proved more
conducive to ITF activities. For instance, in early 1980, ITF
affiliated seafarers' and docker's unions met and decided to form
a Caribbean Maritime Council to promote ITF rates of pay
and training schemes based upon minimum standards set down
in the International Convention on Training and Certification of
Seafarers adopted by the International Maritime Organization in
1978.[34] This meeting was followed in March 1982 with a seminar
held in Antigua by the ITF and the Caribbean Maritime and
Aviation Council. The seminar examined what action to take on
FOC cruise ships in the Caribbean basin.[35]

SECTIONAL ACTIVITIES

Affiliates comprising ITF's various industrial sections are active formulators of ITF policy in various transport sectors. They
meet on the average of once or twice yearly and coordinate
their activities through the section secretaries employed by the
ITF. The recent activities of those outside of the maritime industry are discussed below.

Railwaymen's Section

This thirty-eight member section committee is divided into two
subcommittees which meet between section conferences to formulate policy on rail transport and on working conditions of railway staff. The subcommittee on working conditions of railway
staff met three times between the 1977 and 1979 congresses. The
subcommittee's work in this period included preparation for a
meeting of the ILO Inland Transport Committee and the completion of a secretariat study of the "Human Effects of Technological Change on the Railways." The transport subcommittee,
which is a German-speaking committee, is composed of delegates
from Austrian, German, Swiss, and Benelux affiliates. This subcommittee met five times between ITF congresses and considered
a large number of issues including the possible effects of the

---

[34] *ITF Newsletter*, No. 2 (February 1980), pp. 17-18.

[35] *ITF Newsletter*, No. 4 (April 1982), pp. 37-38.

proposed Rhine-Main-Danube Canal on the railways, how the railways could attract more business, and problems of transport between Eastern and Western bloc countries. In addition to a Railwaymen's Section Conference in London April 3-4, 1979, a large number of lectures and seminars were conducted by the section, particularly in Europe and Asia. The German unions have been particularly active in this area, with five of the fourteen lectures and seminars held between 1977 and 1979 being held in Germany.

The ITF was strongly represented by the Railwaymen's Section at a variety of meetings and hearings conducted under the auspices of the European Conference of Ministers of Transport (ECMT). Finally, the section has published a booklet available in English, French, Swedish and German entitled "What's Happening to the Railways?" [36]

Road Transport Section

The focus of Road Transport Section policy has been centered to a large extent on the formulation of an ILO Convention and Recommendation on Hours of Work and Rest Periods in Road Transport. This convention and recommendation was created to replace the outdated 1939 Hours of Work and Rest Periods Convention (No. 67) which had been ratified by only four countries in thirty-five years.

The section's steering committee, composed of section Chairman Hans Ericson (Sweden), Vice-Chairman Kurt Haussig (Germany), Peter Kung (Switzerland), and A. Kitson (United Kingdom) met twice between ITF congresses, both times to consider what policy should be in regard to the above mentioned convention and recommendation.

Sectional conferences were held in 1977 and 1979. More recent meetings of the steering committee include a joint meeting on transportation policy with the subcommittee for that area from the Railwaymen's Section in October 1980 in Stockholm and a meeting in early 1981 to discuss the question of weights and dimensions of road vehicles and questions of social welfare for truck drivers when their work brings them out of their home country. The steering committee met in September of the same year to consider a paper presented on the road transport of dangerous goods, an area of particular concern. In addition to

[36] ITF, *Report on Activities 1977-1979*, pp. 47-56.

these activities, the ITF Road Transport Section and the American
Brotherhood of Railway and Airline Clerks sponsored an Asian
Road Transport Workers' Conference in February 1979 in
Penang, Malaysia.[37]

Inland Navigation

The Inland Navigation Section, the smallest of ITF's nine sections, has a committee representing affiliates from eleven countries; of these, four constitute the working group on the Rhine-
Main-Danube canal. That proposed canal, the conditions of women
in the inland navigation industry, and proposed changes in manning requirements on the Rhine represent the major concerns of
this group in recent years.

As a result of the projected completion of the Rhine-Main-
Danube canal and of the consequent contact between Rhenish
riparian states and Eastern bloc countries whose standards are
far lower than those of Western European countries, the section
set up a five member working group to study the social implications and to make policy recommendations. The working group
met for the first time December 4, 1974, and has met on a yearly
basis since that time. The section has called upon international
organizations to evolve a policy designed to protect working conditions of employees and owner/boatmen on this canal.

Members of this section also serve as worker delegates of the
European Commission's Joint Advisory Committee for Inland
Navigation and its various working groups.[38]

Civil Aviation Section

One hundred thirty-one affiliates belong to ITF's Civil Aviation
Section. The formulation of statements, resolutions, and policy
objectives constitutes much of the section's work and is performed
largely by three subcommittees set up for technical flight deck
and cabin crew matters and for ground staff personnel including
flight controllers. Position papers are submitted to the meetings
of the appropriate bodies of the ILO and International Civil
Aviation Organization (ICAO). The ITF has also attempted to
influence the policies of various airlines and airline groups but
has met with little success, as described in Appendix D.

---

[37] *Ibid.*, pp. 57-61; *ITF Newsletter*, No. 11 (November 1980), p. 106; No. 2
(February 1981), p. 14.

[38] ITF, *Report on Activities 1977-1979*, pp. 62-68.

Travel Bureau Section

Formerly covering affiliates in allied transport industries and services, this section was restructured in 1975 to include only those affiliates representing staff from the travel trade industry. The section has been recognized by the World Tourism Organization (WTO), an international group promoting protective consumer and worker legislation and training programs for travel bureau staff. The section has undertaken a study comparing legislation and collective agreements affecting travel bureau staff and has urged ITF affiliates involved in the sector to undertake recruitment campaigns. A second study in December 1976 adopted a draft model agreement for the travel industry.[39]

More recently, the section held an International Seminar and Section Conference in Amsterdam in October 1979. The ITF sent a delegation to the World Tourism Conference in Manila in October 1980. This conference was attended by over 700 delegates from more than 100 countries. The Section chairman, Lars Hellman, suggested that some type of licensing and certification be set up for the industry. He said that, ideally, the possession of such a license could be made a prerequisite for employment in the industry.[40] This would, of course, give unions, and possibly the ITF, a large voice in, if not control of, entrance to the trade.

Fishermen's Section

Like other ITF sections, the Fishermen's Section serves primarily as a specialized lobby for transport workers in the fishing industry. Its activities have centered mainly around the ILO's Tripartite Committee on Conditions. Although the group met only once between the ITF's 1977 and 1980 congresses, affiliate delegates are active participants in meetings of various other international groups and agencies.

At a section meeting in Reykjavik, Iceland, in August 1981, a variety of issues were discussed. The discussion centered mainly on safety issues such as training standards, lifeboat requirements, and universal industrial safety training for fishermen. Other issues, such as the desire for a common European Community fishing policy and efforts to limit overcapacity in world fishing fleets, were discussed as well. Interestingly, a statement

---

[39] ITF, *Report on Activities 1974-1976*, pp. 151-153.

[40] *ITF Newsletter*, No. 11 (November 1980), p. 105.

was issued which urged the International Whaling Commission
to preserve whaling employment "on the understanding that such
decisions are compatible with the preservation and enhancement
of the whale stocks." [41]

Seafarers' Section

The combined activities of the Seaferers' and Dockers' Sections
with respect to FOC ships are discussed in Chapter III. The
considerable activity of the Seafarers' Section outside of this area
is discussed below.

The section committee is composed of representatives from
twenty-seven countries, with a geographical balance which is
much more even than that of the ITF as a whole. It is chaired
by K. Mols Sørensen of Denmark. Again, excluding FOC related
meetings, there has been a broad variety to section meetings in
recent years. Three meetings were held with member unions in
preparation for the Inter-Governmental Maritime Consultative Organization's, now the International Maritime Organization (IMO),
Subcommittee on Standards of Training and Certification of Seafarers in 1977, 1978, and 1979. Meetings of radio officers' unions
and European seafarer's indicate that there are both vocational
and geographic working groups within the section.

The Manning Committee consists of seven representatives from
four European countries and the United States. They meet yearly
and have made repeated submissions to IMO (IMCO) on such
subjects as medical personnel at sea.

Aside from the FOC issue, the section is most concerned with
the employment of non-domiciled seafarers (sometimes called
crews of convenience), coordination and financing of international
welfare activities, facilities for seafarers, ship abandonment, and
even piracy.[42]

As with other parts of the ITF, this section is an adept con-
tributor to ILO considerations. For example, the chairman of
the section for the Joint ILO/IMO (IMCO) Committee on Training during meetings in London in June 1977 was an ITF representative.[43] The IMO and the ILO serve as the main international

---

[41] *ITF Newsletter*, No. 9 (September 1980), supplement.

[42] ITF, *Report on Activities 1977-1979*, pp. 76; "ITF calls for end to owners
abandoning ships," *Lloyd's List*, March 5, 1983, p. 1.

[43] ITF, *Report on Activities 1977-1979*, p. 77.

forums for section activity in the areas of regulation and standards.

The extent of the activity of the section is perhaps best emphasized by noting that this section received more than twice as much space as any other section in the ITF *Report on Activities 1977-1979*. Its influence is also shown by the amount of organizational resources put into, and reaped from, the ITF's FOC campaign, as discussed in Chapter IV.

Dockers' Section

Representatives from the ITF's Dockers' Section are active in two main arenas. One is the ILO; the other is the FOC campaign, in which certain affiliated unions are most important to successful embargoing of FOC ships.

The section was largely responsible for the drafting and adoption of an ILO Convention on Protection against Accidents (Dockers), the longest text adopted on safety and health since World War II.[44] The employers' representatives to the ILO wanted a recommendation rather than a convention, but under pressure from the ITF delegation agreed to a convention. Subjects as diverse as certification of lifting equipment, storage and handling of dangerous substances and goods and fire-fighting equipment are covered in the convention, which was adopted in June 1979.

Special Seafarers' Department

The department originally was formed as a section as part of the ITF's FOC campaign. Unlike other sections, the department consists of individual members of the ITF. Affiliates from Seafarers' and Dockers' Sections have formed a Fair Practices Committee to conduct the campaign and govern the department. (See Chapter IV.) Representatives from these groups meet on a yearly basis to formulate ITF policy with respect to flags and crews of convenience and to review the provisions of the ITF collective agreement, as well as to handle the affairs of the department. At the same time, individual seafarers not covered by an ITF-affiliated unions' jurisdiction are enrolled in the ITF via the Special Seafarers' Section. Shipowners signing ITF collective agreements agree to pay yearly membership fees and to make annual contributions in excess of $200 per man per year to the

---

[44] See Appendix C.

ITF's Seafarers' International Assistance, Welfare, and Protection Fund. This fund plays a significant role in the FOC campaign, as discussed in Chapter III and in the evaluation of that campaign made in Chapter IV.

CONCLUDING REMARKS

The operation of the ITF, its structure, government, and finances, exclusive of its FOC activities, are generally like those of the other principal International Trade Union Secretariats (ITSs). The FOC campaign and its implications, however, clearly distinguish the ITF from other ITSs. We now turn to the history, experience, and results of the ITF FOC campaign in key countries throughout the world.

CHAPTER III

The Flag of Convenience Campaign

The flag-of-convenience (FOC) campaign of the ITF is both its most significant activity in terms of impact on world commerce and the major source of contributions to the ITF treasury. The actions pursuant to this campaign also raise very serious and profound issues of public policy for many countries and for international governmental bodies. The FOC campaign therefore deserves careful analysis.

THE ITF AND THE ILO

The ITF's traditional and very successful work on international standards for seamen has occurred in the International Labour Organisation (ILO). Prior to 1948, the ITF maintained contact with shipping industry executives through its participation in the ILO maritime conferences and commissions. Probably no organization, and certainly no ITS, has gained more from ILO participation than has the ITF. Of the 158 conventions passed by the ILO, which become national law when ratified by individual countries, thirty-one have pertained to conditions of work in ocean transport. (See Table III-1) Moreover, five of these—Officers' Competency Certificate, No 53; Holidays with Pay (Sea), No. 54; Shipowners Liability (Sick & Injured Seamen), No. 55; Hours of Work and Manning (Sea), No. 57; and Certification of Able Seamen, No. 73—are, with the exception of the ILO's Final Articles Revision, No. 80, the only conventions ratified by the United States Senate and, therefore, part of American law.[1]

---

[1] Of course, U.S. labor law in these matters is often more protective than the ILO conventions. Because ILO conventions fail to give weight to the special features of American labor legislation, and because ratification would give the ILO convention precedence over the law, opposition to ratification is widespread. For example, convention No. 98, Principles of the Right to Organise and to Collective Bargaining, would if ratified alter the exclusive representation and majority rule concepts of the National Labor Relations (Taft-Hartley) Act.

TABLE III-1

International Labour Organisation
Conventions Pertaining to Seafarers

Title	Number	Year Enacted	In Force (* Indicates Convention In Force)
Minimum Age Seamen	7	1920	*
Unemployment Indemnity (Shipwreck)	8	1920	*
Placing of Seamen	9	1920	*
Medical Examination of Young Persons (Sea)	16	1921	*
Seamen's Articles of Agreement	22	1926	*
Repatriation of Seamen	23	1926	*
Officers' Competency Certificate	53 a	1936	*
Holidays with Pay (Sea)	54 a	1936	*
Shipowners' Liability (Sick & Injured Seamen)	55 a	1936	*
Sickness Insurance (Sea)	56	1936	*
Hours of Work and Manning (Sea)	57 a	1936	
Minimum Age (Sea) (Revised)	58	1936	*
Food and Catering (Ships' Crews)	68	1946	*
Certification of Ships' Cooks	69	1946	*
Social Security (Seafarers)	70	1946	
Seafarers' Pensions Convention	71	1946	
Paid Vacations (Seafarers)	72	1946	
Medical Examination (Seafarers)	73	1946	*
Certification of Able Seamen	74 a	1946	*
Accommodation of Crews	75	1946	
Wages, Hours of Work and Manning (Sea)	76	1946	
Paid Vacations (Seafarers) (Revised)	91	1949	*
Accommodation of Crews (Revised)	92	1949	*
Wages, Hours of Work and Manning (Sea) (Revised)	93	1949	
Seafarers' Identity Documents	108	1958	*
Wages, Hours of Work and Manning (Sea) (Revised)	109	1958	
Accommodation of Crews (Supplementary Provisions)	133	1970	
Prevention of Accidents (Seafarers)	134	1970	*
Continuity of Employment (Seafarers)	145	1976	*
Seafarers' Annual Leave with Pay	146	1976	*
Merchant Shipping (Minimum Standards)	147	1976	*
U.S. ratified 5	Total 31		In force 21

Source: Adapted from Table C-1, Appendix C.
a Indicates U.S. ratified.

Most of the developed maritime nations, however, have ratified all these ILO conventions and, in addition, have enacted legislation providing for equivalent or superior protection of, and conditions for, seamen than is called for by the ILO standards. The ITF has also successfully supported many ILO recommendations regarding conditions of work for seamen and has utilized such recommendations as standards to judge shipboard conditions.

The key role played by the ITF and its coordination of national seafarers' unions in promoting and winning these ILO maritime conventions and recommendations gained it respect throughout the world as a supporter of the rights of seafarers and as a spokesmen for seamen safety and fair treatment. The ITF's role as the effective leader of maritime workers' delegations to the ILO gave it access to governments and shipping concerns and the opportunity to form a relationship with both. The ITF experience in the ILO as the worldwide spokesmen for, and protector of, seamen's rights won it an immediate audience when it began its FOC campaign, which it initially based upon claims that FOC ships were substandard and that conditions for seamen thereon were not only inferior but well below any rule of decency or fairness. As has always been the case, however, the substitution of lower paid Third World seafarers for the much higher compensated ones from the developed countries was, as it is now, undoubtedly a compelling factor in the ITF's motivations. (The ITF's activities in the ILO are discussed in greater detail in Appendix C.)

EXTENT AND BACKGROUND OF FOC SHIPPING

During World War II, seamen greatly advanced their wages and working conditions because of the increasing importance of their work and because they were in short supply. The United States was at this time by far the largest maritime power and had the highest paid seamen. Thousands of ships were sold by the U.S. government following the war, and shipowners looked for ways to man them at lower wages and with less stringent working conditions than those required by the then extremely powerful U.S. maritime unions.[2] Additional and sometimes more

---

[2] For analyses of U.S. maritime union policies from different points of view, see Joseph H. Ball, *The Government-Subsidized Union Monopoly: A Study of Labor Practices in the Shipping Industry* (Washington, D.C.: Labor Policy Association, Inc., 1966) ; and Joseph P. Goldberg, *The Maritime Story: A Study in Labor-Management Relations* (Cambridge, Mass.: Harvard Uni-

significant factors motivating ship registry in other countries
were, and still are, tax considerations and flexibility of investment. In any case, by 1948, the situation of ships effectively
owned by companies in one country being registered in another
was expanding rapidly. The ITF called this situation a "flag of
convenience." The shipowners termed it a "flag of necessity."
It is the former name that prevailed in the literature, and this
is the one which we use without invidious connotation.

Background of FOC Shipping

Flag of convenience shipping is not a new post-World War II
phenomenon. According to Doganis and Metaxas, "There is ample
historical evidence . . . that shifts of maritime activity from one
flag to another are as old as modern national states and that in
some cases they have even preceded their creation."[3] Carlisle
details the post-World War I history of the development, noting
that Panama's legislation and special relation to the United
States, plus the U.S. government's desire to maintain American
ownership of vessels in the face of legislation that made the U.S.
flag noncompetitive, facilitated the use of the Panamanian flag.
Avoiding prohibition against the use of alcoholic beverages also
contributed to passenger and cruise ship transfers, as did further
legislation in Panama when it became apparent that this was a
source of revenue for the small republic. As a result, other
nations also transferred ships to this flag.[4] International maritime law has quite consistently supported the theory that the
registry, not the ownership—which historically as now is often
difficult to discern—determines the country to which the ship
belongs.[5] The growth of the maritime flag "is an undoubted
attribute of sovereignty."[6]

---

versity Press, 1958). For a case study of how these unions helped to destroy
jobs in the industry, see David Kuechle, *The Story of the Savannah: An
Episode in Maritime Labor-Management Relations* (Cambridge, Mass.: Harvard University Press, 1971).

[3] R.S. Doganis and B.N. Metaxas, *The Impact of Flags of Convenience*
(London: Polytectronic of Central London and Ealing Technical College,
1975), Transport Studies Group, Research Report No. 3, p. 7.

[4] Rodney Carlisle, *Sovereignty for Sale* (Annapolis, Md.: Naval Institute
Press, 1981), Chapters 1 and 2.

[5] For a detailed analysis of the development of maritime law in this
regard, see B.A. Boczek, *Flags of Convenience, An International Legal Study*
(Cambridge, Mass.: Harvard University Press, 1962).

[6] Quotation on chapter head from Carlisle, p. iv.

By 1939, *Lloyd's Register of Shipping* showed 159 ships under the Panamanian registry, as compared with 24 in 1924. These included not only American, but British, German, Greek, Norweigan, and Spanish, among others, the last as a "flag of refuge" from Spain's Civil War.[7] World War II saw an expansion of the FOC fleet as Europeans sought refuge and as Americans, with the active support of the Roosevelt Administration, acted to avoid U.S. neutrality legislation. A total of 267 vessels of over 1,000 gross registered tons (GRT) were transferred from the U.S. flag: 126 to Britain; 63 to Panama; and the balance to France and neutrals.[8] Throughout the war, Panamanian-registered vessels worked both sides, but the extent to which American control was exerted is demonstrated by the fact that many vessels were armed and over 150 ships were sunk or captured with more than 1,500 crewmen lost. The most valuable of the ships lost were twenty-five Esso (Exxon) tankers.[9] Meanwhile, Honduras, "which in the 1920s and 1930s had developed a small fleet largely under the ownership of United Fruit Company and other banana companies, vied with Panama to attract the flood of shipping" by recodifying its laws.[10]

The war period demonstrated the efficiency of FOC, and especially Panamanian registry. After the war, the Panamanian registry grew; American tanker owners, in particular, expanded their use of it. U.S. unions vigorously protested the flag transfers and were soon joined in their opposition by European unions. Meanwhile, the U.S. Maritime Commission was anxious to dispose of the huge surplus fleet built up during the war and needed foreign sales, including Panamanian, to do so. Because labor opposition to the FOC registries was concentrated on Panama, however, and because Panama was undergoing an internal upheaval, a new FOC country was sought. Former Secretary of State Edward R. Stettinius, Jr., long an advocate of aiding underdeveloped countries, persuaded Liberia to enact appropriate legislation and petroleum companies to register their ships there. The Greek owner, Stravos Niarchos, registered the first ship under the new Liberian code in 1949, although two other vessels had

---

[7] Carlisle, *Sovereignty for Sale*, pp. 56-70.

[8] *Ibid.*, p. 83.

[9] *Ibid.*, pp. 74-77.

[10] *Ibid.*, p. 99.

been registered by special arrangements in 1948. From its inception, tankers have occupied the majority of the Liberian registry.[11]

Extent of FOC Shipping

Table III-2 and Figure III-1 show the growth of FOC shipping since 1939 and particularly since World War II, together with the principal countries of FOC registry. Between 1947 and 1982, the FOC vessels increased their share of gross registered tonnage (GRT) from approximately 3 percent to 27 percent. Also as shown in Table III-2 and Figure III-1, Liberia rapidly relegated Panama to second place in ship registries as it grew impressively in this regard. Honduras' registry grew "from 27 ships in 1939 to 82 in 1949, but the core of the registry remained United Fruit Company vessels." [12] Later, Honduras eliminated the fiscal attractiveness for ship registry:

> Because Honduras expected actual manning of its ships by Hondurans, organized in a government-recognized union, and also required ownership to be vested in a Honduran corporation, the system had drawn only a scattering of owners besides the United Fruit Company, which had considerable interests in Honduras.[13]

Costa Rica was an important FOC registry during and immediately after World War II; but it became a haven for drug and arms smugglers, causing it to abolish the system by 1982.[14] Somalia and Lebanon opened their doors to FOC registry, but wars eliminated their attractiveness. Singapore, Cyprus, and some Pacific, Asian, Caribbean, and other countries have joined the FOC nations, and other countries have attempted to do so without success.[15]

Table III-3 attempts to demonstrate the "details of the real ownership and management of vessels flying flags of convenience," [16]

---

[11] *Ibid.*, Chapter 7.

[12] *Ibid.*, p. 132.

[13] *Ibid.*, p. 136.

[14] *Ibid.*, p. 132.

[15] Doganis and Metaxas, *The Impact of Flags of Convenience*, p. 16, mention Morocco, San Marino, Haiti, and Sierra Leone in the tried but failed category. St. Vincent and the Grenadines, St. Lucia, Bahamas, Caymen Islands, Netherland Antilles, Vanuatu (formerly New Hebrides), and most recently, Uruguay and Sri Lanka have all entered the field, but none is a significant factor except Bahamas and Sri Lanka.

[16] "Flags of Convenience: Who Owns What?," *Lloyd's Shipping Economist*, May 1982, p. 5.

TABLE III-2
FOC Shipping, 1939-1982

| Year | Liberia | | Panama | | Honduras | | Cyprus | | Singapore | | FOC Total ** | World Total | FOC as % of World Tonnage |
	Ships	Million GRTs	Ships	Million GRTs	Ships	Million GRTs	Ships	Million GRTs	Ships	Million GRTs	Million GRTs	Million GRTs	
1939	—	—	159	0.72	32	0.06	—	—	—	—	0.80	69.44	1.2
1947	—	—	372	1.71	78	0.28	—	—	—	—	1.99	—	—
1948	—	—	518	2.72	93	0.32	—	—	—	—	3.04	80.29	3.8
1949	5	0.05	536	3.02	123	0.41	—	—	—	—	3.47	82.57	4.2
1950	22	0.24	573	3.36	142	0.52	—	—	—	—	4.12	84.58	4.9
1951	69	0.59	607	3.61	152	0.51	—	—	—	—	4.71	87.24	5.4
1952	105	0.90	606	3.74	145	0.47	—	—	—	—	5.11	90.18	5.7
1953	153	1.43	593	3.91	146	0.47	—	—	—	—	5.96	93.35	6.4
1954	245	2.38	595	4.09	130	0.44	—	—	—	—	7.11	97.42	7.3
1955	436	4.00	555	3.92	117	0.43	—	—	—	—	8.69	100.57	6.6
1956	582	5.58	556	3.92	106	0.39	—	—	—	—	10.40	105.20	9.9
1957	743	7.47	580	4.13	94	0.37	—	—	—	—	12.49	110.27	11.3
1958	975	10.08	602	4.26	89	0.34	—	—	—	—	15.27	118.03	12.9
1959	1085	11.94	639	4.58	78	0.20	—	—	—	—	17.01	124.94	13.6
1960	977	11.28	607	4.23	59	0.15	—	—	—	—	16.01	129.77	12.4
1961	903	10.93	601	4.05	58	0.12	—	—	—	—	15.65	135.96	11.5
1962	853	10.57	592	3.85	54	0.11	—	—	—	—	15.28	139.98	10.9
1963	893	11.39	619	3.89	49	0.10	—	—	—	—	16.29	145.86	11.2
1964	1117	14.55	691	4.27	46	0.09	—	—	—	—	19.76	153.00	12.9
1965	1287	17.54	692	4.46	47	0.08	—	—	—	—	22.86	160.39	14.3

TABLE III-2 (continued)

Year	Liberia		Panama		Honduras		Cyprus		Singapore		FOC Total **	World Total	FOC as % of World Tonnage
	Ships	Million GRTs	Ships	Million GRTs	Ships	Million GRTs	Ships	Million GRTs	Ships	Million GRTs	Million GRTs	Million GRTs	
1966	1436	20.60	702	4.54	43	0.07	35	0.18	—	—	26.13	171.13	15.3
1967	1513	22.60	757	4.76	45	0.07	60	0.36	—	—	28.39	182.10	15.6
1968	1613	25.72	798	5.10	45	0.07	109	0.65	73	0.13	32.17	195.15	16.5
1969	1731	29.22	823	5.37	51	0.07	134	0.77	112	0.23	36.25	211.66	17.1
1970	1869	33.30	886	5.64	52	0.06	207	1.14	153	0.42	41.11	227.49	18.1
1971	2060	38.55	1031	6.26	54	0.07	277	1.50	185	0.58	47.68	247.20	19.3
1972	2234	44.44	1337	7.79	58	0.07	394	2.01	281	0.87	56.17	268.34	20.9
1973	2289	49.90	1692	9.57	57	0.07	589	2.94	387	2.00	66.29	289.93	22.9
1974	2332	55.32	1962	11.00	56	0.07	722	3.39	511	2.88	74.70	311.32	24.0
1975	2520	65.82	2418	13.67	60	0.07	735	3.22	610	3.89	90.44	342.16	26.43
1976	2600	73.48	2680	15.63	57	0.07	765	3.11	722	5.48	101.70	372.00	27.33
1977	2617	79.98	3267	19.46	63	0.10	800	2.79	872	6.79	111.70	393.67	28.37
1978	2523	80.19	3640	20.74	70	0.13	793	2.60	954	7.48	113.80	406.00	28.02
1979	2466	81.52	3803	22.32	99	0.19	762	2.35	1031	7.86	116.87	413.02	28.29
1980	2401	80.28	4090	24.19	124	0.21	688	2.09	988	7.66	117.06	419.91	27.87
1981	2281	74.90	4461	27.65	143	0.20	588	1.81	828	6.88	113.13	420.83	26.88
1982	2189	70.71	5032	32.60	172	0.23	557	2.14	849	7.18	115.05	424.74	27.08

Source: Lloyd's Register of Statistical Tables, 1975-1982.
** Each figure includes statistics for the following countries: Costa Rica, Lebanon, Somalia, Bahamas, Bermuda, Malta, Cayman Islands, Sri Lanka, St. Vincent, Vanuatu (New Hebrides), St. Lucia.

FIGURE III-1
Growth of Liberian and Panamanian Fleets

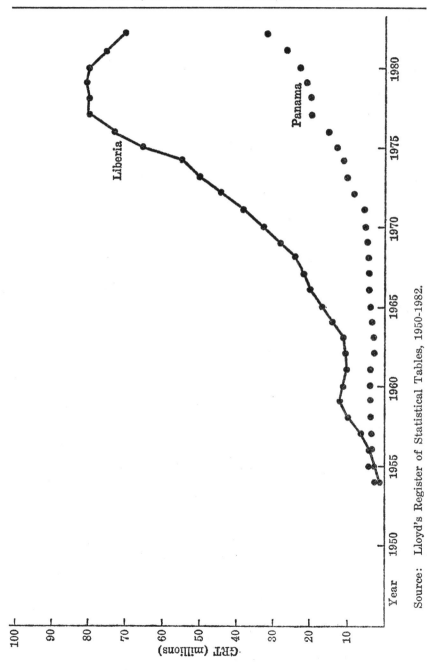

Source:　Lloyd's Register of Statistical Tables, 1950-1982.

TABLE III-3

True Management and Beneficial Ownership of Open Registry Fleets, 1981

Country of Manager/ Beneficial Owner	Liberia (i)*		Liberia (ii)*		Panama (i)		Panama (ii)		Cyprus (i)		Cyprus (ii)		Others (i)		Others (ii)		TOTAL (i)		TOTAL (ii)	
	no.	m. dwt	no.	m. dwt	no.	m. dwt	no.	m. dwt	no.	m. dwt	no.	m. dwt	no.	m. dwt	no.	m. dwt	no.	m. dwt	no.	m. dwt
US	521	50.8	552	53.7	262	3.9	304	7.4	1	*	1	*	8	*	26	0.1	792	54.7	883	61.2
Hong Kong	584	36.1	542	34.5	621	11.6	430	8.5	3	*	3	*	7	0.1	2	*	1,215	47.8	977	43.1
Japan	207	9.6	211	10.7	606	7.8	674	8.4	251	1.5	267	1.7	2	*	2	*	818	17.4	885	19.1
Greece	94	8.7	215	18.1	218	2.6	223	2.8	21	0.1	11	0.1	25	0.5	2	*	560	12.8	707	22.6
UK	141	9.3	40	2.1	89	1.0	11	0.6	—	—	—	—	1	*	12	0.4	276	10.9	141	9.1
Monaco	67	6.6	22	1.4	37	3.7	—	—	—	—	—	—	1	*	1	*	104	10.3	38	1.8
W. Germany	72	2.3	74	2.6	158	2.8	160	2.8	68	0.4	73	0.4	1	*	—	—	299	5.4	308	5.8
UK Based Greek	59	4.0	—	—	16	0.5	—	—	16	0.2	—	—	1	*	1	*	92	4.8	110	4.2
Switzerland	57	3.7	55	3.5	67	0.8	52	0.7	2	*	2	*	1	*	1	*	127	4.6	147	5.3
Norway	72	2.3	116	4.9	23	0.3	26	0.4	3	*	3	*	2	—	2	*	100	2.6	117	2.5
Netherlands	23	1.6	26	1.7	88	0.8	89	0.8	2	*	2	*	2	—	—	—	115	2.5	94	1.9
S. Korea	12	1.2	10	0.8	95	1.2	84	1.1	—	—	—	—	—	—	—	—	107	2.4	84	2.2
Italy	18	1.4	24	1.7	42	0.4	52	0.4	4	*	4	*	3	*	4	*	67	1.9	94	2.0
Israel	16	1.5	24	1.7	7	0.2	7	0.2	—	—	1	*	1	*	1	*	24	1.7	33	—
Singapore	19	0.6	—	—	120	0.7	—	—	1	*	—	—	—	—	—	—	140	1.3	—	—
US Based Greek	25	1.2	—	—	8	0.1	—	—	1	*	—	—	—	—	—	—	84	1.2	77	1.2
Indonesia	21	0.4	26	0.5	54	0.7	51	0.7	—	—	—	—	4	*	—	—	75	1.1	—	—
Canada	13	1.0	—	—	8	*	—	—	—	—	—	—	—	—	—	—	25	1.0	—	—
China	—	—	1	*	—	—	107	2.1	—	—	—	—	—	—	—	—	108	2.1	108	2.1
France	28	1.0	12	1.1	—	—	21	0.1	—	—	—	—	—	—	—	—	—	—	33	1.3
Unidentified	76	2.7	28	1.0	211	2.0	211	2.0	42	0.2	42	0.2	7	*	7	*	288	3.3	288	8.0
Unspecified	—	—	107	4.0	171	1.9	176	1.9	—	—	—	—	—	—	—	—	247	4.6	283	5.9
60 countries managing less than 1m. dwt each	92	3.5	—	—	286	1.6	—	—	32	0.2	—	—	21	0.2	—	—	431	5.5	—	—
64 countries beneficially owning less than 0.5%	—	—	182	5.5	—	—	426	3.2	—	—	38	0.2	—	—	27	0.2	—	—	623	9.1
TOTAL	2,217	149.6	2,217	149.6	3,182	44.5	3,182	44.5	447	2.6	447	2.6	85	1.0	85	1.0	5,981	197.7	5,981	197.7

Source: Reproduced from Lloyd's Shipping Economist, May 1982, p. 5.

Note: Column totals may not add exactly due to rounding.

(i)* True management of opening registry fleets.

(ii)* Beneficial ownership of open registry fleets.

* Total less than 0.05m. dwt.

also termed "open registry" fleets. The data were prepared by A & P Appeldare Ltd., consultants to the United Nations Conference on Trade and Development (UNCTAD). According to *Lloyd's Shipping Economist:*

> True manager is defined as the person, company or organization responsible for the day-to-day husbandry of the ship concerned (as distinct from the manager of the company nominally owning the vessel). The country of management is assumed to be the country of domicile of the true manager. The beneficial owner is the person, company, or organization which gains the pecuniary benefits from the shipping operations.[17]

In fact, these data should be regarded as considered estimates rather than definitive. Such ownership is often difficult to pinpoint because of numerous interlocking corporate layers. An additional factor here is that Singapore is excluded as an FOC country. "This is a result of the statement by the Singaporean representative of the third special session of the UNCTAD committee on shipping that the Singapore registry would effectively become a closed registry when new regulations entered force in 1981." [18] In fact, as discussed below, Singapore remains an FOC country, albeit a carefully regulated one.

Table III-3 therefore probably both understates the extent of FOC shipping and contains inaccuracies. Nevertheless, it does reveal interesting data. The United States, Hong Kong, Japan, and Greece are the major countries using FOC registries, with the United Kingdom fifth and the balance scattered. We shall discuss situations involving ITF action in these and other major areas below.

Crews of Convenience

Parallel to the growth in size of flag-of-convenience fleets and also attracting the ITF's interest has been the growing employment of seamen from developing countries at lower rates of pay. Although the absence of restrictions concerning the employment of national crews has facilitated their employment aboard these vessels, these crews of convenience are not employed exclusively aboard flag-of-convenience vessels. British flag vessels, for example, have traditionally employed Asian seafarers, at Asian rates, on Far Eastern and later, world trade routes. In fact, the

---

[17] *Ibid.*

[18] *Ibid.*

lack of a sufficient number of national seamen has at times necessitated the employment of foreign crews.[19] This practice has
been accepted during periods of merchant fleet expansion by
North European maritime unions whose wages and benefits are
on the average considerably higher than the rest of the world;
yet, in a severely depressed and contracting industry, the employment of Asian seafarers raises problems for unions whose declining membership is largely unemployed.

The ITF's policy on crews of convenience has been formulated
to affect vessels flying what are considered traditional maritime
flags as well as those flying "convenience" flags: "any shipowner
who, without prior consultation and agreement with the bonafide
seafarers' trade union(s) recognized as such by the ITF, in the
country flag of the vessel(s), departs from the practice of manning his vessel(s) with the seafarers of that country, shall be
deemed to have engaged a crew of convenience."[20] Despite the
inclusion of traditional maritime flag operators in this definition,
and occasional boycott activity taken against them,[21] the major
thrust of the ITF's campaign has been directed toward flag-of-
convenience operators employing crews of convenience.

The ITF's claims that it represents these crews, which have on
occasion solicited portside intervention by ITF-affiliated unions,
have been disputed both by unions and governments of developing nations, as well as by shipowners signing valid articles of
agreement with national maritime boards of the crews' home
countries. The development of the ITF policy on flags and crews,
case studies of companies' responses to the ITF's campaign, the
legal responses in various countries, and the current status of the
ITF campaign are all discussed in the balance of this chapter.

---

[19] S.G. Sturmey, *British Shipping and World Competition* (London: The
Athlone Press, 1962), pp. 14, 297. This competition between developed country
and Third World country seamen continues. In December 1982, the British
National Union of Seamen announced: "Fresh attempts are to be made to
end the problem of low paid Asian and African seamen on UK flag ships."
The Seamen, December 1982, p. 1.

[20] International Transport Workers' Federation, *Report on Activities: 1971-
1973* (London, 1974), p. 161. (Hereafter cited as *ITF Reports 1971-73*.)

[21] The ITF reported that the Swedish motor vessel *Delos* was boycotted in
Sydney, Australia, by Australian unions until the owners agreed to pay the
twenty-six member Papuan and New Guinean crew at Swedish rates, increas-
ing wages 633 percent. Swedish maritime unions reportedly boycotted the
British flag *Clan Robertson*, employing a Zulu crew, in Gothenburg, Sweden,
March 18, 1973. *Ibid.*, p. 112.

DEVELOPMENT OF THE ITF CAMPAIGN AGAINST FOC SHIPS

Prior to 1948, contact between ITF affiliates and management representatives in the shipping industry was limited, as has already been noted, to participation in the International Labour Organisation's Maritime Conferences and Joint Maritime Commissions. By the time of its second postwar congress, held in Oslo in July 1948, however, the ITF favored direct and independent action. At the urging of the Dockers' and Seafarers' Sections, the Oslo congress passed a resolution condemning the registration of ships in Panama and Honduras and calling for "an international boycott of Panama and Honduras ships . . . [to] be applied by both seafarers and dockers, . . . [since] it is only through such drastic action that the menace can be eliminated." [22] A boycott committee was subsequently appointed by a joint seafarers' and dockers' conference that met in London in February 1949.[23]

The Panamanian government requested an ILO inquiry into its maritime affairs, and the ITF boycott was not implemented. Following the release of the ILO committee's report in June 1950, a number of shipowners signed collective agreements with the ITF. These may have been the first agreements ever signed between employers and an international trade secretariat. Shipowners generally agreed that many Panamanian vessels in the early postwar period were substandard. Surplus tonnage and low freight markets encouraged a transferral of obsolete tonnage from traditional maritime flags to the Panamanian government, which, by 1947, had registered two million tons of shipping, had ratified no International Labour Conventions, and had no administrative machinery for the conclusion of collective contracts.

These first agreements set for crews of mixed nationality minimum acceptable standards at the level established by the British National Maritime Board and provided for union organization of crews of flag-of-convenience ships and contributions to a seafarers' international welfare fund. In cases where the majority of the crew was of a single nationality, minimum acceptable standards were to be those set by national maritime board agree-

---

[22] Text of the resolution cited in Erling D. Naess, *The Great PanLibHon Controversy* (Epping, Essex: Gower Press, 1972), p. 10.

[23] International Transport Workers' Federation, *Reports 1950-51 and Proceedings of the Stockholm Congress, 1952* (London, 1952), p. 74. (Hereafter cited as *ITF Reports 1950-51*.)

ments of the majority's home country if those levels were higher than those set by the British National Maritime Board.[24] A Special Seafarers' Section was set up to act as bargaining agent for crews employed aboard Panamanian, Honduran, Liberian, and Costa Rican vessels. The ITF's three-pronged campaign policy is outlined in the secretariat's 1950-1951 report:

1. Organization of the crews of Panamanian and suchlike ships in a Special Seafarers' Section to the ITF;

2. Conclusion of collective agreements with owners who are prepared to apply the wage and other standards formulated by the ITF;

3. Compilation of an index of substandard ships against which action shall be taken at every possible opportunity.[25]

A permanent International Fair Practices Committee composed of affiliated seamen's and dockers' union representatives was set up by the ITF's 1954 Congress to replace the original boycott committee. In 1955, a comparison of northern European collective agreements was completed, and studies to examine agreements from additional countries were planned.[26]

Documentation concerning the significance of this early ITF affiliate boycott activity is sketchy. Erling Naess reports only twenty-one separate actions between October 1952 and May 1957. Except for one in Belgium, all of these were taken in the United Kingdom, the United States, and Scandinavia.[27] ITF reports for these years, however, indicate that the number of collective agreements continued to grow. According to one report,

> It has been possible to negotiate the appropriate agreements direct with some shipowners without any recourse to disturbing action or indeed threats of action. These owners, during negotiations, have expressed themselves to the effect that they wished to apply reasonable wages and conditions and they had no objection to entering into collective agreements for this purpose.[28]

---

[24] International Transport Workers' Federation, *Reports 1954-1955 and Proceedings of Vienna Congress, 1956* (London, 1956), p. 77. (Hereafter cited as *ITF Reports 1954-55.*)

[25] *ITF Reports 1950-51*, p. 73.

[26] English translations of Danish, Finnish, Norwegian, German, and Swedish agreements were included in this ITF study. *ITF Reports 1954-55*, p. 74.

[27] Naess, *The Great PanLibHon Controversy*, pp. 13-14.

[28] *ITF Reports 1954-55*, p. 79.

By 1956, much of the obsolete tonnage registered under flags of convenience in the postwar years had been scrapped. Flag-of-convenience tonnage, however, had continued to grow from four million tons in 1950 to over eight and one-half million tons by 1955. The ITF acknowledged this rapid growth and reported in 1955 that fully one-third of the tonnage registered under the flags of Panama, Liberia, Honduras, and Costa Rica was less than six years old.[29] Concerned primarily with the maintenance of its active Northern European and United States affiliates' wage standards, ITF policy underwent further change;[30] except for speculation about "what conditions on board will be like in a few years' time . . .," protests about obsolete and substandard vessels yielded to charges of unfair economic competition.[31]

Coalition of Interests

With their own maritime economies and interests affected by increasing tonnage under the flags of Panama, Honduras, and Liberia, the governments and shipowners of traditional maritime countries, such as the United Kingdom and the Scandinavian countries, joined the ITF in opposition to their continued growth, although for different reasons. Until late 1958, the ITF actively courted the favor of these groups, appointing a delegation to discuss the effect of flag-of-convenience registry "with other interested parties in the international shipping industry" and publishing a pamphlet "stating the problem in terms of the shipping industry itself, the economic effects on maritime countries, and its relation to Western defense through NATO." Prepared in nine languages, this ITF pamphlet was distributed by seafarers' affiliates in November 1957 to legislators, shipowners, embassies, and the press.[32] The adoption of the "genuine link" concept by the International Law Commission in 1956, its subsequent in-

---

[29] *Ibid.*, p. 77.

[30] The close collaboration of United States unions in this phase of the ITF's campaign is evidenced by the opening of a New York office "to co-ordinate the activities of the special section on the North American continent with the activities being pursued in Europe." *Ibid.*, p. 81.

[31] See Boczek, *Flags of Convenience*, p. 69. The Preparatory Technical Maritime Conference, which met in 1956 to discuss the question of flag transfers, noted the change in the nature of the complaints against flags of convenience ships. *ITF Reports 1954-55*, p. 79.

[32] *ITF Reports 1954-55*, pp. 79-81; Boczek, *Flags of Convenience*, pp. 64, 74-75; International Transport Workers' Federation, *Reports 1956-57* (London, 1958), pp. 73, 76-78.

corporation as article 5 in the 1958 United Nations Convention on the High Seas, and the adoption of the Seafarers' Engagement (Foreign Vessels) Recommendation (No. 107) and the Social Conditions and Safety (Seafarers) Recommendation (No. 108) by the Maritime Session of the 1958 International Labour Conference marked the most significant achievements of this temporary coalition of interests.[33]

The idea of a "genuine link," which has never been clearly defined and the validity of which is not recognized in the United States,[34] sought to establish an effective bond of control between a state and ships registered under its flag as a principle of international law. Specifically, article 5 of the UN Convention on the High Seas states, "there must exist a genuine link between the state and the ship; in particular the state must effectively exercise its jurisdiction and control in administrative, technical and social matters over ships flying its flag." [35]

The ILO's recommendation concerning the social conditions and safety of seafarers incorporated the UN conference's formula into the body of its own resolution. The recommendation went further, however, by incorporating many of the proposals first forwarded by the seafarers' group at the Preparatory Technical Maritime Conference in 1956. The Seafarers' Engagement (Foreign Vessels) Recommendation, on the surface also a clear victory for the ITF position, advised states to discourage seamen from crewing foreign flag vessels without collective contracts or provisions comparable to the minimum already recognized by shipowners' and seafarers' groups of European maritime countries.[36] These recommendations, however, proved to lack any real influence or effect. The ITF boycott in December 1958, particularly the ensuing actions by American unions (discussed below) supposedly on behalf of the ITF, dissipated whatever support the ITF had among governments and shipowners of certain maritime European countries.

---

[33] See the discussion in the previous chapter.

[34] See Walton J. McLeod, "The Flags of Convenience Problem," *South Carolina Law Review*, Vol. 16 (1964), pp. 413-16, for discussion of United States position at that time. See also Carlisle, *Sovereignty for Sale*, pp. 154-55.

[35] Text of article 5 of UN Convention on the High Seas quoted in Boczek, *Flags of Convenience*, p. 73.

[36] *Ibid.*, pp. 68-72; International Transport Workers' Federation, *Report on Activities: 1958-59* (London, 1960), pp. 60-61. (Hereafter cited as *ITF Reports 1958-59.*)

1958 Boycott

In conjunction with its portside campaign to conclude collective contracts and its diplomatic activities before international agencies, the ITF's Fair Practices Committee encouraged direct pressure by national affiliates upon the governments of traditional maritime states. When these union representations proved ineffective, the committee, influenced by Scandinavian and United States affiliates, recommended and the ITF congress approved plans for a four-day boycott of all flag-of-convenience ships not carrying agreements acceptable to the ITF.[37]

The ITF's 1958 boycott, beginning at midnight November 30 and lasting until midnight December 4, marked the first attempt by an international trade secretariat to coordinate industrial action by its affiliates on a world scale and to solicit support from other international trade secretariats.[38] Its effectiveness was spotty. The single notable exception was the support received in the United States, where an estimated 42 percent of flag-of-convenience tonnage was effectively owned in 1958 and where American maritime unions were concerned about the consequent reduction in jobs available to their members.[39] The ITF's two largest United States maritime affiliates, the National Maritime Union (NMU) and the Seafarers' International Union (SIU), brought nearly twenty years of jurisdictional disputes to an end and won the support of sixteen other United States unions during the four-day boycott. There is some discrepancy in the numbers of vessels claimed to have been boycotted in the United States. The ITF initially reported that 192 vessels had been detained worldwide, 143 of these in United States ports. NMU and SIU figures, however, indicate only 129 stoppages in nineteen ports picketed. Twenty-five of these were reported in New Orleans, where the boycott was most successful.[40]

---

[37] *ITF Reports 1958-59*, p. 64.

[38] According to Omar Becu, then ITF general secretary, "The International Federations of oil workers [the now defunct IFPCW], metal workers [IMF], and factory workers [presently ICEF] . . . called on their members to take appropriate action to ensure that the boycott also applied to the loading and unloading of tankers and ship repairing." Omar Becu, "Fighting the pirate flags," *Free Labour World*, February 1959, p. 60.

[39] Edward A. Morrow, "72 vessels tied up by boycott in U.S.," *New York Times*, December 2, 1958, p. 27.

[40] Edward A. Morrow, "129-ship boycott is ordered ended," *New York Times*, December 5, 1958, p. 62; ITF General Secretary Omar Becu reported that final tabulations showed "over 200 vessels" affected by the boycott in seventeen countries. Becu, "Fighting the Pirate Flags," p. 61.

Exact figures for Europe are even less complete. *Lloyd's List*
reported that nine ships were affected in the United Kingdom,[41]
one in Sweden, and several in Belgium.[42] Key nonaffiliated
Christian and Communist unions in three important maritime
countries—France, Italy, and the Netherlands—refused to co-
operate with the ITF's boycott.[43] There was no boycott in West
Germany.[44] Asia, except for the Philippines, and Latin America,
except for Cuba and Uruguay, were unaffected. There was no
boycott in Africa.[45] Despite the fact that boycott headquarters
were located in the Dutch seafarers' building in Rotterdam,
Dutch affiliate support was insignificant for reasons discussed
below. The boycott received no backing from either shipowners
or governments. The International Shipping Federation refused
to support it "because it involved a breach of national collective
agreements and, in some cases, a breach of national law." [46]

The Legal and Public Policy of the 1958 Boycott

Whatever success the 1958 boycott had was lost to the ITF in
legal and public policy challenges thereafter. In the United States,
such legal action, combined with the steady erosion of American
flag ships and therefore membership in American seamen's
unions, ended the efforts of the ITF to utilize United States boycotts and labor law in support of its FOC campaign. Likewise,
the ITF found a hostile legal reception in West Germany, the
Netherlands, and Norway. On the other hand, the ITF found no
legal penalties in its path in Sweden and Finland, and later a
Labour government removed obstacles to ITF action in Britain.
Still later, however, the conservative Thatcher government considerably altered the British labor law framework. Our discussion
of the legal situation in various countries is best presented with
the concrete case examples which are set forth below on a
country-by-country basis.

---

[41] According to the *New York Times*, the boycott was ignored only in Hull
because of high unemployment there. "British unions press boycott," December 2, 1958, p. 27; Morrow, "72 Vessels Tied Up," p. 27.

[42] Naess, *The Great PanLibHon Controversy*, p. 62.

[43] Becu, "Fighting the Pirate Flags," p. 61.

[44] Morrow, "72 vessels tied up," p. 27.

[45] Naess, *The Great PanLibHon Controversy*, p. 62.

[46] OECD Maritime Transport Committee, "Flags of Convenience," *Journal
of Maritime Law and Commerce*, Vol. 4, No. 2 (January 1973), p. 251.

PROTECTING UNION STANDARDS IN THE 1960s

The employment of Third World crews aboard flag-of-convenience vessels was an increasing concern of the ITF in the 1960s; indeed, it has always been a concern. In 1959, the then ITF general secretary, Omar Becu explained what was apparent to most sophisticated observers, namely that the protection of union (that is, European and North American union) standards had always been at the heart of the ITF's anti-FOC campaign:

> The main reasons for the growing concern on the part of seafarers' and dockers' unions were that they saw in this growing fleet of merchant ships . . . a strong threat to established standards; and because they recognized that continued development would ultimately threaten the very jobs of their members.[47]

In an effort to respond to the foregoing threats, a joint meeting of seafarers' and dockers' sections held in London, January 22, 1959, evolved a new formula for the conclusion of ITF agreements. The new policy's most important provision stated that "such agreements [are] to be concluded through the affiliated unions of the country in which actual control of the shipping operation is vested and, where necessary, by the I.T.F. Seafarers' Section through its Fair Practices Committee."[48] The Fair Practices Committee met from April 13 to 14, 1959, unanimously endorsed the joint sections' resolution, agreed to implement the new policy, and announced the termination of all previously acceptable ITF agreements. This shift in policy reflected the experience of American maritime unions within ITF councils. Joseph Curran and Paul Hall, then presidents of the two largest United States maritime unions, had been appointed to the Fair Practices Committee in 1958. Because a majority of foreign flag operators were subsidiaries of American-owned companies, the new policy provided for increased organization of foreign crews by American unions. Agreements, previously acceptable to the ITF, had been based upon the wage level agreed to by the national maritime board of the home country of the majority of the crew—for example, Italian wage levels for crews aboard those flag-of-convenience ships employing primarily Italian nationals.

Under the new policy, if effective control was determined to lie in the United States, an Italian crew's wage levels could

---

[47] Omar Becu, "Memorandum on Panlibhonco Shipping," January 1959, p. 2, in authors' possession.

[48] *ITF Reports 1958-59*, p. 64.

be negotiated by American unions.[49] Hall and Curran cooperated in establishing an International Maritime Workers' Union to coordinate their efforts to organize crews of FOC and foreign ships. Their efforts collapsed when key litigation was decided in the maritime employers' favor.

United States Litigation and Its Impact

Initially, United States labor laws seemed to favor the ITF campaign and to provide the U.S. maritime unions with the necessary immunity and legal protection to pursue their aims. Twelve Liberian and three Panamanian corporations were denied injunctions to prevent union participation in the ITF's four-day 1958 boycott. The courts reasoned that injunctions in such labor disputes were prohibited by the Norris-LaGuardia Anti-Injunction Act of 1932.[50] Moreover, in a series of cases, the National Labor Relations Board (NLRB) ruled that the National Labor Relations (Taft-Hartley) Act, as amended, gave it jurisdiction over FOC ships and crews of convenience, and that its role would be defined by the "weight of foreign vs. American contacts" of the subject company.[51] (This was at a time when the U.S. State Department and the Maritime Commission were opposing "the genuine link" which was grounded philosophically on the same reasoning.)

The NLRB's fling into international waters was halted in 1963. The FOC interests had selected cases which presented the best picture from their viewpoint and by intelligent legal tactics obtained the precedent-setting United States Supreme Court review of the NLRB's right to assert jurisdiction over FOC ships and crews. Two of the cases brought before the Supreme Court involved United Fruit company vessels, registered in Honduras, carrying Honduran crews and calling regularly in Honduran ports where United Fruit had major interests. The crews were covered by agreements with a Honduran labor

---

[49] Edward B. Shils, " 'Flags of Necessity,' 'Flags of Convenience,' or 'Runaway Ships'?", *Labor Law Journal*, Vol. 13 (December 1962), p. 1017.

[50] Guy L. Heinemann and Donald C. Moss, "Federal Labor Law and the Foreign-Flag Vessel—An Inversion of the Doctrine of Preemptive Jurisdiction," *Journal of Maritime Law and Commerce*, Vol. 1, No. 3 (April 1970), pp. 430-31. Naess describes the American shipping industry's legal response to American union activity, *The Great PanLibHon Controversy*, pp. 47-83.

[51] West India Fruit and Steamship Co., 130 N.L.R.B. 343 (1961); and United Fruit Co., 134 N.L.R.B. 287 (1961).

union. The third case involved an Italian-owned, Italian-manned, Liberian-registered ship.[52] Rather than follow the regular and more time-consuming NLRB appeal procedure, the American Committee for Flags of Necessity (later known as the Federation of American Controlled Shipping—FACS) and the Honduran seamen's union sought and obtained injunctions from lower courts in the Honduran cases on the rarely used, and even more rarely granted, premise that the NLRB had exceeded its authority in taking jurisdiction over the FOC ships and crews.[53]

The U.S. Supreme Court consolidated the three cases and unanimously ruled in the Honduran ones that it found "no basis for a construction [of the Taft-Hartley Act] which would exert United States jurisdiction over and apply its laws to the internal management and affairs of vessels here flying the Honduran flag." Moreover, the court declared that its "attention is called to the well-established rule of international law that the law of the flag state ordinarily governs the internal affairs of a ship." It noted the discord that would result if Honduras certified one union and the NLRB another, each under different legislation. The Supreme Court concluded that, absent a clear, affirmative direction from Congress, it could not "sanction the exercise of local sovereignty" in such cases.[54]

The third case, that of the Incres Steamship Company, reached the Supreme Court on appeal from New York State's highest court. The latter judiciary had overturned a lower New York court which had granted an injunction to the shipowner to restrain picketing. The Supreme Court did not rule on this aspect; rather, it remanded the case to the New York court on the grounds that the reason for the New York court's opinion, preemption by federal law, did not apply because federal law,

---

[52] Carlisle, *Sovereignty for Sale*, pp. 157-166. Carlisle has an interesting discussion of how the then new Kennedy Administration attempted to support their union friends by inducing the court to distinguish these cases from others in which "a genuine link" was really absent.

[53] The precedent for such cases was Leedom v. Kyne, 358 U.S. 184 (1958), in which the NLRB was enjoined from failing to adhere to the provision of the Taft-Hartley Act which requires that professional employees be given the opportunity to determine whether they desired a separate bargaining unit. Injunctions under this precedent are rarely granted by the courts.

[54] McCulloch v. Sociedad Nacional de Marineros de Honduras, 372 U.S. 10 (1963), affirming both Empresa Hondurena de Vapores, S.A. v. McLeod, 300 F.2d 222 (2nd cir. 1962), and Sociedad Nacional de Marineros de Honduras v. McCulloch, 201 F.Supp. 82 (D.D.C. 1962).

specifically the Taft-Hartley Act, had no jurisdiction over a Liberian flag ship.[55]

In 1970, the Supreme Court seemed to backtrack from this view in the *Ariadne Shipping Co.* case,[56] which involved picketing of a foreign flag ship by a United States union protesting alleged substandard wages thereon. Here the court ruled that the picketing was "arguably" protected activity under the Taft-Hartley Act and therefore state court jurisdiction was preempted. The court ruled that, as the picketing union members were longshoremen (dockworkers), no conflict with the ship's internal order and discipline was involved.

Four years later, however, the Supreme Court laid to rest any hopes of an American seamen's union bid for power over FOC ships. In the *Windward Shipping* case,[57] the court held that picketing of foreign flag vessels by American seamen was not an activity protected by the Taft-Hartley Act, and therefore a state court suit to enjoin such picketing was not preempted by federal law. The court in effect used the same rationale as in the above noted United Fruit cases: absent a clear direction from Congress, it would decide the case in a manner that would avoid international disputes or conflicts in sovereignty.

Finally, in the *Mobile Steamship* case,[58] the Supreme Court ruled that, even though some of the plaintiffs included American grain shippers and an association of stevedores, the NLRB was without jurisdiction over picketing because a foreign flag ship was involved. Hence, the action of a Texas court in granting an injunction against the picketing was affirmed.

Taken together, these cases have effectively ended affirmative support in the United States for ITF boycotts or direct actions against FOC shipping. As a result, American seamen's unions, now greatly weakened by the decline of United States shipping, have concentrated their efforts on political action. The president of the U.S. International Longshoremen's Association is a vice-president of the ITF but his union's power to fight FOC

---

[55] Incres Steamship Company Ltd. v. International Maritime Workers Union, 372 U.S. 24 (1963).

[56] International Longshoremen's Association, Local 1416, AFL-CIO v. Ariadne Shipping Company, 397 U.S. 195 (1970).

[57] Windward Shipping (London) Ltd. v. American Radio Association, 415 U.S. 104 (1974).

[58] American Radio Association v. Mobile Steamship Association, 419 U.S. 215 (1974).

shipping is, of course, directly curtailed by the Supreme Court's interpretation of American labor law.

Expanded Definition of FOC

The activities of the United States unions prior to their legal setbacks, together with "measures taken at this time by the Greek government, to transform the Greek flag into a 'quasi-flag of convenience'," [59] lured many ships to the Greek flag and led to the registration of many newly-built American ships under the British flag. In November 1960, Liberia announced that it had lost some two hundred ships to Greece and other nations in an eighteen-month period. (See Figure III-1 above.) Similarly, American owners, who had placed only 9.7 percent of their investments under British flag in 1959, placed more than 36.9 percent under that flag in 1961.[60] Shipowners threatened to transfer additional tonnage to traditional maritime flags.[61]

In response, a September 22, 1961, Seafarers' Section conference resolved that "flag of convenience registration is not limited to the Panlibhon nations, but applied to registration under any flag for such purposes." [62] For the first time, the ITF declared its right to conclude collective contracts with vessels flying any flag other than that of the country in which effective control resided. Even the British flag, with stringent safety codes, a respected inspection service, strict licensing requirements, and whose National Maritime Board agreement levels had been accepted by the ITF since 1952, was considered a "convenient" registry subject to ITF boycott activity if American owners employed it to remain competitive. The objectives of the ITF were clearly stated in a 1963 Fair Practices Committee press statement: ". . . ITF unions are determined to pursue their efforts to ensure that wages and conditions of seafarers on flag-of-convenience ships are adequate and to continue to work towards the aim of

---

59 Doganis and Metaxas, *The Impact of FOC*, p. 10.

60 Shils, " 'Flags of Necessity,' " p. 1026; Edward B. Shils, "The Flag of Necessity Fleet and the American Economy," *Labor Law Journal*, Vol. 13 (February 1962), pp. 156-57; International Transport Workers' Federation, *Reports: 1960-61* (London, 1962), p. 69. (Hereafter cited as *ITF Reports 1960-61*.)

61 *ITF Reports 1960-61*, p. 67.

62 *Ibid.*

forcing all ships back to the flags of countries in which genuine control lies." [63]

Shortage of staff, difficulty in securing dockworker (longshoremen) cooperation, and the prospect of lengthy and costly legal action prevented implementation of ITF policy except in Sweden and Finland, where boycott activity was legal, the seamen's unions had the full cooperation of militant transport workers' unions, and nonunion labor was relatively unavailable.[64]

The 1963 statement of the Fair Practices Committee is interesting also because it established for the first time the ITF's position on the employment of Asiatic seafarers at lower rates of pay aboard vessels registered in traditionally maritime countries. The press release proposed

—improvement of the extremely bad wages and working conditions applying to seafarers in the Southeast Asian region; and

—prevention of the adverse effects of these substandard conditions on the wages and working conditions of seafarers in European maritime countries.[65]

A proposal to appoint an ITF Southeast Asian representative was passed by the executive board in 1963. A 1964 meeting of the Asian Advisory Council appointed Charles Blyth special ITF representative to Hong Kong to stimulate the development of trade union activity there. Blyth later served as secretary of the Special Seafarers' Section, assistant general secretary, and general secretary of the ITF. He is now retired.

The ITF adopted a policy for Asian seamen in November 1965. The policy, which was reaffirmed by the Fair Practices Committee in March 1968, insisted that Asian seafarers serving on nonflag-of-convenience ships belong to an ITF-affiliated union in the country of the flag and enjoy wages and other conditions negotiated by the union not less than those provided by ILO Recommendation No. 109.[66] When the Fair Practices Committee at-

---

[63] ITF Press Statement, 1963, in authors' possession.

[64] From 1965 to 1968, twenty-seven Panlibhon ships signed agreements with the ITF, all in Sweden and Finland. Naess, *The Great PanLibHon Controversy,* pp. 111-16; International Transport Workers' Federation, *Proceedings of the 29th Congress* (London, 1968), p. 37.

[65] ITF Press Statement, 1963, in authors' possession.

[66] "Employment of 'Crews of Convenience'" (Special Seafarers' Section), *Report on Activities: 1968, 1969, and 1970* (London, 1971), p. 140. See Chapter III, above, for details for this recommendation of the ILO.

tempted to pass a similar resolution in 1972, however, they met with opposition from Indian and Philippine affiliates, who apparently were concerned that the wage rates negotiated by European unions were unrealistic for seafarers from low wage areas and would threaten their employment opportunities.[67] This opposition has continued and is discussed in a later section of this chapter.

The policy for European flag vessels placed Asian seafarers in the same position in which European unions had found themselves when the 1959 policy for flag-of-convenience vessels temporarily gave American unions the power to negotiate wages for European crews aboard vessels controlled by American company subsidiaries. Conflicting interests of unions from disparate wage areas resulted in similar strains in international union solidarity. In recognition of this fact, the ITF revised its policy on both flag-of-convenience and crew-of-convenience vessels, permitting its affiliates to "adopt a flexible approach to the problems of wages and conditions." [68] In no instance, however, are wages, hours, and manning levels to be less than those specified by ILO Recommendation No. 109.[69]

THE CAMPAIGN OF THE 1970s AND EARLY 1980s

Under pressure from Scandinavian unions backed by a powerful and newly affiliated Australian Waterside Workers' Federation (dockworkers or longshoremen), and supported in some measure by public opinion following the widely publicized collision of two Liberian tankers in 1971, the ITF campaign entered a new phase in 1972. In January 1972, the Fair Practices Committee directed a subcommittee composed of representatives of the British National Union of Seamen (NUS), Swedish Seamen's Union, and Federrazione Italiana Lavoratori del Mare, an affiliate of the

---

[67] Kingsley Laffer, "Australian Maritime Unions and the International Transport Workers' Federation," *Journal of Industrial Relations* (Australia), Vol. 19 (June 1977), p. 124. (Reproduced below as Appendix A.)

[68] *ITF Reports 1971-73*, p. 107. The ITF's collective agreement later employed two wage scales for flag-of-convenience vessels, one for European affiliates and one for Far East Asia. These scales, which established basic monthly pay for various occupational groups from master to catering boy, set the rate for able seamen at U.S. $483 per month and U.S. $343 per month, respectively (effective September 1975). See below for a discussion of this issue.

[69] At the time, Recommendation 109 provided for a minimum wage of £25 ($100). The ILO minimum is raised regularly.

Confederazione Italiana Sindacati Lavoratori (CISL), to draft a new ITF collective agreement and requested affiliates in ten key ports to appoint officials to inspect conditions on flag-of-convenience ships on a regular basis. The growth in the number of vessels signing ITF agreements, the steady expansion of the ITF inspectorate, and the increase in the size of the Seafarers' International Assistance, Welfare, and Protection Fund reflect both the renewed interest in and increased effectiveness of the ITF's campaign since 1972.

By March 1979, the ITF claimed in its *Newsletter* that 1,720 vessels carried blue certificates indicating that a special agreement with the ITF had been signed. In addition to certain wages (including rates for overtime, Saturdays, Sundays, and public holidays and for cash compensation for unclaimed leave), hours, and conditions, the special agreement also then provided for a contribution of $144 per man per year to the ITF's Seafarers' International Assistance, Welfare, and Protection Fund. In cases where the crew was of mixed nationality or belonged to a union not affiliated to the ITF, additional fees were levied for enrollment in the ITF's Special Seafarers' Section ($12 per man) and payment of annual membership dues ($24 per man per year).[70] Activities leading to special confrontations and agreements with the ITF are discussed in the following sections country by country. (See Chapter IV for the current fee and contribution rate.)

Port Activities in Scandinavia

Since 1972, when the first ITF inspectors were appointed, portside activity has become increasingly effective. In January 1976, the ITF's Fair Practices Committee announced the appointment of an increasing number of inspectors, and in March 1979, the committee reported the appointment of "a number of new ITF ship inspectors . . . including those in Portugal, Spain, Iceland, and the U.K.," bringing the number of countries with inspectors up to eighteen.[71] These have since been added to as shown in Appendix B.

---

[70] These rates, effective as of September 1, 1975, represent a substantial increase in 1972 rates, previously expressed in pounds, which were as follows: £4 enrollment fee, £8 dues payment, £48 contribution to ITF's welfare fund. A further 7 to 8 percent increase was planned for 1976. See Chapter IV, Table IV-1, for rates over the years.

[71] "New ITF drive on free flags," *Lloyd's List*, January 29, 1976, p. 1; and *ITF Newsletter*, March 1979, p. 33.

These inspectors, who in some cases assume ITF responsibilities in addition to their national union duties, are paid at least in part from welfare fund contributions. When a flag- or crew-of-convenience vessel arrives in port, inspectors board the vessel and request the captain to show an ITF blue certificate as proof that his vessel meets the standards accepted by the ITF. Often no further inspection of the vessel is made. If the vessel does not carry a blue certificate, the inspector informs the ship's officer that portside unions intend to boycott the vessel until an ITF special agreement is signed, regardless of wages and conditions on board. Boycott activity of this type has been most effective in Finland, Sweden, Australia, Canada and, at least until recently, the United Kingdom. The ITF leadership has acknowledged that conditions aboard FOC ships vary tremendously. Thus Charles Blyth, since retired as ITF general secretary, stated: "Among extremes associated with Flags of Convenience, making generalization hazardous, is that some owners are among the best employers in the world, e.g., the U.S. oil companies, while others are certainly the worst." [72]

Nevertheless, the ITF's policies, from the 1970s to the present day, have almost exclusively directed pressure against the flag-of-convenience ships regardless of conditions thereon when the vessel in question does not hold a blue certificate and have almost equally ignored national flag ships even when conditions on such ships are decidedly inferior to those on comparable FOC ships that have been boycotted. The exceptions, as discussed below, occur either where ITF agents have been approached by seamen for assistance or, as shipowners claim often occurs, where ITF agents have induced seamen to press for additional compensation. Despite the ITF's acknowledgement that conditions aboard United States oil company-owned tankers are among the best in the world, these tankers have been targets of the ITF under its anti-FOC policies.

Gulf Oil Corporation. Shortly before the Fair Practices Committee met to reorganize the ITF campaign in 1972, an incident involving Gulf Oil Company occurred in Skoldvik, Finland. On December 29, 1971, a representative of a Finnish ITF affiliate boarded the *J. Frank Drake,* a Gulf tanker docked at Skoldvik to discharge crude oil at the Neste refinery, and requested to inspect the vessel's ITF blue certificate. The vessel was manned

---

[72] Charles H. Blyth, address to Company of Master Marines, London, December 3, 1975.

by a nonunion Italian crew covered by wage standards superior to the ITF minimum at that time. Because the ship held no blue certificate, the Finnish Seamen's Union threatened a blockade in port "until the necessary affiliation fees to the ITF had been made." A local union official at Skoldvik, however, "told Gulf's local agents that the ship could sail on the condition that a letter be forwarded to the Union stating that the required fee payment would be forthcoming." Upon promise of payment, the ship was permitted to sail December 30, 1971. The union threatened to shut down Fingulf's marketing operation unless a check for the fee was submitted by January 5.

Alhough a check totalling $3,230 was forwarded to the Finnish Seamen's Union, Gulf refused to recognize ITF jurisdiction over its nonunion crew or to sign an ITF special agreement. Once more, Fingulf's marketing operations were threatened by strike. A meeting between Gulf officials and ITF representatives was held in London on January 7, 1972. At that meeting, the ITF sought no major confrontation, and it appeared that the action of their Finnish affiliate "could well be an embarrassment to them." Gulf signed no agreement with the ITF, and the Finnish union, apparently under pressure from secretariat headquarters, cancelled the threatened shutdown action "after the Company made assurances that all seamen on the *J. Frank Drake* were paid wages and benefits equal to the Italian standards set by the union," standards which were already in effect and superior to the minimum set by the ITF.[73]

Phillips Petroleum Company. In August 1972, a vessel belonging to Philtankers Inc., a subsidiary of the United States Phillips Petroleum Company, was detained in the Swedish port of Malmo. While discharging its cargo of carbon black feedstock on August 22, 1972, the *Phillips Texas*, which carried a crew of nonunion Italian nationals, received an ultimatum from the ITF-affiliated Swedish Seamen's Union. The union, according to Phillips' Malmo agent, "acting on behalf of International Transport Workers' Federation, London," demanded that Phillips sign a "collective agreement" with the ITF requiring Phillips to contribute to the ITF's welfare fund and receive in return a blue certificate assuring the *Phillips Texas* of immunity from further ITF boycott. This demand was made despite the company's position that wages and working conditions aboard Philtankers' vessels "exceed in every aspect . . . these (ITF) minimum stand-

---

[73] Letter from Gulf Oil Corporation to the authors, September 16, 1974.

ards" and aboard the *Phillips Texas* specifically are "in every way in compliance with the Italian union's standards," and that any payment into a union fund was merely "tribute money." The ITF representative threatened that the ship's master's non-compliance with the Swedish demands would result in the withholding from the *Phillips Texas* of the pilots required by law when leaving the harbor and the tugs that were needed that day because of high winds.

Because litigation procedures would have involved several days, at greater final cost to the company than the initial amount demanded (£1,740, or about $4,350), the company signed the ITF agreement. The agreement was signed August 22, and the *Phillips Texas* sailed the following morning with less than an hour's delay.

The *Phillips Texas'* blue certificate was allowed to expire at the end of a year, and Phillips has had no further contact with the ITF. Interestingly enough, Philtankers had routed one of its Liberian flag tankers, the *Phillips New York*, to Malmo in 1971, and it discharged its cargo and proceeded without incident. Subsequent to the 1972 boycott, the company sent the *Phillips New Jersey*, also of Liberian registry, to Malmo in July 1974 and July 1975; again, the vessel discharged its cargo and departed without incident.[74]

Texaco and Standard Oil of California. Texaco Panama Inc., a subsidiary of Texaco, first encountered the effects of a toughened ITF campaign in the Swedish ports of Malmo and Stockholm in 1972. While docked in the port of Malmo on November 2, the Panamanian *Texaco Missouri* was boarded by two union officials requesting that the ship's master enroll the nonunion Italian officers and Indian crew in the ITF's Special Seafarers' Section. The master refused and was threatened with a boycott by local tugboat crews. A protest note was issued by the master "holding the ITF responsible for their illegal intrusion and for any delay or damage to the vessel or third parties as a result of this boycott." The *Texaco Missouri* sailed with pilots on board but without tugboat assistance.

At Stockholm, union officials were denied access to the *Texaco Missouri*. The ITF representatives then informed the terminal that, unless the required ITF enrollment fees and membership dues were paid, the *Texaco Missouri* would be refused tug assist-

---

[74] Information received from Director of Marine Operations, Phillips Petroleum Company, April 2, 1975.

ance. Nevertheless, the vessel shifted berth the following day, November 5, with tug assistance. The 29,340-deadweight-ton vessel was berthed with a downstream heading in case further tug assistance was denied. Union demands were reduced, requiring payment only for Indian crewmen. On November 6, Swedish union officials announced that no further action would be taken against the *Texaco Missouri,* which departed the next day after generator repairs.

The Swedish newspaper *Arbelet* reported that Texaco had agreed to ITF wages for all Indian crewmen employed on the *Texaco Missouri.* Company officials denied the report, maintaining that, "except for the initial boarding in Malmo when the Master refused to discuss their demands, the ITF was completely denied access to the vessel and no discussions were held with ITF representatives." [75]

In 1974, Finnish maritime unions simultaneously boycotted another Texaco tanker, the 43,000-deadweight-ton *Texaco Iowa,* registered in Panama, and a 78,000-deadweight-ton crude carrier, the *Chevron Frankfurt,* operated by Standard Oil Company of California and registered in Liberia.

On April 29, 1974, the *Texaco Iowa,* which had just completed loading a full cargo of gasoline destined for the United States, was informed that it would face boycott by Finnish maritime unions responsible for the vessel's departure unless an ITF blue certificate were signed for Texaco's entire Panamanian fleet. As the *Chevron Frankfurt* approached its dock at the Neste Oy facility at Porvoo Roads the following day, company officials were similarly informed that, unless Chevron, a division of Standard Oil of California, signed an ITF agreement covering all of their flag-of-convenience vessels, the *Chevron Frankfurt* "would not be given tugs, pilots, and similar services to sail following discharge of cargo." Following negotiations with Texaco lawyers, demands were reduced to cover the two vessels in port only. Both companies, however, still refused to sign an ITF agreement.

Since wages and working conditions on Texaco Panama vessels, including the *Texaco Iowa* which carried an all-Italian crew, already exceeded ITF standards, Texaco officials believed the sole objective of the Finnish action to be "to force the company to pay dues to the ITF and recognize their jurisdiction." Standards for Chevron's Indian crew were established by Indian National Mari-

---

[75] Information received from Marine Department, Employee Relations Division, Texaco, Inc., May 11, 1976.

time Board agreement and negotiated with the National Union of Seafarers of India, an ITF affiliate. For these reasons, Chevron officials also maintained that the Finnish action was illegal and that the ITF affiliates had "no authority to collect funds or establish wages on their [the crew's] behalf." [76]

Finnish unions refused to provide either the pilots or tugs required by law for ships navigating in Finnish waters. Lawyers for the companies applied twice in writing to the Finnish Maritime Board for permission to sail without a pilot. Permission was subsequently granted. The *Texaco Iowa* sailed May 3 without a pilot. A pilot did board the *Chevron Frankfurt*, which also obtained tug assistance, and guided the ship to sea. A total of three days' time was lost.

The International Federation of Petroleum and Chemical Workers, the now defunct petroleum industry trade secretariat, reported that the ITF was asking for the support of refinery workers in a boycot of all Texaco and Chevron tankers. It also reported that the Finnish union wished to call public attention to "irresponsible actions of the operators of the Panamanian flagship, *Texaco Iowa*, and the Liberian-flag, *Chevron Frankfurt*," which "not only risked the lives of the crews of the two ships concerned and the safety of other vessels and their crews, but also risked the possibility of a major pollution disaster." [77]

The actions of the operators in this instance were in fact most responsible. The fully loaded *Texaco Iowa*, which had been shifted from dockside to anchorage, was in an extremely hazardous position at Porvoo Roads. For this reason, the Finnish Maritime Board waived the requirement that the vessel sail with a pilot in Finnish waters. The departure was accomplished before darkness, as the board required, and under excellent weather conditions. The *Chevron Frankfurt* sailed with the assistance of both pilots and tugs. No international action of any kind was taken against Texaco or Chevron vessels by refinery or other petroleum workers. In Australia, however, maritime unions detained a British flag Texaco tanker "for just a little while," according to then ITF General Secretary Charles Blyth. [78]

---

[76] Information received from Manager, Labor Relations, Texaco, Inc., December 31, 1974, and Manager, Labor Relations Department, Standard Oil Company of California, October 22, 1974.

[77] *IFPCW Petrogram*, No. 74-23 (June 7, 1974).

[78] Christopher Hayman, "ITF Hots Up the Flag War," *Seatrade*, Vol. IV, No. 9 (September 1974), p. 4.

Exxon. An Exxon oil tanker, the *Esso Yokohama,* was boycotted in Norrkoping, Sweden, between September 26 and October 4, 1975. The vessel carried a Panamanian flag and a Filipino crew led by four senior Italian officers and several Filipino junior officers. Upon arrival in Norrkoping on September 25, 1975, the *Yokohama* was boarded by a local member of the Swedish Seamen's Union who acted as an ITF representative in demanding that the ship's master sign an ITF agreement and pay initiation and other fees. When the master refused to sign the agreement, the terminal workers, employed by the Port of Norrkoping, entered into a sympathy action with the Swedish Seamen's Union and halted the discharge of the cargo. The master issued a "Note of Protest" to the harbor master on September 26 stating:

> Before all of the cargo which my ship came to deliver was discharged, the operation was stopped by your representatives. Since 1730 hours on 25th September, I have approximately 2,500 Tons of cargo remaining on board my ship. I consider this a hazardous situation and hold you responsible for any damage to my ship and its personnel that may arise from not having been able to fully discharge.
>
> I request that you make the necessary arrangement to receive the rest of the cargo.[79]

The note was ignored, and the ship attempted to leave port. It was, however, refused essential tugboat assistance. Exxon representatives from New York and Gothenburg met in Norrkoping on September 28 to discuss the matter with the ITF union representative and the harbor master. A second "Note of Protest" was issued by the ship's master raising the question of the vessel's safety in port because of weather conditions: strong winds threatened to blow the ship off the pier, and the master warned that the harbor master would be "responsible for any damage to [the] vessel unless [it was] permitted to leave before strong winds again occur[red]." [80]

Subsequent to the foregoing warning, Exxon's New York representative went to London and joined his European colleague for a meeting with then ITF General Secretary Charles Blyth. Blyth's immediate response was that the matter was a local affair and that he had no authority to enter into it; however, when Exxon insisted that there was a safety factor involved in having

---

[79] Note of Protest issued to the harbor master, Port of Norrkoping, by the captain of the *MV Esso Yokohama,* September 26, 1975, in authors' possession.

[80] Copy of second Note of Protest also in authors' possession.

the ship detained in port, Blyth agreed to have one of his assistants in London contact the ITF Swedish affiliate for an investigation. This action presumably led to the end of the boycott on October 4, 1975. When Exxon officials returned to Norrkoping from London, tugboat assistance was made available, and the ship left port still carrying about twenty-five hundred tons of oil.

Interestingly enough, the tugboats were manned by personnel from three different unions, only one of which was the Swedish Seamen's Union. The latter covers the deckhands who stated that they would not participate in assisting the ship's exit, although they did appear for work on the morning of the exit. No ITF agreement was signed, nor were any commitments made on the part of the company concerning future activities.

Swedish Law. The incident raises the question of whether the company could recover damages in court. Such action has never been taken by shipowners in Sweden. Exxon's local affiliate and company counsel advised that it would be futile to institute legal action in the Swedish Labor Court. Although the Swedish legislation then governing collective agreements did not address the question of sympathetic actions supporting foreign primary conflicts, the Swedish Labor Court had determined that such support is not illegal provided a primary conflict does not exist abroad. The amended Swedish labor law, which was heavily influenced by the unions, now permits unions to take sympathy action without restriction concerning previously existing or legal primary conflicts.[81]

In Sweden, the law does require a seven-day notice prior to a work stoppage. Whereas in Norway, neglecting to give proper notice makes boycott action illegal, as discussed below, notice in Sweden is merely an order of instruction, and failure to issue such notice constitutes a misdemeanor. A special clause inserted in the law upon the urging of the Swedish Labor Federation, Landorganisationen i Sverige (LO), however, provides that the obligation to give notice does not apply to unions planning to boycott flag-of-convenience vessels unless the ship's arrival is announced sufficiently in advance to make such notice feasible.[82] There is no legal relief for boycotted shipowners. The only alternative for those companies that desire to discharge cargo in

---

[81] Ake Bouvin, "Sympathetic Action in Support of Foreign Conflicts" (Address at Los Angeles Conference, November 7, 1975).

[82] Folke Schmidt, *Politska strejker och fackliga sympati atgarder* (Stockholm: P. A. Norstedt & Sojers Forlag, 1969), p. 43.

Sweden without ITF certification appears to be that of going into ports where exit is possible without union assistance.

Finnish Law. Shipowners are equally helpless to obtain relief in Finland. In July and August, 1978, the Finnish Seamen's Union and the Pilot Federation boycotted the Lebanese-flag, Greek-owned ship, *Eurabia Sky.* Despite a payment of $25,000, the boycott was not lifted. The company sued in Helsinki Town Court for the lifting of the boycott and the return of the money. The court agreed that the pilots' boycott was illegal since they were government employees, but ruled that the seamen's action was legal since they were demanding a contract with ILO minimums. The fact that the Lebanese-flag ship carried a Lebanese crew with a Lebanese labor agreement was found immaterial, and the demands for the return of the money and the lifting of the boycott were denied.[83]

Regional Boycott in Scandinavia. It is not surprising that Swedish and Finnish trade unions led the movement for an intensified ITF campaign. ITF officials report that, in 1975, 110 ships were stopped in Sweden alone. Since then, any ship without an ITF-approved blue certificate is certain to be boycotted in Sweden and Finland. In an effort to intensify the campaign along regional lines, the Scandinavian Transport Workers' Federation (STWF)—a loosely knit organization of Nordic trade unions, most of which are also affiliated with the ITF, headed by the president of the Swedish Transport Workers' Federation—has for several years attempted to organize a Scandinavia-wide boycott of all flag-of-convenience vessels. The failure of this group to implement a successful boycott illustrates further the critical importance of national policy to the ITF campaign.

In May 1974, the Scandinavian Transport Workers' Federation congress, meeting three months before the ITF congress, announced a Nordic boycott of all flag-of-convenience vessels to be enforced by Swedish, Norwegian, Finnish, Danish, and Icelandic trade unions. *Lloyd's List* reported in July that the boycott, scheduled to begin September 1, would "effectively exclude all black sheep owners from a sizeable portion of Europe." [84] In fact, no such boycott ever took place, although, of course, iso-

---

[83] Translation of court decision in author's possession.

[84] "Convenience flags to face major boycott," *Lloyd's List,* July 11, 1974, p. 1; "ITF launches combined campaign," *Fairplay International Shipping Weekly,* October 31, 1974, p. 9.

lated actions continued in Sweden and Finland unsupported by unions of other countries.

Another effort to launch a regional Nordic campaign occurred on May 1, 1976. Announced by the STWF Executive Board on November 16, 1975,[85] the action sought "to persuade shipowners of vessels sailing under flags of convenience to conclude collective agreements with their crews in order to eliminate the threat to the international wage level which underpayments could contain." [86] The late Folke Schmidt, professor of law at the University of Stockholm, formulated the boycott's legal strategy: "The laying down of work by the dockers should . . . not be regarded as a sympathy measure in support of the crew on a vessel sailing under a flag of convenience. It is primarily a question of a measure intended to support the Nordic Seamen's Union in their effort to obtain acceptable wage and employment conditions for *their* members." [87]

The boycott marked one of the STWF's several attempts to test the legality of sympathy boycotts in Norway and Denmark since 1959, when court settlements in those countries had seriously circumscribed union actions.[88] Potential problems arose in both countries in two areas: the legality of the boycott itself and strict notice requirements. In Norway, the wording of the ITF's collective agreement posed further difficulty.

After consulting with ITF officers, the STWF drew up a "notice of warning" to be issued to all shipowners. The notice informed shippers planning to send vessels to Scandinavian ports after May 1:

> Should you refuse to sign an Agreement acceptable to the ITF and the Scandinavian Transport Workers' Federation, your ship will be placed under boycott when she has entered a Scandinavian harbour. Consequently, the Scandinavian Transport Workers' Federation will call all appropriate members of the affiliated unions mentioned below to take industrial action. You will not be allowed to hire any person

[85] "Convenience ship boycott," *Financial Times*, November 18, 1974, p. 7; excerpt from Swedish Press Bureau, Stockholm, November 17, 1975, in authors' possession.

[86] Scandinavian Transport Workers' Federation, *Nordic Action Programme for Trade Union Measures Against Ships Sailing Under Flags of Convenience*, Circular No. 5, 1974, p. 4.

[87] *Ibid.*, p. 33 (emphasis added); see also "World Roundup: Scandinavia," *Business Week*, December 8, 1975, p. 41.

[88] *Svenska Dagbladet* (Stockholm), November 6, 1975. The ITF reportedly offered to assist the STWF by drawing up a register of shipowner addresses. See below for further discussions of Norwegian law.

to supplement the crew. Your ship will not be handled, towed, loaded or unloaded by any member of these unions or by any worker joining in a sympathetic action.[89]

Four Danish unions, three Finnish unions, three Norwegian unions, and six Swedish unions were listed as supporting the boycott. Copies of ITF policy guidelines on flags of convenience, the ITF's collective agreement, and the special agreement to be signed by owners which promised payment to the ITF's welfare fund and enrollment of nonunion seafarers in the ITF's Special Seafarers' Section, were enclosed with the letter. In Denmark, this letter was supplemented by union-issued notices informing various Danish employer associations of the intended date of boycott in accordance with the provisions of Denmark's Collective Agreement of 1973. Similarly, Norwegian unions were to inform the Norwegian Employers' Association and the Steamship Forwarding Employers' Association of the intended boycott action.[90] Because trade union membership in Norway is voluntary (a position upheld by the Norwegian courts in the 1959 *San Dimitris* ruling discussed below), article 24 of the ITF's special agreement was amended to read as follows in Norway: "All seafarers covered by this agreement who are not members of an appropriate national trade union affiliated to the ITF *may voluntarily* become members of the Special Seafarers' Section of the ITF." [91]

Denmark: Industrial Court Case No. 7745. Despite these precautions by the Danish unions, the Danish Employers' Federation challenged both the lawfulness of the boycott and the legality of the notices of intended sympathy action issued by the Danish Federation of Special Workers' Unions, the Danish Federation of Employees' Unions, and the Trade Unions in Denmark (LO).[92] The Industrial Court held its first hearing May 6, 1976, five days before sympathy action was scheduled to begin in Denmark.[93]

---

[89] Text of letter from Scandinavian Transport Workers' Federation, Stockholm, April 20, 1976.

[90] Scandinavian Transport Workers' Federation, *Nordic Action Programme*, pp. 21, 35-37.

[91] *Ibid.*, p. 39 (emphasis added).

[92] Landsorganisationen i Danmark.

[93] Section 2, article 4 of the Collective Agreement of 1973 stipulated that, prior to a lawful work stoppage, dual notice must be given to the employer or employer group affected. The first notice must be given fourteen days prior to the intended stoppage; the second, one week prior to the stoppage. *Ibid.*, pp. 21-22. Since the first notices were not sent until April 22 and April 23, respectively, and since the Danish LO did not send its second notice until

In Denmark, a conflict between unions or union groups affiliated to LO and employers organized in the Danish Employers' Federation (DAF) was then subject to regulation under the Collective Agreement of 1973. Because foreign shipowners do not belong to the DAF, a boycott of flag-of-convenience vessels by seamen's groups did not fall within rules prescribed by Danish labor law. Boycott action by the Danish Union of General and Semiskilled Workers, the Danish Federation of Special Workers' Unions, or the Danish Federation of Employees' Unions in support of such action was, moreover, subject to the provisions of the Collective Agreement of 1973, including the notice requirements, because the workers involved were affiliated through their unions to the LO and employed by groups affiliated to the DAF.

In its legal action, the DAF maintained that no lawful main conflict could be initiated simply through the issue of four to six thousand letters, that the Danish unions could not demand collective agreements for an entire ship complement, and that the unions could not argue that they desired agreement for their own members because not one member served on the flag-of-convenience vessels concerned. The action, then, was completely outside the scope of the traditional accommodations covered by Danish labor law and could not be declared legal. The court rejected this contention.

In addition, the DAF argued that there was no basis for sympathy action, whether the main conflict was legal or not. Among its arguments, the employers' group cited the January 1959 court settlement that had outlined conditions under which future sympathy actions against flag-of-convenience vessels would be deemed lawful.[94] Assuming a lawful main conflict, the settlement provided:

> the Danish Employers Federation recognizes that the Federation of Trade Unions in Denmark shall be entitled, subject to observance of the notices prescribed in paragraph 2 of the September Settlement, to declare sympathetic conflicts where requested to do so by the International Transport Workers' Federation (ITF) to such an

---

April 30, the Danish boycott could not have begun until May 7 at the earliest. Transcript of the Judgment of 1st July, 1976 of Industrial Court Case No. 7745 (office copy), p. 2, in authors' possession. The 1981 agreement, now in effect, contains the same provisions.

[94] The events leading to this 1959 settlement have been discussed earlier in connection with the ITF's "worldwide" boycott in 1958. The September settlement referred to below preceded the collective agreements of 1960 and 1973, but its provisions regarding notice were substantially the same.

extent and for such period as the ITF might decide. . . . The Danish Employers Federation further recognizes that the Federation of Trade Unions in Denmark shall be entitled to carry through such sympathetic conflicts *to the same extent as they are in fact carried through in the other countries or in a substantial number of Western European countries which are affiliated to the ITF.*[95]

The DAF maintained and the court upheld that not all the conditions of the settlement were fulfilled. In particular, the court ruled: "Since it has not been contested that no parallel actions decided by the ITF have been started in the Federal Republic of Germany, Holland, and England, the notified sympathetic conflicts cannot consequently be lawfully established." [96]

As a result of this action on the part of the Danish Employers' Federation, the STWF boycott failed in Denmark, and also in Norway as discussed below. Actions continued in Sweden and Finland as usual. No action took place in Denmark, and it seems likely that the court's decision has restrained any significant union participation in future regional boycotts. Apparently it is legal for Danish seamen's groups to prevent their members from signing on board flag-of-convenience vessels, but it is unlikely that any Danish seamen are currently employed on such vessels anyway. Without the support of dock and refinery workers, the seamen are powerless to prevent loading and unloading of flag-of-convenience ships calling at Danish ports. The unions in Norway adopted a "wait and see" attitude from May 6 to July 1, 1976, when the Danish case was finally resolved. Flag-of-convenience ships entered and left Norwegian ports unaffected by the much publicized STWF boycott. In Norway, such boycotts have also run afoul of the law ever since the 1950s.

The Norwegian Legal Situation. Unlike the situation in Sweden and Finland, the law in Norway is antagonistic toward ITF boycotts, although Norwegian unions have actively fought the FOC ships. Between 1930 and 1939, fourteen Norwegian-owned vessels were registered in Panama.[97] Norwegian owners, however, "worked out agreements with Norwegian sailors' unions in which the Norwegian scale would be supplemented with extra pay to cover social security payments lost by transfer out of

---

[95] Text of the settlement cited in transcript of the Judgment of 1st of July, 1976 of Industrial Court Case No. 7745 (office copy), p. 7 (emphasis added).

[96] *Ibid.,* p. 16.

[97] Carlisle, *Sovereignty for Sale,* p. 61.

Norwegian registry." [98] Such arrangements have typified relations in Norway. Although boycott action has occurred there, it is inhibited by the Boycott Act, December 5, 1947, Section 2(d), which has effectively blocked much ITF activity. In 1959, the Norwegian high court ordered the Norwegian Seamen's Union and the Transport Workers' Union to pay jointly the equivalent of £ 2,894.9 plus 4 percent interest from June 15, 1955, and an additional NKr 2,000 to the Cia Naviera Somelga because of an illegal stoppage of that company's ship, the *San Dimitris*. In particular, failure to give proper notice makes boycott action illegal. [99]

Norwegian unions made another major effort to expand their boycott privileges with the *Nawala* case. The Norwegian Seamen's Union, the Transport Workers' Union, and other unions, backed by the STWF, boycotted the Hong Kong-owned and United States-managed ship the *Nawala* at Narvik from June 30 to July 19, 1979. A Hong Kong crew covered by a Hong Kong agreement was in effect. The ship had previously been boycotted in the United Kingdom. Both the Narvik Municipal Court and the Court of Appeal found that boycott illegal because 1) the demand for an ITF agreement with back pay covered periods before the *Nawala* arrived in Norway, and 2) the two-months notice of a change in wages required by the Norwegian shipping labor agreement was not given. The shipowners were awarded damages of NKr 36,673. [100]

After the decision in this case, Norwegian unions announced that they would seek to have the governing laws amended, but no legislative changes occurred. Then, in February 1983, the Norwegian Parliament reduced manning levels by 25 to 30 percent on all of that country's flag vessels of 200 GRT or more. The object was to make such vessels more competitive. The Norwegian unions protested but accepted the regulations. At an ITF European Seafarers' Conference a statement was issued recommending that the new Norwegian law be fought for fear

---

[98] *Ibid.*, p. 69.

[99] English translations of the Oslo City Court's decision (December 21, 1957), the Eidsivating Court of Appeal's decision (January 24, 1959), and the Supreme Court of Norway's decision (November 5, 1959), are in the Industrial Research Unit library. See also Naess, *The Great PanLibHon Controversy*, p. 13.

[100] English translations of the Municipal Court and Court of Appeal decisions are in the Industrial Research Unit library.

that other nations would follow suit. (The Greek government, as we note below, is in fact moving similarly in regard to manning levels.) Despite boycott threats however, it is unlikely that any ITF action will occur as long as the Norwegian seafarers do not strike.[101]

Boycotts are thus not likely in Norwegian ports. They do occur, but not often. When they do, it is usually because shipowners are unwilling either to risk the time and money loss caused by being delayed or to risk reprisal elsewhere if they fight for their rights.

Netherlands Law and Cases

Legislation in the Netherlands is also hostile to ITF boycotts. The first key case arose out of the 1958 ITF general boycott. The Dutch affiliate of the ITF, a member union of the then socialist federation Nederlands Verbond van Vakvereinigingen (NVV),[102] requested dockworkers to refuse to handle cargo on FOC ships and thereby to observe the boycott. Although few dockworkers actually refrained from work, the employer associations petitioned for an injunction which, after numerous appeals, was granted by the High Court (Hoge Raad).[103] The court ruled that the strike violated the employees' contractual obligations and that violations thereof were subject to injunctions and suits for damages except in certain exceptional cases, of which this was not one. As a result of this case, it is relatively unusual for the ITF to take boycott action against FOC vessels in Dutch ports unless the crew of the vessel authorizes it directly. Two more recent cases illustrate the Dutch situation.

Lynda. In February 1981, the ITF inspector in Amsterdam gave notice to the captain of the *Lynda*, a Liberian flag ship,

---

101 "Norway to reduce ships' crews," *Financial Times*, February 22, 1983, p. 20; Tony Gray, "Action is threatened over manning plan," *Lloyd's List*, February 25, 1983, p. 1; Victor Smart, "Crew cuts protests fade in Norway," *Lloyd's List*, March 1, 1983, p. 4; Smart, "ITF pledges to fight Norway's manning cuts," *Lloyd's List*, March 10, 1983, p. 1; Ray Farndon, "Owners reject threats over manning levels," *Lloyd's List*, March 11, 1983, p. 1; and "Norwegians' stand causes confusion," *Lloyd's List*, March 15, 1983, p. 3.

102 The NVV has since merged with the Dutch Catholic Federation, (Nederlands Katholiek Verbond—NKV) to form the Federation of Dutch Trade Unions (Federatie Nederlandse Vakbeweging—FNV).

103 This discussion is based upon John P. Windmuller, *Labor Relations in the Netherlands* (Ithaca, N.Y.: Cornell University Press, 1969), pp. 321-25. The case is cited in Dutch legal references as H.R. 15-1-1960, N.J. 1960, 84.

that it would not be permitted to leave its berth unless the crew was covered by an "I.T.F. acceptable agreement." The ship's agents advised the owners that, because there was no dispute between the crew and the owners and because the crew was not on strike, the ITF could not undertake any action. To make certain nothing would happen, however, the crew was "pacified" by the distribution of a bonus totalling $30,000. The vessel discharged its cargo on schedule and sailed "without any problem." [104]

Saudi Independence. This vessel was flying the Saudi Arabian flag. It had a Philippine crew and was operated by a company headquartered in Greece. In 1981, at Rotterdam, the crew, claiming poor quality food, contacted the ITF which, in turn, called a strike demanding that the crew's grievances be corrected, that an ITF agreement be signed, and that back wages, membership dues, and the welfare fund contribution be paid. The Rotterdam District Court granted an injunction to the owners ordering both the end of the strike and the end of the ITF action. The court ruled on the grounds, first, that the crew-ship relationship was covered by Philippine law which forbids ITF participation or such action and, second, that the employees were under proper employment contracts and had not given proper notice for change. The appeals court affirmed and, as to the ITF role, stated:

> the question arises whether the I.T.F. ought to be treated differently from the crew and especially, whether the I.T.F. contrary to the crew should be judged under Dutch law. In this respect it is important that also according to Dutch law it must be considered unlawful to provoke or stimulate unpermitted strikes and that, since the subject strike was unpermitted [unlawful] . . . . and said strike was provoked or stimulated by the I.T.F., the tort of the I.T.F. is established. It is quite immaterial that the unlawfulness of the subject strike has to be judged according to Philippino [sic] law.
>
> The I.T.F. is engaged at the international level and will therefore have to reckon with rules on strikes of the system of law she penetrates into.[105]

The appeals court also considered the claim that the ITF action was lawful because the wages of the crew were below ILO standards. The court noted, however, that the wages were in accord with ILO recommendations at the time that the employment contracts were made and that it was not relevant that the

---

[104] Agents' reports of events in authors' possession.

[105] Translation of the district and appeals court decision in the Industrial Research Unit library.

ILO had recommended increases during the tenure of the employment contracts. Whether the Dutch court would have found that wages below ILO recommended minima could be a determining factor in such a case is not clear.

French Cases

The largest maritime workers' unions in France are affiliated with the Communist-controlled Confédération Générale du Travail (CGT) and are therefore not affiliated with the ITF, although there has been occasional ITF-CGT cooperation. Unions affiliated with the Confédération Française Démocratique du Travail (CFDT) and the Force Ouvrière (CGT-FO or FO) are ITF affiliates and work closely with it. Although there does not appear to be a regular systematic check on FOC ships calling on French harbors, they often encounter ITF agents. To avoid injunctions against boycotts, ITF inspectors in France work to encourage strikes by FOC crew members for ITF conditions. Such tactics apparently were implemented in the following exemplary cases.

Globtik Venus. In 1977, this ship was threatened with a boycott in England and left the English port for LeHavre, France. The CGT, cooperating with the ITF, boycotted the ship, which was under an FOC flag with a Philippine crew. The owner, an Indian living in England, hired persons from England who went on board and drove off the striking Filipino crew, who were sent home by plane. The ship remained under boycott until $200,000 was given to the ITF for the displaced crew. A new British crew was installed, the vessel sailed under the British flag, and the owner sold his home in England.[106]

Global Med. This Liberian-flag ship was boycotted in 1979 at Boulogne-Sur-Mer by the CFDT working with the ITF and the crew sitting in. The vessel was Greek-owned and carried an Indian crew. Despite a lower court injunction, the French police refused to interfere. The shipowner finally conceded, provided backpay totalling $116,126 for the thirty-two crewmen, repatriated the crew at his expense, and put a new crew on at ITF rates.[107] The CFDT termed the results "une victoire totale." [108]

---

[106] *ITF Newsletter*, March/April 1977, Supplement No. 3/4, p. 1.

[107] Ian Hargreaves, "Liberians attack France over ship boycott incident," *Financial Times*, April 2, 1979, p. 3.

[108] "Boulogne-Sur-Mer: Pavillons De Complaisance: Pas Pour Tout Le Monde," *CFDT Magazine*, No. 28 (Mai 1979), p. 6.

After the release of the ship, the Court of Appeal confirmed the lower court's judgment that the physical violence used to enforce the boycott was illegal. The court ordered the refund of union dues and of the detention damages sustained during the course of the boycott and ruled that the owner could recover any additional wages paid to the crew by the owner under duress to obtain the vessel's release. The court also ruled that, since the ITF agreement was signed under duress, it was totally void under Article 1112 of the French Civil Code.[109] Whether the shipowner did recover the funds is not known. In many such cases, the funds are not sought because the owners fear further retaliation.

Good Faith. This Liberian-flag vessel was boycotted at St. Naire and held up for less than two days in June 1981. Ten crew members, in cooperation with the ITF and the CFDT, demanded improved conditions, ITF standard rate of wages, and the signing of an ITF agreement with back wages, dues, and welfare fund contributions. Discharging of cargo was not affected, as the dockworkers, members of the CGT, did not respect the CFDT picket lines. When, however, the ship attempted to leave, demonstrators prevented it from doing so. The shipowner then appealed to the courts, which ordered the CFDT to cease its boycott under penalty of fines of 100,000 French francs per day for non-compliance. The court also ordered that a survey be conducted to ascertain the amount of damages sustained by the shipowner as a result of the detention.[110]

Sofina Reefer. This vessel was boycotted at Brest in the summer of 1981. Hong Kong-owned, with a Filipino crew, the ship docked on June 15. Almost immediately, eighteen crew members demanded an ITF agreement, retroactive wages, and other such gains. The ITF and the CGT sailors' union supported them. Counsel for the company assured the owners that an injunction would be obtained promptly, not only because of the strike, but because of illegal acts by the strikers, who had placed derrick masts as barricades in front of the holds. Although proceedings were begun, the ship's charterers preferred to settle and did so, for about $125,000 (FF 697,387).[111] As we shall note later, char-

---

109 Summary of decision in Industrial Research Unit library.

110 Translation of court decision in Industrial Research Unit files.

111 Summary obtained from shipowner representative.

terers are usually a force for settlement even at high costs in order to avoid more costly delays.

West German Cases

Although West German law is not favorable to boycotts, the Public Service, Transport and Communications Workers' Union there (Gewerkschaft Öffentlicher Dienste, Transport und Verkehr-im DBG—ÖTV of the German Trade Union Confederation DGB) is a strong supporter of ITF. It has on many occasions assisted (in its words) or fomented (in the shipowners' words) strikes by FOC crews, and if a crew is on strike the German courts will often not interfere.

In December 1978, the *Singapura,* a Singapore-flag ship, was detained in Bremen when three Indian officers complained to the ITF representative (an ÖTV official) that they were being paid low wages. It was released after ten days when the company signed an agreement with the Singapore Marine Officers' Union (SMOU). In November 1979, another Singapore-flag ship, the *Pangani,* was detained in Hamburg but released when the Singapore Organization of Seamen, an ITF affiliate, lodged a vigorous protest. A third Singapore-flag ship, the *Newcastle,* was held up at Hamburg because it had no union agreement. It signed with the SMOU and was released.[112]

Liberian, Panamanian and other FOC ships have been halted with increasing frequency in German ports in recent years. For example, in April 1982, the ÖTV supported a strike, which lasted for several weeks, by crewmen aboard the Liberian flag vessel *Cer Alachrity* at Bremen. The Bangladesh and Pakistani crew demanded ITF wage rates.[113] In early 1983, the Greek-owned Liberian-flag vessel *Glafki,* with a Filipino crew, was halted for over a month at Brunsbuttel at the Kiel Canal. According to the ÖTV, crewmen of this ship, on charter to the Soviet Union to transport Cuban sugar, were demanding £ 67,000 in back pay to meet ITF wage standards. The Liberian Shipowners' Council advised members to avoid the Kiel Canal because of the ÖTV members' control of the locks.[114] At the same time that the

---

[112] Information from Singapore unions, companies, and government officials, interviews, Singapore, July 12, 1982.

[113] Jess Lukomski, "Crew of Liberian Vessel Strikes for Higher Wages." *Journal of Commerce,* April 14, 1982.

[114] "Filipino seamen strike for back pay," *Lloyd's List,* January 13, 1983; "Liberia urges Kiel boycott over ship row," *Lloyd's List,* February 5, 1983, p. 1.

Glafki was being boycotted, an ÖTV boycott was holding another FOC ship in Hamburg, the *Balsa I,* which had a Filipino crew. Here the demands were for backpay of $288,000 to meet ITF standards.[115] This boycott action, however, was set back by decisions of the German labor courts in mid-1983. An injunction forced the release of the *Glafki.* Then the Hamburg Labour Court ruled that the actions of the ITF and the ÖTV in the *Balsa I* case were illegal. The court specifically outlawed any occupation of ships by striking crew members, and strikes over claims of unfair wages by the ITF or ÖTV were found invalid where there is a union contract in existence covering the crew and negotiated in another country. The court declared that if there were wage issues arising from such agreements, the court, not a strike, was the forum to be used. Thus, back pay and welfare fund contribution demands of the ITF would seem contrary to German law in most situations involving FOC ships.[116]

The Greek Situation

The merchant marine is one of the great economic assets of Greece. At its peak in 1981, some 4,000 ships totaling 42,005 gross registered tonnage (GRT) were found in the Greek fleet, making it at the time second only to the Liberian registry in size.[117] As the data in Table III-3 show, Greek shipowners are also major users of open registries. Greek shipowners take a pragmatic attitude toward the ITF, frequently signing agreements and carrying the ITF blue card. Special agreements have also been made between the National Union of Seafarers of India (Bombay), and the Union (Association) of Greek Shipowners governing the employment of Indians on Greek ships. Similar arrangements have been made by the Greek shipowners with other Third World groups,[118] and allegedly the shipowners

---

[115] Edelgard Simon, "ÖTV backs seamen in fight over pay," *Lloyd's List,* February 16, 1983, p. 10.

[116] Press release of German Shipowners' Association (Verband Deutscher Reeder—VDR), April 12, 1983; Edelgard Simon, "Owners welcome strike ruling," *Lloyd's List,* April 14, 1983, p. 2.

[117] *Maritime Transport 1981* (Paris: Organisation for Economic Cooperation and Development, 1982), p. 67; and Victor Walker "Foundering Greek shipowners win vital breathing space," *Financial Times,* February 2, 1983, p. 4.

[118] A copy of the 1979 agreement is in the Industrial Research Unit files.

once suggested to the ITF that an overall agreement be signed between the Greek shipowners and the ITF which would make all Greek ships eligible for the blue card.[119] Nevertheless, Greek-owned, FOC flag vessels have been involved in many ITF boycott incidents, some of which are described in this chapter. A Greek government decree of December 1980, however, provided that foreign seamen serving on Greek-flag vessels could be replaced by Greek seafarers. Moreover, Greek-flag shipowners must pay $30 per month per foreign seaman to a workforce fund for the benefit of Greek seamen.[120]

One hears little of any boycott activity in Greece. The Panhellenic Seamen's Federation (PNO) is very strong but is primarily concerned about jobs on Greek ships. Representing as many as 80,000 seafarers, it has succeeded in raising wages and instituting rules which have made many Greek ships high-cost and noncompetitive.[121] The Greek fleet was particularly hard put by the 1981-83 recession and by the concomitant drop in ocean transport demand. By September 1982, the Greek registry had lost 7.72 percent of its ships and 7.96 percent of its tonnage. This meant a loss of 303 ships and 3.4 million tons, contracting the totals to 3,620 ships and 39.2 million tons.[122]

As a result of this crisis, the Greek socialist government enacted new legislation in June 1983 which provides that only Greek citizens can serve as officers on Greek-flag ships, reduces ship manning, and permits foreigners to serve as seamen up to 25-30 percent of ship crews when Greek seamen are not unemployed. Where that occurs, the foreign seamen's pay is to be based upon his country's wage levels as set forth in agreements between the seamen's union of the foreign crew members' country and the Union of Greek Shipowners. Payment from owners to the welfare fund for Greek seamen and other benefits are also required. The aim was to lighten the owners' costs and to decrease unemployment of seamen; but the legislation also provides

---

[119] This was in the early 1970s. According to the account which we received, the ITF declined the arrangement fearing that it could not be policed.

[120] Leo Barnes, "LDC Seamen Have to be Competitive," *Is ITF Right?* (London: Lloyd's of London Press, Ltd., 1981), p. 11. Dr. Barnes is General Secretary, National Union of Seafarers of India (NUSI) (Bombay).

[121] Walker, "Foundering Greek shipowners . . ."

[122] Victor Walker, "Greek Flag's Survival Tied to Owners Parley," *Journal of Commerce*, December 6, 1982, pp. 1B, 3B.

for compulsory rotation of seamen, to which the shipowners have taken strong exception.[123]

Proposals for this legislation, at first apparently accepted by the PNO, were opposed by one ship officers' union and one deck union, both of which precipitated a series of strikes, and by the ITF. As will be described below, the ITF is very much opposed to agreements giving a lower rate of pay to non-domiciled seafarers and is attempting to phase out such agreements in the United Kingdom and the Netherlands. To that end, an ITF assistant general secretary met with the Greek government and unions to try to alter the proposed legislation.[124] (For more on Greek relations, see South Korea below.)

Other European Continent Situations

Italy, like France, does not feature systematic ITF inspections, but boycotts do occur irregularly. For example, in 1982, the Liberian-flag ship *Revere* was boycotted during cargo discharge at Ravenna. This resulted in the payment to the ITF of $79,563 for alleged back wages, the ITF welfare fund, etc. The crew was composed of Spanish officers and some Spanish members but was predominantly Colombian. In the opinion of the company's counsel, redress under the law in Italy required too much time to be effective.[125]

Among the other European countries, Belgian unions do not encourage boycotts, allegedly because they fear loss of jobs in their ports. Occasional action occurs in Portugal; but because of the political difficulties there, legal redress can be obtained but cannot always be enforced. In Spain, as noted in Appendix B, ITF activity is increasing and the legal situation is unclear, as new legislation has not been fully interpreted.[126] Because of the owners' success in the courts in Norway, Germany, and other

---

[123] An English copy of the proposed legislation is in the Industrial Research Unit library. See also, "Special Report—Greece," *Lloyd's List*, June 7, 1983, pp. 5-6; and Gillian Whittaker, "Owners angered as Greek bill passes," *Lloyd's List*, June 24, 1983, p. 3.

[124] Gillian Whittaker, "Greek cheap crews may be blocked," *Lloyd's List*, February 12, 1982, p. 1; "Special Report—Greece," pp. 5-6; and "Strike begins to affect Greek fleet," *Lloyd's List*, June 16, 1983, p. 1.

[125] Memorandum in the Industrial Research Unit library.

[126] See Mario Gobbo, *The Political, Economic, and Labor Climate in Spain*, Multinational Industrial Relations Series, No. 10A (Philadelphia: Industrial Research Unit, The Wharton School, University of Pennsylvania, 1981), Chapter IV.

countries, and because of the new legislation in the United Kingdom (as discussed in the next section), the ITF may attempt to increase its boycott activities in these other European countries.

Port Activities in the United Kingdom

In 1976, the then Labour government of the United Kingdom enacted amendments to the Trade Union and Labour Relations Act (TULRA). Included therein was a change in section 29(3) which made international sympathy strikes and boycotts lawful. Before the act was changed, a labor dispute constituted protected activity "even though it relates to matters occurring outside Great Britain" if the British workers "are likely to be affected" by the outcome of the dispute with respect to their own employment. (To be lawful, a trade dispute must have concerned one of the subject matters enumerated in section 29(1) (a-g), e.g., terms and conditions of employment.)

Under the original legislation, certain international sympathy boycott actions would normally have been lawful since the terms and conditions of British workers' employment could appear to be affected by the outcome of the dispute. An example of this would be British seamen protesting the fact that a foreign ship employs seamen at wages below the ITF minimum where British seamen compete in the same job market. In many instances, however, it was doubtful that the required nexus could be so easily established.

This situation changed sharply when the amendment to section 29(3) took effect. The amendment eliminated the proviso to section 29(3) so that there was no longer a requirement that the British workers' employment be affected. As a result, the frequency of international trade union sympathy action increased significantly, especially where British union leaders supported the activities of the ITF.

Even before the TULRA was amended, the attitude of the Labour government undoubtedly emboldened the ITF and its affiliates to increase their pressure. Milford Haven, Britain's most important oil terminal, has long been troubled by boycotts. The port's tug operators, who are members of the ITF-affiliated Transport and General Workers' Union (TGWU), issued an ultimatum to oil tanker owners flying flags of convenience in January 1975. The tugmen apparently threatened to refuse to handle ships unless wage scales of the tankers' crews were approved by either the National Union of Seamen (NUS) or the ITF, regardless of crew nationality or articles of agreement already in effect.[127] This type of boycott is effective particularly at Milford Haven, which is located on the southwest tip of the Welsh coast and can be approached only through a narrow, shallow, six-mile long channel from Angle Bay.

Nereide and Nemeo. These two 18-000-ton Greek-owned tankers of Liberian registry on charter to Esso were among the first vessels "blacked" in January 1975 at Milford Haven. These British coastal trade vessels had recently switched to the Liberian flag. Coastal trade is reserved normally for local union standards, if not national flag standards. The ITF contacted the secretary of the NUS's Milford Haven branch, Joe Barlow, who refused to allow the *Nereide* to berth until the vessel registered under a Greek flag. The *Nereide* left Milford Haven for the British east coast without unloading but returned January 22, still under Liberian flag. Boycott was reimposed and was extended to the *Nemeo,* which had arrived the same day. The owners arrived in Milford Haven on January 24 to discuss the situation with Barlow, as well as with the local secretary of the TGWU. The owners apparently paid £700 in back wages to the crew and "gave a written assurance that they would change to the Greek flag and pay the crews under the country's pay scales which are almost in line with international agreement." No ITF agreement was signed.[128]

Exxon. In November 1975, a 250,000-ton Exxon carrier, the *Esso Singapore,* was detained in Milford Haven by the NUS. The vessel was permitted to unload and leave port after a verbal understanding that the company was paying its Italian crew at Italian rates of pay, rates which were 99 percent of the then ITF minimum of $483 basic monthly pay. A company official met officers of the NUS in London and was told that, in the future, more definitive information regarding terms and conditions of employment would be required. NUS officers later approached Esso petroleum officials in London promising not to detain Exxon's ships in the United Kingdom if Exxon's crews, which are not composed of British nationals, would join the NUS. Exxon has always maintained that the conditions on board Exxon

---

[127] "Tugmen in free flag boycott," *Lloyd's List,* January 30, 1975, p. 1; "ITF blackings spread to Britain," *Fairplay International Shipping Weekly,* February 6, 1975, p. 15.

[128] "Underpaid crews—ships are 'blacked,'" *Western Telegraph—South/ West Wales,* January 27, 1975.

vessels match those of the country of the crew's origin and has refused to consider the NUS's approach.[129]

Universe Ranger. In December 1975, a Liberian carrier, owned by Universe Tankships and transporting 273,000 tons of crude oil from the Persian Gulf to Milford Haven for Texaco Refining, was prevented from entering Milford Haven by the refusal of tugmen to assist the vessel until owners agreed to meet with the ITF. Although the *Universe Ranger,* which can enter Milford Haven only several times a month when the tides are high enough to handle the vessel's draught, was under boycott for only two days, unfavorable tides and bad weather resulted in a total of nine days lost at a reported cost of $300,000.

Universe Tankships' representatives met with ITF representatives, including General Secretary Blyth and Brian Laughton, at a hotel in London, January 20-21, 1976. An agenda drawn up by the shipper included safety, manning capabilities, and terms and conditions of employment. The company's strategy was to exhaust the conference by discussing the first two matters and, when the time came to discuss terms and conditions of employment, by maintaining that there was nothing to discuss. After exploring the question of safety, the ITF conceded that there was no complaint about the *Universe Ranger,* which was less than two years old. A long discussion followed concerning manning capabilities, but the company was able to demonstrate that, because their crews had long service records, there was essentially no crew complaint regarding company policy in this respect. The ITF, too, agreed that Universe Tankships had demonstrated good conditions in that area.

Regarding terms and conditions of employment, company representatives maintained that, since the mixed West Indian crew employed aboard the *Universe Ranger* was already represented by a union, the ITF had no right to negotiate terms and conditions for them. The ITF, arguing that the union was little more than a company union, persisted in its demands that the crew be affiliated with the ITF's Special Seafarers' Section and be paid according to the terms of the ITF's collective contract. Company representatives refused to negotiate on these matters. General Secretary Blyth requested that the company consider the ITF demand and respond within thirty days. The company responded by letter nearly a month later, maintaining that it could not

---

[129] Information received from Manager, Fleet Employee Relations Division, Exxon International Company.

speak for the *Universe Ranger*'s union, that it held the ITF responsible for damages, and that further harassment would lead to court action.[130] The ITF, however, persisted against Universe Tankships, resulting in the key litigation discussed below.

New Breeze. Milford Haven has not been the only United Kingdom port troubled by ITF-related union activity. Two further actions took place in 1976 at Cardiff and Eastham. The latter, which led to court action, greatly enhanced the ITF's legal position against owners seeking injunctions in the United Kingdom until later legislation and further litigation altered the situation.

On January 23, 1976, Bank Line Limited, a British company, sold its small dry goods vessel *Rosebank* to Transocean Shipping Company Limited of Monrovia, Liberia. At the time of purchase, the vessel, which was berthed at Cardiff, was renamed *New Breeze* and placed under Liberian flag. The British officers and Indian crew already employed aboard *Rosebank* were retained by the new owners at the same rates of pay. These rates, established by a new contract negotiated prior to the vessel's sale, provided for payment of the nonunion British officers at rates higher than British National Maritime Board rates. Similarly, the Indian crew members were compensated at the highest rates allowed by Indian government policy. The new owners made additional payments to an Indian Seafarers' Welfare Fund.

Before the vessel could be delivered to Transocean Shipping's London agent, Associated Shipping Services Limited, representatives of the NUS at Cardiff approached agency representatives at the port and demanded that the owners of the now Liberian flag vessel produce an ITF blue certificate or be "blacked." *Rosebank*, as a British flag vessel, had not been required to carry a blue certificate. The vessel was prevented from sailing by the sympathy action of the port's lock operators, who are members of the National Union of Railwaymen, the ITF's second largest British affiliate.

Directors of Associated Shipping Services Limited met with union officials in Cardiff on Saturday, January 24, 1976. Interestingly enough, union representatives present at the meeting were district officers of the Merchant Navy and Airline Officers' Association (MNAOA), a smaller ITF affiliate than the NUS.

---

[130] "Supertanker held up by pay row," *Financial Times*, December 23, 1975; "ITF sponsors boycott of VLCC," *FACS Forum*, February 1976, p. 2; and conversations with various company officials, March 2 and 11, 1976.

The union refused to alter its position that the owners must sign an ITF special agreement, despite the company's contention that wages and conditions aboard the *New Breeze* were equal or superior to recognized Indian and British rates and the same as those aboard the *Rosebank*. In addition, the union demanded that the company enroll the six nonunion British officers in the MNAOA at a cost of £20 per man. Associated Shipping Services' director signed the ITF special agreement under protest and paid £2,990.35 to the ITF's welfare fund. No Special Seafarers' Section enrollment or membership fees were required because the Indian crew already belonged to an Indian ITF affiliate and because Associated Shipping did enroll the *New Breeze*'s officers in the MNAOA. Following enrollment in the MNAOA, *New Breeze*'s officers demanded to be paid ITF rates. The company agreed to pay the officers a 20 percent increase in basic wages in lieu of overtime pay. At the following port, the entire crew complement was discharged and a new crew hired. The owners also have considered changing the ownership of the *New Breeze* to invalidate the ITF special agreement and bring pay scales back to normal.[131]

Because the issues of substandard wages and working and safety conditions are not involved, it is difficult to understand the ITF's position in cases like the above, except insofar as this position secures contributions to the ITF welfare fund. The Liberian vessel was not forced back to British flag. Nor did the British officers or Indian crewmen receive long-term improvement in wages. Nor will it be likely that unionized British seamen will in any way gain from the dismissal of *New Breeze*'s officers and crew. The ITF campaign did, however, receive a substantial boost from another 1976 United Kingdom stoppage which resulted in court action granting the ITF and its officers immunity from injunction until the law was amended.

The Role of the Public Policy in the United Kingdom—The Camellia. The *Camellia*, a 30,000-ton oil tanker owned by the Panamanian Camellia Tanker Ltd., S.A. and managed by Wing On Enterprises, a Hong Kong group, was detained by British unions at the Queen Elizabeth II docking complex at Eastham during the period January 29 to February 9, 1976. The vessel was registered in Panama and carried a mixed crew of Pakistani, Indian, and Chinese seamen.

---

[131] Affidavit sworn by director of Associated Shipping Services, Ltd.

Upon arrival at Eastham, the *Camellia* was boarded by an ITF representative who made certain demands regarding previous ITF-related incidents at Haifa, Israel, in which the *Camellia* had been involved. The British ITF representative insisted that the owners pay wages due a Filipino crew discharged at Haifa in June 1975, drop disciplinary action against them, and provide for their reemployment. The following day, John Nelson, secretary of the Manchester branch of the NUS and official ITF inspector, boarded the *Camellia* with a solicitor and received permission to speak with the crew. Upon employment, crew members had signed affidavits promising to have nothing to do with the ITF. On January 20, Nelson returned to demand that the owners sign an ITF agreement, pay the crews at the rates prescribed by the ITF agreement, provide the difference in back pay amounting to $142,987, and reimburse the crew members signed at Piraeus who had paid $400 apiece to a recruiting agency prior to employment. Nelson informed the ship's master that the vessel would not leave the docks until these demands were met. Apparently both tugmen and lock operators were prepared to support these ITF demands.

By the evening of January 20, 1976, the *Camellia's* cargo of crude oil from Venezuela had been discharged; a formal port clearance notice was issued by the port authority the following day. On January 22, the crew refused to allow the vessel to sail or change berth. Following intervention by Nelson, the crew did permit the *Camellia* to shift berth.

Faced with mutiny and with threats of boycott by TGWU-affiliated tug and lock operators, the owner first applied in High Court, Chancery Division, for an injunction restraining ITF-affiliated unions or representatives from preventing the *Camellia's* sailing. The plaintiffs named the ITF and John Nelson as codefendants. In a judgment rendered February 6, Justice Templeman held that the incident constituted a trade dispute within the meaning of section 29 of the Trade Union and Labour Relations Act (TULRA) 1974. Immunity from tort was granted to the ITF under section 14 and to Nelson under section 13 of that act as then in effect.

Section 14 granted immunity from tort to trade unions where the actions giving rise to litigation are "done in contemplation or furtherance of a trade dispute." [132] Section 13 conferred immunity from tort liability upon those persons who have induced

---

[132] Trade Union and Labour Relations Acts 1974 and 1976, c. 52, S14.

a breach of contract of employment if they were acting "in contemplation or furtherance of a trade dispute." [133] As already noted, a trade dispute, for the purposes of the act, was then defined as extending "to matters occurring outside Great Britain." [134]

The court of appeal found it unnecessary to consider whether Nelson was acting "in contemplation or furtherance of a trade dispute." The justices found that Nelson had not induced breach of contract but had merely passed on information regarding the *Camellia's* presence in port. The court based its opinion on the findings of *Thomson v. Deakin* (1952), where inducement was defined as involving "pressure, persuasion, or procuration." Lord Justice James held that although "Mr. Nelson hoped for and expected support from members of affiliated Unions [sic] . . . [those] affiliated Unions were autonomous and not bound to follow ITF policy." [135]

Even more importantly, the court of appeals' decision seemed both to mark a significant departure from previous judicial thinking regarding the granting of interlocutory relief and to make injunctions increasingly diffcult to obtain. In Britain, unlike the United States, the test applied in determining whether an injunction should be granted was not defined by the statute until the passage by the Labour government of the Employment Protection Act (EPA) in November 1975, when section 17(2) of the TULRA was incorporated in schedule 16. Section 17(2) as then written clearly stated that a judge, before granting an injunction against union defendants, must "have regard to the likelihood of that party's succeeding at the trial of the action in establishing the matter or matters which would, under any provisions of section 13, 14(2) or 15 [of TULRA] . . ., afford a defence to the action." [136] Under this law, if the trial court found that the employer could not succeed on the merits of the case because the TULRA then gave the union or the union officers a defense to an action in tort, the court could not grant an injunction. In contrast, the judicial standard, established prior to the passage of the EPA by a 1975 patents case, *American Cyanamid v. Ethican*,

---

[133] *Ibid.*, S13(1).

[134] *Ibid.*, S29(3).

[135] Judgment in the Supreme Court of Judicature, the Court of Appeal (Civil Division), Royal Courts of Justice, February 17, 1976, Camellia Tanker Limited S.A. and International Transport Workers' Federation (A Corporate Body) and John Nelson, p. 19.

[136] Employment Protection Act 1975, Chapter 71, Sch. 16, pt. III, para. 6.

had required only that the plaintiff show "a serious question to be tried," [137] regardless of his chances of winning the case. In the *Camellia* case, the court held that the plaintiff must show "a good arguable case." [138] This standard approaches the United States prima facie case standard. When 1976 British labor law is considered, especially section 13 of the Trade Union and Labor Relations Act, which became law in March 1976, it becomes apparent that employers found in most instances that it was more difficult to get an injunction when "a good arguable case" standard was applied.

The difficulty that shipowners continued to face in Britain in their efforts to obtain injunctions against ITF action is further highlighted by a decision of the House of Lords on July 27, 1979, which upheld a court of appeal decision to overturn a lower court ruling that granted an injunction in the case of the Chinese-owned ship the *Nawala*,[139] the same ship boycotted in Norway, as already described.

Nawala. In June 1979, the ship, flying the British flag and containing a crew of thirty-one Chinese, was designated by the ITF to be boycotted at the British port of Redcar, Cleveland. Dockers and tugmen refused to carry out the boycott and the ship sailed to Narvik, Norway, where it was detained for two weeks before being released under a court order.

In Britain, the shipowners sought an injunction against further "blacking" of the carrier. A High Court judge granted an injunction against ITF action, but this decision was set aside on appeal, and the court of appeal upheld the judge's refusal to grant an injunction.[140] On July 26, 1979, the House of Lords, without citing reasons, dismissed the appeal against the ship's "blacking." Harold Lewis, ITF General Secretary, said, "We have always believed that we were acting lawfully and now we have been vindicated in that belief." Lewis also indicated that, in regard to the flags-of-convenience campaign, "we shall continue to prosecute that campaign with all our vigour." [141] The

---

137 American Cyanamid Co. v. Ethicon Ltd. [1975], Appeal Cases 369.

138 Judgment in the Supreme Court . . . Camellia Tanker Ltd. and ITF and John Nelson, p. 4.

139 "Lords dismiss appeal against ship blacking," *Financial Times*, July 27, 1979, p. 8; see also Ian Hargreaves, "Law Lords ruling this week on international seamen's boycotts," *Financial Times*, July 23, 1979, p. 4.

140 "Lords dimiss appeal," p. 8.

141 *Ibid.*

ITF has indeed done this, but British law is no longer stacked in its favor.

Marina Shipping and the 1980 Employment Act.[142] The Conservative government began its overhaul of British legislation by enacting the Employment Act of 1980. Among this law's provisions were sections 16 and 17 which limit the right of unions to engage in secondary picketing and boycotts. After the 1980 Act had received Royal Assent, a ship docked at Hull and was boycotted pursuant to the ITF's program. A significant difference in this ordinary occurrence was that the contract with the Hull Port Authority was made for the charterers, not the shipowners. Because the dispute was between the shipowners and the boycotting union, while the contract for seamen was between the Port Authority and the charterer, the court ruled the boycott an illegal secondary one.[143] By having a charterer make berthing and service arrangements, a shipowner can thus have a legal remedy in the United Kingdom for ITF boycotts, or he can utilize the provisions of the Employment Act of 1982, as described below.

Universe Tankships v. ITF.[144] As noted above, the ITF and its British affiliate, the Transport and General Workers' Union (TGWU), determined to bring Universe Tankships into line. The result was a surprising legal setback in 1982 for the ITF and one which preceded the Conservative government's 1982 overhaul of the TULRA's boycott sections.

The facts in the case reveal typical ITF action.[145] The Milford Haven tugmen refused to allow a Universe tankship, the *Universe Sentinel,* to depart until $71,720 was paid to the ITF for distribution to the crew members; $1,800 was paid for subscriptions (memberships) of the crew to the ITF (the crew were already members of their country's seamen's union); and $6,480 was paid to the ITF welfare fund. Universe Tankships paid the money, but then filed suit in British courts demanding that the money be

---

142 Marina Shipping Ltd. v. Laughton [1982] (All E.R. 48).

143 The analysis of the Marina Shipping case follows M.J. Sterling, "Actions for Duress, Seafarers, and Industrial Disputes," *Industrial Law Journal,* Vol. 11, No. 3 (September 1982), p. 166.

144 [1982] All E.R. 67.

145 This analysis has benefited greatly from the Sterling article, "Actions for Duress . . .," pp. 156-169.

returned "on the grounds, *inter alia*, that it was paid under duress and was money had and received to their use." [146]

In the House of Lords, to which the case was eventually appealed, the ITF admitted duress but claimed immunity under the TULRA. The House of Lords, however, determined that section 14 and 15 of the TULRA did not apply because this action was charging economic duress, a cause of action in restitution, whereas sections 14 and 15 apply to tort. The question of whether the ITF actions had immunity under section 29(4) of the act was also considered by the House of Lords. It was decided that the demands for back pay of $71,720 and for membership subscriptions of $1,800 were ones in furtherance of a labor dispute involving terms and conditions of employment and therefore protected by section 29(4).

> However, as regards the payment of the $6,480 to the Welfare Fund, the majority were of the opinion that because there was nothing to suggest that a member of the crew of the Universal [*sic*] *Sentinel* would have a right to benefit from the fund, because payments out of the fund did not depend on the relationship of employer and employee, between the shipowner and the crew, the payment was not connected with the terms and conditions of employment of the employees.[147]

Under these circumstances, the House of Lords, in effect, ruled that the ITF demand for the $6,480 payment to the welfare fund was illegitimate and wrongful and that duress occurred. Not only did this contribution to the welfare fund have to be returned, but the case raised a potentially greater problem for the ITF: owners who have yielded to the ITF demand and contributed $200 per crew member to the ITF welfare fund in the United Kingdom can presumably file court actions within the six year limit prescribed by British law and regain the payments made to the welfare fund. No such cases had been filed by early 1983, undoubtedly, again, because of the fear of ITF retaliation. Nevertheless, our information is that the ITF is deeply concerned about this possibility and is no longer requesting welfare fund contributions in British ports.

The Employment Act of 1982. This act seeks to make fundamental changes in the law of industrial disputes in Great Britain. Trade unions are now no longer immune from actions in tort and may be liable for damages and have injunctions issued against

---

[146] *Ibid.*, p. 156.

[147] *Ibid.*, pp. 163-64.

them. Section 29 of the TULRA is amended to define a legitimate labor dispute as one that "relates wholly or mainly to" certain specified matters instead of, as formerly, one that "is connected with" such issues. Moreover, only disputes between "workers and their employer" are now termed "trade" (labor) disputes, and a dispute to which a union or employer association is a party is no longer treated as a dispute of this nature.

These clauses raise the question of whether the ITF may insert itself into a dispute. It could, of course, induce an affiliated British union to do so; but if the employees do not join in the action, the newly amended law does not make clear whether the matter is a trade dispute. If not, there would seem to be no bar to the granting of an injunction and damages. The language of the law would also seem to strengthen the *Universe Tankships* decision in ruling out contributions to the ITF welfare fund.

The 1982 act was in part designed to limit the activities of the ITF.[148] The ITF is in fact rarely the chosen representative of the employees of the ship which it is boycotting, but as in the *Universe Tankships* case, "the dispute is essentially between the ITF itself and the shipowners. The ITF acts through its tugmen and represents, not necessarily the crew of the blacked [boycott] ship, but those seafarers who would be employed if the ITF standard rates of pay were agreed." [149] Clause 18(2) of the 1982 Act defines a trade (labor) dispute as one "between workers and their employer." Since in the *Universe Tankship* case no dispute existed "between workers and their employer," and the tugmen were not employees of the shipowner, it appears obvious that if that dispute had occurred after the 1982 act became law, the shipowner could have secured an injunction in the case and possibly won damages. The combination of the Employment Act of 1980, the Employment Act of 1982, and the House of Lords' decision in the *Universe Tankship* case has virtually eliminated boycotts in the United Kingdom. None occurred during the first half of 1983. These factors also increase the difficulty of collecting money for the welfare fund unless employees of the boycotted ship duly designate the ITF, or its affiliate, as their representative and unless the shipowners contribute to the fund without duress.

---

[148] *Ibid.*, p. 165, noting remarks of the Under-Secretary of State Employment in the Parliamentary debates on the proposed Act.

[149] *Ibid.*, p. 165. See also "The IRS Guide to the Employment Act 1982," *Industrial Relations Review and Report 285* combined with *Industrial Relations Legal Information Bulletin 222*, December 1, 1982.

Australia

Australia deserves special attention in any discussion concerning FOC ships. Not only does this country rank with Finland and Sweden as the most ardent supporters of the ITF campaign, it also boasts an avowedly communist-led seamen's union which, by virtue of its control of the tug boat operators, maintains a campaign of its own that is at least as unrelenting as that of the ITF. The Australian Waterside Workers' Federation (dock workers, or longshoremen) is the key ITF affiliate enforcing the ITF anti-FOC campaign in that country, sometimes cooperating with the seafarers, sometimes working at cross purposes. The background and experience of ITF activity in Australia is reproduced in Appendix A from an earlier Wharton Industrial Research Unit study.

Boycotts in Australia have traditionally been protected by law, and even today the potential for legal redress against them is neither assured nor, often, even likely. Prior to 1974, the only hope for an employer who was being boycotted was to seek relief under the common law of contracts, or trade disputes. A few such cases provided relief, but they were the exception to the rule.[150] Then in 1977, the Conservative government amended the 1974 Trade Practices Act, Australia's antitrust legislation, to permit action against secondary union action; in 1978 this law was strengthened. Because employers in Australia often fear massive union retaliation if they invoke this law, the number of cases brought under it have been limited. Nevertheless, as described below, relief pursuant to this statute has been critical in some situations. The election of a Labour government in March 1983 may result in a change in the law affecting this avenue of relief since immediately after the election the unions began pressing to have sections 45D and 45E of the Trade Practices Act repealed, thereby ending restrictions on secondary boycotts.[151]

Utah International. This company grew from a construction organization to the largest mining concern in Australia, with

---

[150] For an analysis of legal action prior to the 1977 amendments, see J.H. Portus, "Civil Law and the Settlement of Disputes," *Journal of Industrial Relations* (Australian) Vol. 15, No. 3 (September 1973), pp. 281-95. For an account of a successful case brought under this procedure, see Herbert R. Northrup and Richard L. Rowan, *Multinational Collective Bargaining Attempts*, Multinational Industrial Relations Series No. 6 (Philadelphia: Industrial Research Unit, The Wharton School, University of Pennsylvania, 1979), pp. 257-261.

[151] See *Workforce* (Australia) No. 433, March 9, 1983, p. 1.

interests in other counrties. In the 1970s, it was acquired by the General Electric Company, which in 1983 sold it to Australia's largest concern, Broken Hill Properties. Utah maintains its headquarters in San Francisco. Its experience demonstrates the difficulties of operating non-Australian flag ships in Australia. Its subsidiary in that country, Utah Development Company, had a multi-year dispute with the communist-led Seamen's Union of Australia (SUA) over whether Australian seamen should be employed on Utah-operated bulk carriers.

Utah employs Spanish seamen under the Liberian flag on the carriers involved, which, among other activities, transport coal from Queensland, Australia, to European steel mills. According to the company, if Spanish crews were replaced by Australians, annual operating costs would rise by $23,000 for each Australian seaman employed. Utah has negotiated a labor agreement covering the seamen with Euzko Langileen Alkartasuna-Solidaridad de Trabajadores Vascos (Basque Workers' Solidarity), an affiliate of the ITF.[152]

The dispute began in May 1977, when members of the SUA employed on tugs used to berth carriers at Hay Point, Queensland, refused to handle *Lake Berryessa*, a Utah ship. The company then agreed to a number of SUA demands, which, it claimed, increased benefits above ITF standards. At this point, according to the company, the SUA demanded that the Spanish crew be replaced by Australians. After considerable legal maneuvering, Utah filed for an injunction in the Federal Court of Australia, pursuant to section 45D of that country's Trade Practices Act. The Australian government filed an action supporting Utah's request. On December 22, 1977, an injunction was granted forcing the SUA to lift the boycott. An attempt by the SUA to have section 45D set aside was denied by the High Court of Australia on November 28, 1978.[153]

As part of its defense against the SUA's actions, Utah appealed to the ITF to obtain a blue certificate for its ships. It

---

[152] "Utah Development Company and the Seamen's Union of Australia: A Position Paper" (Utah Development Company, July 1978), pp. 2, 4; "Utah's Consortium—The Basic Facts," *The Seamen's Journal* (Australia), February 1978, pp. 38-39; and Larry Kornhauser, "Seamen's Union unlikely to ban Utah vessel," *Financial Review* (Australia), January 6, 1978, p. 1.

[153] The Seamen's Union of Australia v. Utah Development Company, High Court of Australia, 53 ALJ 83 (November 28, 1978). The opinions herein contain a thorough review of the case. For an analysis thereof, see Brian Brooks, "Decisions Affecting Industrial Relations in 1978," *Journal of Industrial Relations* (Australia), Vol. 21 (March 1979), pp. 90-91.

pointed out that it had a contract with an ITF affiliate covering its seamen and that it was paying wages and benefits considerably above the ITF minimum. According to the company, ITF officials responded that they would give the company the certificate, but that no guarantee could be made that the SUA would recognize it. Utah ships experienced no difficulty in Europe during this period.

Despite their successful court fight, Utah continued to experience problems with the SUA. For four years, the company did not send any of its own ships into Australia because the ITF could not guarantee that the Waterside Workers' Federation and the SUA would recognize the blue certificate. Instead, the company chartered out its ships and chartered others, which held a recognizable blue certificate, to enter Australian ports. Finally, in 1982, Utah won a contract to sell coal to India. The company chartered an Australian flag ship which picked up rock from a quarry on Christmas Island, an Australian dependency and therefore an area coming under Australian regulations requiring Australian ships. This ship carried the coal to India and picked up the rock on its return trip. This so pleased the SUA that it ceased harassing the company. Utah could again use its own ships. Meanwhile, however, the recession had induced Utah to reduce its ship complement from thirteen to five.[154]

Prompt Shipping. For almost six months, a number of ships carrying coal, iron ore, and oil to Japan from Australia were idled and/or held up by boycotts. In New South Wales, which includes Sydney, all FOC ships were banned. Finally, in May 1982, Prompt Shipping, a Hong Kong-based company allegedly Japanese controlled, agreed with the Australian unions to put one Australian-manned vessel in the coal trade for every four FOC ships used. Since Australian crews receive six month vacations, this in effect means two such crews receive work for each four FOC ships. The cost is met by a charge of fifty-five cents (Australian) on each ton of cargo shipped on FOC vessels. The agreement specifies that the Australian unions will continue their campaign to phase out FOC ships in the Australian trade.[155] We understand that the real purpose of the fifty-five-cent charge was to put the accrued funds in a new company (Hong Kong/

---

[154] Interviews, San Francisco, March 1, 1978, and February 10, 1983; London, May 7, 1978; and Hong Kong, July 15, 1982.

[155] Interviews, Hong Kong, July 13-15, 1982; "Australians to Man Ships in Coal Trade," *Journal of Commerce*, May 20, 1982.

Australia) which will operate Australian-flag vessels. One vessel apparently began operating under the Australian flag, but the agreement has apparently lapsed.

Ship Repair Demand. On June 10, 1982, an inspector from the SUA, which maintains its own inspection activity while the Waterside Workers Federation handles ITF inspections, boarded the Singapore-registered vessel *Pacific Viking* and conducted an inspection. The vessel's seamen were covered by a Singapore Organization of Seamen (SOS) agreement; the SOS is an ITF affiliate. The SUA inspector identified 100 changes and repairs which were declared necessary to be done by SUA-approved unions before the ship would be allowed to depart. These changes included cutlery, more televisions, a dartboard and darts for the crew, and a complete fumigation. There were no charges that the ship was unseaworthy or unsafe or that the crew was either underpaid or not properly represented. Moreover, an Australian government inspector found no fumigation was needed. In fact, the demands of the SUA seemed to concern "quality of life" issues that could not be their real concern—Singapore sailors do not use darts.[156]

What was apparently behind this obvious exercise in legal extortion was the demand of the Australian unions that a larger share of ship repair work be diverted to Australian ports. Singapore has been quite successful in taking such work, and the Australian unions have demanded more of it. The Waterside Workers have held up ships for the same reason. For example, one Japanese ship, the *Ibaraki-Maru,* had an accident in Port Kembla, Australia, had minor repairs done there, but was held for two more months while Australian unions tried to force its owners to have a complete overhaul. The Australian unions have sent requests to all shippers that use their country's ports notifying them that they expect a share of repair to be done there. Companies that fail to comply with this demand and have all repairs done elsewhere can expect difficulties in Australian ports.[157]

---

[156] Comment of the General Secretary, National Trade Union Congress to one of the authors, Singapore, July 12, 1982.

[157] Interviews, Singapore, July 12, 1982; Kingsley Wood, " 'Viking' owner accepts union repair demand," *Lloyd's List,* June 26, 1982; Vincent W. Stove, "Australian Unions Press for Yard Work," *Journal of Commerce,* January 13, 1983, pp. 24B, 3B; and Kingsley Wood, "ACTU to remind Knutsen over repair campaign," *Lloyd's List,* February 9, 1983, p. 10.

Retaliation for Ship Layup. Early in 1983, the Australian National Line containership *Australian Enterprise* was taken out of service. The SUA promptly put a ban on ships trading from Australia to Hong Kong, Taiwan, the Philippines, and Singapore charging that ships with cheap labor were responsible for the loss of business by the Australian company. First affected were seven ships of the Zim Israeli Navigation Company; five of the Panamanian-flag Hong Kong Islands Line; and four of the Russian Fesco Line. German, British, and Japanese owned ships were soon also involved. The SUA was demanding Australian crews on some of these vessels. The Australian Labour government then pledged $90 million (Australian) to the state-owned Australian National Line if it would reduce manning levels. The unions surprisingly agreed to an average 2.5 person reduction on the line's ships. Negotiations were in progress as this study went to press.[158]

Australia—Final Comment

Australian maritime unions have carried the campaign against FOC shipping—and in several cases, all non-Australian shipping—to the extreme point. The ITF blue certificate or an agreement with an ITF affiliate is no guarantee of boycott-free acceptance in an Australian port. Demands of all sorts which result in expensive settlements are the rule rather than the exception.

In addition, the SUA frequently boycotts ships for political reasons. Thus a ship bound for Chile was held in Brisbane for two weeks to protest against "the Fascist . . . country and its persecution of unionists." [159] Neither the Soviet maritime fleet nor those of its satellites have been boycotted for political reasons, despite the absence of free unions in these countries.

Besides the activities of the SUA and the Waterside Workers' Federation, an Australian Royal Commission has found that some Australian maritime union officials have demanded payoff funds

---

158 Kingsley Wood, "Unions block E. Asia ships," *Lloyd's List,* March 14, 1983, p. 3; *ibid.,* "Australian unions step up blacking campaign," *Lloyd's List,* March 25, 1983, p. 2; and *ibid.,* "Unions agree to crewing cutbacks in ANL fleet," *Lloyd's List,* May 9, 1983, p. 1.

159 "Unions warn on ships bound for Chile," *Lloyd's List,* January 13, 1983, p. 3.

and that unlawful activities are common at some ports.[160] The FOC ships entering ports of this country are certainly at risk.

Japan

The All-Japan Seamen's Union (KAIIN) is unique among Japanese labor organizations in that it is dominant in its industry, rather than being a loose federation of enterprise unions, and in that it has engaged in eleven national strikes. KAIIN and four associations of shipping corporations have long engaged in industry-wide bargaining. As a result, Japanese seamen's wages and working conditions have risen substantially above those of less well-developed Asian countries, and Japanese shipowners (as the data in Table III-3 demonstrate) have become important FOC operators. Since 1972, Japanese companies have increasingly turned to FOC registry to reduce their costs, a move which, along with technological development, has continued to reduce the number of Japanese seamen.[161]

KAIIN has long been a major affiliate of the ITF. The ITF maintains a regional office in Tokyo staffed by a full-time representative who, at this time, is a former Japanese railroad union official. Nevertheless, virtually no actions are ever taken against FOC ships in Japanese ports. The ITF representative recalls delaying at least two ships over the years—one Norwegian and one Israeli—but these delays involved disputes between a national union and a national employer and the ships both sailed after short stoppages.[162] There are several reasons for the absence of ITF effectiveness against FOC ships in Japan.

The ITF has no dockworker or tugboat union affiliates in Japan. Unions in these areas are splintered, some not affiliated to a national federation. Therefore, it is not easy for the ITF or KAIIN to interfere with a ship's sailing.

---

[160] See, e.g., Richard Ackland, "Union pay-offs should be recoverable," *Australian Financial Review*, May 26, 1976, pp. 1, 8; Neil Mooney, "Murder, fires in dock report," *Melbourne Herald*, May 26, 1975, p. 1; and "Union demands on ship agents 'grossly improper'," *The Age* (Melbourne), May 26, 1976, p. 1.

[161] K. Okochi, B. Karsh, and S.B. Levine, *Workers and Employers in Japan* (Tokyo: University of Tokyo Press, 1973), pp. 297-301; and H. Sasaki, *Strategic Factors in Industrial Relations Systems: The Shipping Industry in Japan*, Research Series No. 3. (Geneva: International Institute for Labour Studies, 1976), esp. pp. 28-43.

[162] Interview, E. Masuda, ITF representative, Tokyo, June 30, 1982.

Perhaps more important, Japanese seamen, even when laid off, are paid. They are guaranteed jobs to their retirement at age fifty-five. So, although KAIIN is shrinking in size, its members are not nearly as concerned about the impact of FOC vessels upon their jobs as are their European counterparts.

Japanese shipping companies are, however, very concerned about the high costs of their non-seafaring seamen. They utilize some for dockside jobs and, since 1976, have negotiated with KAIIN for the use of some Japanese seamen on FOC-flag vessels. In return for guarantees that a proportion of the vessels of a company will utilize a Japanese flag crew, KAIIN has agreed to mixed crews, e.g., part Japanese, part Filipino, on FOC ships. In such cases, the Japanese seamen are paid the Japanese wage scale, the Filipinos their wage scale. Since the company is paying the Japanese seamen whether or not they work, it is cheaper to utilize them than to pay them for not working and another crew to work.[163]

The ITF obviously is displeased with the fact that Japanese ports are so open. Their displeasure is compounded by the fact that much of Japan's trade involves Third World countries and the United States, where boycotts are not legally feasible. ITF officials have no doubt been pressuring KAIIN to try to close this opening in the net. At its November 1981 congress, KAIIN discussed the matter and decided to have a study made of the feasibility of having inspectors at its ports. One year later it was reported that KAIIN had decided to appoint a network of inspectors to monitor crew conditions on FOC ships.[164] Because its prime purpose is to increase the employment of Japanese seamen, it is apparent that, at least initially, KAIIN's interest will be directed principally toward Japanese owned FOC ships.[165]

Whether the ITF blue certificates will henceforth be required in Japan and whether KAIIN's new program will succeed are both open questions, however. In the first place, the ITF and KAIIN both lack the support of the dockworkers and tugboat operators, either of whom would seem to be necessary to effectuate a boycott. If the dock or tugboat unions do not cooperate, a KAIIN's inspector's only recourse would be to find something

---

[163] "2 shipping concerns reach agreement on use of seamen," *The Japan Economic Journal*, November 16, 1976, p. 14; and "Japanese seamen offered convenience flag jobs," *Lloyd's List*, February 23, 1983, p. 2.

[164] "Japanese boost for ITF," *Lloyd's List*, December 13, 1982, p. 1.

[165] *Ibid.*

paraticularly amiss on the FOC ship and to appeal to the government for a formal inspection and ban on departure. Our information is that the Japanese government would be loath to take such action.

Second, the law in Japan is antagonistic to boycotts. The boycott of an FOC vessel by a dock or tugboat union would be illegal unless the ship and dock or tug facilities were owned by the same company. In this latter case, a boycott could be legal because the company would then be in a position to alter terms and conditions of employment.

Contrary to press reports, KAIIN appointed one inspector who was approved by the ITF, not "a network." [166] According to our information, the plan is to inspect FOC vessels and then to notify other countries' unions, e.g., Australian ones, so that the boycotts can be handled outside of Japan. Meanwhile, given FOC problems in Australia and the prospective problems at home, Japanese shipping concerns have been transferring registry from FOC countries to Hong Kong,[167] whose unique status is discussed later in this chapter.

ITF AND THE "ASIAN PROBLEM"

The ITF began the decade of the eighties with an affiliated membership of approximately 4.4 million. Almost 20 percent of that membership came from its Asia/Pacific region, and a sizable portion of this 20 percent came from Asian underdeveloped or Third World countries.[168] A large percentage of seamen from these countries are employed on FOC ships, but seamen from India, Bangladesh, and Pakistan also work on British, Dutch, and other European ships, as they have since the early eighteenth century.[169] As seafaring jobs have declined, the European seamen's unions, led by the British National Union of Seamen (NUS), have attempted to force European-flag owners to pay Asiatic seamen the same rates as are paid European ones. This has been resisted not only by the shipowners, but also by the governments and the seafaring unions of the three Asian nations.

---

[166] We have been in contact with governmental and legal authorities in Japan who have provided this information on a confidential basis.

[167] James Brewer, "Japanese owners in bid to beat free flag curbs," *Lloyd's List*, January 26, 1982.

[168] See Table II-4, Chapter II.

[169] Leo Barnes, "LDC Seamen Have to Be Competitive," pp. 1-2.

The role of the ITF in this controversy is discussed below, followed by an analysis of the situation in other Asian countries.

The Indian Subcontinent

As noted, the ITF's strong support of the drive of European unions to equalize the wages of Indian, Bangladesh, and Pakistani seamen has caused serious controversies with affiliated unions from the Indian subcontinent and from several other Asiatic countries. During the 1973-78 period, however, this internal disagreement was partially ameliorated by a unique agreement between the ITF and the International Shipping Federation (ISF).

The ISF-ITF Agreement. The London-headquartered ISF is the shipowners' counterpart of the ITF. Founded in 1909 as a European organization, it went worldwide in 1919. Its membership comprises the shipping federations of the major maritime countries.[170] It maintains regular, if informal, contact with the ITF and is the key employer representative, as ITF is the key union one, at United Nations agencies and at other international governmental bodies such as the ILO.

In May 1973, the ITF Asian Seafarers' Conference declared its concern for the disparity between rates paid to Asian and other Third World country seamen and rates paid to seamen from developed countries. They warned of the "danger of multinational shipping companies holding down the level of wages in Asian countries . . ." Indian and Pakistani union delegates to the conference, however, expressed concern that a significant increase in crew costs might endanger the employment of their members.[171]

At that time, the ITF was demanding that wages on all ships be no less than the then ILO recommended minimum of £48 ($110.36) per month for able-bodied seamen and appropriate differentials for other seagoing personnel. The governments of India, Bangladesh, and Pakistan, however, forbade domestic shipowners registered in their countries from offering more than £32

---

[170] This account of the ISF's functions is based upon an ISF pamphlet and an interview with Mr. R. Brownrigg, Secretary, London, May 5, 1982. Country associations with membership in ISF as of October 1981 were those from Argentina, Australia, Belgium, Brazil, Canada, Denmark, West Germany, Finland, France, Greece, Hong Kong, India, Ireland, Italy, Japan, South Korea, Kuwait, Liberia, Netherlands, New Zealand, Norway, Pakistan, Philippines, Portugal, Spain, Sweden, United Kingdom, United States, and Zaire.

[171] *Maritime Worker*, August 5, 1973.

per month and even threatened to withhold crews from companies that offered employment at the ILO rates.

Caught in this crossfire, European shipowners extricated themselves through an agreement between the ISF and the ITF. This agreement, as revised in 1974 and subject to renegotiation on six months' notice by either party, provided that the ITF would recommend that "no action should be taken concerning matters covered by this understanding" where

1. Asian crews except those from the Indian subcontinent were paid at least the £48 rate;

2. Ships employing Indian subcontinent seafarers and registered in one of the three countries therein "pay the appropriate rate agreed by the National Maritime Boards of those countries";

3. Ships managed by companies that are members of associations affiliated with the ISF which employ Indian subcontinent seafarers but are not registered in one of the three countries pay a rate less than £48 and then pay the difference between that rate and £48 to a welfare fund which was to be established in each country.

The ITF made it clear that it did not regard this understanding as applying to ships which it classified as FOCs.[172]

It is, of course, unusual for governments and unions to insist on lower wages for their constituents. The concern of the Indian subcontinent authorities and unions is, however, easily explained. In a region already plagued by unemployment and underemployment in huge proportions, they fear the additional loss of jobs which would result if wages were placed on parity with those of European seamen. Moreover, they are concerned that wages for seamen—already high compared with those of the bulk of their population—if raised to European levels would create untenable "Islands of Elite" within their countries and cause serious supply distortions and considerable ill will. Finally, they believe that if Indian seamen's wages are raised on European ships, the pressure will be great to do likewise on Indian vessels, thus making the Indian merchant marine noncompetitive. For these reasons, neither the governments nor the unions in the Indian

---

[172] *Revision of Text of Terms of Understanding between ISF and ITF on Asian Crews,* 22nd April 1974. Copy in Industrial Research Unit library.

subcontinent would permit their seamen to be employed by ship-owners proposing to pay such seamen European union rates. Thus, the tensions between ITF and the Indian subcontinent unions have continued to be severe.[173]

The ISF-ITF agreement was in effect from January 1, 1974 to June 1, 1978.[174] The funds turned over to Pakistan were used to create a bipartite charitable trust for the welfare of seamen and their families. Bangladesh developed a deferred credit system for individual seamen. In India, the funds were deposited in the already existing tripartite Seafarers' Welfare Fund, amounting to Rs. 120 million ($116,325).[175]

The ISF-ITF agreement was terminated by the ITF. By 1978, wages of Indian subcontinent seamen exceeded £48 per month, and the ILO recommended minimum had been raised to £102 ($187 at the May 1978 exchange rate). The ITF demanded that all Asian seamen be paid "flag rates"—that is, rates prescribed by the country of registry. The ISF offered a gradual increase in rates for Asian seamen to £102, which the ITF refused to consider.[176] Thus ended a multinational agreement that was probably unique, with possible parallels only in the European broadcasting and recording industries.[177]

ISF-ITF Agreement Postscrpt. Before the ISF-ITF agreement expired, a British government study recommended that the wages of "non-domiciled" seamen be brought to parity with British ones by 1982 "on the basis of three non-domiciled seamen equalling two British seamen."[178] After the agreement expired, the British shipowners agreed for the rest of 1978 to deposit the differential for Indian seamen in that country's Seafarers' Welfare Fund. More than Rs. 16 million ($15,132) was put into the

---

[173] Barnes, "LDC Seamen . . .," contains an excellent presentation of these arguments. See also "British wages for seamen opposed," *Overseas Hindustan Times* (New Delhi), November 23, 1978, p. 5.

[174] Barnes, "LDC Seamen . . .," p. 13; and "ISF/ITF Understanding," ISF press release, May 5, 1978.

[175] Barnes, "LDC Seamen . . .," pp. 12-13.

[176] "ISF/ITF Understanding."

[177] For the situation in broadcasting and entertainment, see Northrup and Rowan, *Multinational Collective Bargaining*, Chapter XVI; and Philip A. Miscimarra, "The Entertainment Industry: Inroads in Multinational Collective Bargaining," *British Journal of Industrial Relations*, Vol. XIX, No. 1 (March 1981), pp. 49-65.

[178] Barnes, "LDC Seamen . . .," p. 13.

fund, but since January 1, 1979, such contributions have been withheld pending a final settlement.[179] Then several events occurred which almost severed Asian country-ITF relationships.

This unusual position of Indian seamen has led to serious conflicts within the ITF's campaign against FOC ships. The relationship between the Indian government and the ITF deteriorated further when the ITF protested the arrest of George Fernandes, former president of the All-India Railwaymen's Federation (an ITF affiliate), under the "emergency" rule of Indira Ghandi on June 10, 1976. The Indian affiliates protested strenuously against the ITF's action and statements. Representatives of four affiliates met in Bombay on August 26, 1976, and adopted a resolution calling for the suspension of the ITF general secretary.[180]

It is in this context that the suspension of the National Union of Seafarers of India (NUSI) from the ITF on October 17-18, 1978, took place. A boycott organized by the ITF against the Liberian-registered *Camilla M* and *Anna M* during September at the port of Glasgow (see the discussion in regard to the United Kingdom) was resisted by the original Indian crew, which refused to sign the ITF contract calling for higher wages.[181] The owners brought a court injunction (later overruled) and were allowed to sail. This action prompted the ITF to demand of the officials of the NUSI whether they had suggested to the owners to bring a court injunction for release of the vessels. A strongly worded telegram from the NUSI to the ITF saying that the NUSI "appreciated the glorious boycott at Glasgow, resulting in loss of employment to Indian seamen on two vessels" led to the NUSI's suspension from the ITF.[182] The NUSI, with twenty-four thousand members, was the largest Indian affiliate of the ITF, and the suspension weakened the ITF's representation of seamen from developing countries.[183]

---

[179] *Ibid.* About £15 million was held by UK shipowners by early 1983 still waiting a determination of this issue. See Victor Smart, "India to be consulted on Asian scheme," *Lloyd's List*, February 25, 1981.

[180] *ITF Reports 1974-1975-1976*, pp. 48-50.

[181] "Camilla M 'still blacked in spite of owners offer'," *Financial Times*, October 11, 1978, p. 11.

[182] Leo Barnes, general secretary, NUSI to ITF, Bombay, December 27, 1978.

[183] Interestingly, another Indian ITF affiliate, the Port and Dock Workers Federation, used the ITF leverage by threatening the Indian government with global boycott of ships visiting Indian ports during the November 1978 major

The ITF then faced the problem of evolving a strategy that, without endangering its campaign against FOC ships, could accommodate the unique and paradoxical problem of seamen of Asian countries like India, Bangladesh, and Pakistan. In the meantime, the Asian Seafarers' Conference met in Singapore on April 28 and 29, 1979, to establish a pro-tem Secretariat of Asian Seafarers, which "will ensure that policies and actions of the International Transport Workers' Federation do not adversely affect the interest and welfare of Asian Seamen." [184] At the Asian meetings, the delegates demanded that "Asian unions be given full and adequate representation on the various committees of the ITF including its Executive Board"; that the ITF flag-of-convenience policy be reviewed "in consultation with unions whose members are engaged on such vessels"; that the ITF Fair Practices Committee be restructured to include "appropriate representation from these unions"; and that NUSI be reinstated.[185]

The Asian conference emphasized that it sought a strengthened ITF and that it did not want to undermine wage standards. Nevertheless, it demanded that ITF policies be carried out so as not to contribute to the shrinkage of employment and not to undermine national collective agreements. The delegates declined to go to a special ITF congress in Stockholm to meet with ITF leaders.[186] The Asians did, however, hold a second conference in August 1979, also in Singapore, which "called upon the ITF to redesign its policies and campaigns and to provide adequate representation to Asians on its various committees including the Executive Board." [187]

Neither the Europeans nor the Asians were anxious for an organizational split with the ITF. The ITF executive committee, after some maneuvering called a meeting of its Asian affiliates in Hong Kong, March 1980. At this meeting, the suspension of NUSI

---

nationwide port strike. See "Global boycott of Indian ships threatened," *Statesman Weekly* (Calcutta), November 25, 1978, p. 7.

184 "Asian seamen to set up secretariat," *Asian Wall Street Journal*, May 6, 1979, p. 7.

185 "Boycott Trade with Vietnam," *Labour News* (National Trade Union Congress, Singapore), Vol. 8, No. 15, mid-August 1979, pp. 1, 16. Despite the title, this article is primarily concerned with the conference of Asian seamen.

186 *Ibid.*

187 Barnes, "LDC Seamen . . .," p. 16.

was lifted, and an Asian Seafarers' Regional Committee was formed which, according to Asian union officials, has improved their relations with the ITF.[188] Nevertheless, three issues continue to exacerbate ill-feelings between the Asian and European affiliates of the ITF: 1) the continued push by the ITF for a worldwide wage standard; 2) the large increase in Asian seamen, particularly in the Philippines, but also in South Korea, Taiwan, Hong Kong and elsewhere; and 3) the obvious and widespread evasion and avoidance of supposedly controlling ITF wages and working conditions. Although the first issue involves Indian subcontinent seamen to a great extent, all three issues also pertain to other Third World countries, some particularly to the Philippines, South Korea, Singapore, and Hong Kong.

ITF's Worldwide Wage Push

As the discussion above has demonstrated, in order to impose Western standards on FOC vessels, the ITF has attempted over the years to substitute either itself or the unions of a vessel's owner's country in place of the flag country's union (if any) as the bargaining agent for FOC crews. Sometimes this has even meant shouldering aside an ITF affiliate acting as bargaining agent (union) for the seafarers involved. Catering to its European affiliates, the ITF has also opposed lower than European wages and conditions for Asiatic seamen serving on European-flag vessels.

The Asiatic seafarers' unions have always opposed the ITF single wage scale demand. The Asian Maritime Committee, which was formed following the ITF Hong Kong meeting of March 1980, recommended a minimum ITF Asian rate of $500 per month for an able bodied (AB) seamen on FOC vessels trading worldwide. The ITF Fair Practices Committee, however, set the rate for an AB at $703 per month worldwide and $499 for Far East trading. The Asian group then accepted the latter as the worldwide rate and proposed periodic increases so that parity would be achieved with worldwide rates in 1986.[189] Effective January 1, 1983, however, the ITF raised its AB worldwide minimum rate to $821 per month, an increase of 4.6 percent, and raised its Far East rate to $698 per month, an in-

---

188 Interviews, Southeast Asia, July 1982.

189 Barnes, "LDC Seamen . . .," pp. 17-19; and Michael Fox, "Unions demand single scale for seamen," *Lloyd's List*, June 18, 1981.

crease of 25.3 percent.[190] As we shall note below, given the economic situation of shipping and of the Third World countries, the net effect is likely to be more evasion and double accounting.

Whether parity will be achieved in these worldwide rates is doubtful. The ITF does not negotiate: it develops policies and then attempts to force ship operators to accept them. As will be discussed below, there is now a tremendous and possibly growing surplus of seamen. The willingness of Third World seamen to work at wages substantially below ITF minima will therefore undoubtedly continue, especially since these so-called substandard wages are also considerably above wages for alternative employment, if any, in their home countries.

Meanwhile, the ITF, under pressure from its European affiliates, and particularly, the British NUS, announced a policy in early 1983 of prohibiting any differentials between the pay of European and Asiatic seamen on European-flag vessels. Specifically, the ITF proposed that effective July 1, 1983, Asiatic seamen's pay should equal 63 percent of European pay and that this percentage should rise so that by 1985 the differential would be eliminated. About 5,000 mostly Indian subcontinent seamen were then involved on British ships, a sizable number of Asiatics on Greek ships, and others on Dutch ones. The ITF then attempted without success to negotiate a new arrangement with the ISF to solve the "non-domiciled seamen problem," but the ISF member associations have declined to do so.[191]

European countries and unions had already taken steps to control the use of "non-domiciles" (mostly Asian, but also West Indian and others) seamen.[192] Thus the NUS agreement prohibits existing British-flag ships manned by British seamen from changing to non-domiciled seamen, and provides that no new ships will be manned by the latter. In addition, this agreement

---

[190] Copy of ITF wage "agreement" in author's possession. See Chapter IV, IV-1.

[191] Victor Smart, "ITF seeks full rate for Third World seamen," *Lloyd's List*, March 1, 1983, p. 1; *ITF Newsletter*, No. 3 (March 1983), supplement, p. 4. *Lloyd's List* reported that the ISF was seeking a new agreement with the ITF (see "ISF seeks international employment agreement," *Lloyd's List*, June 15, 1983, p. 1), but this the ISF vigorously denied upon our inquiry; see also *ISF Press Release*, "ITF Policy Misguided, Says International Shipping Federation," June 2, 1983.

[192] The term "non-domiciles" is now used by the ITF and European unions because the Asians understandably found that "crews of convenience" had for them an invidious connotation.

requires shipowners to pay the NUS or other involved British unions £30 per year for each non-domiciled seaman employed.[193] Likewise, we have noted Greek government restrictions on use of non-domiciled seamen and requirements for a payment of $30 per month to a welfare fund for Greek seamen for each non-domiciled seamen employed.[194]

The payment by the General Council of British Shipping of these fees to the NUS has provided the latter with a substantial sum—over £1.5 million since 1975—during a period when its membership, now about 30,000 has been steadily declining. Until given considerable publicity in late 1982 and early 1983 and earmarked for the assistance of non-domiciled seamen, these funds were commingled with dues and other income and in some years provided over 50 percent of the NUS income. As far as can be determined, it was not spent for the benefit of Asian seamen. (In December 1982, the Asiatic AB seaman rate on British ships was £79 per month compared with £320 for his British counterpart.) Rather, the funds for use of Asian seamen were spent on such things as rehabilitation of NUS headquarters, trips to Moscow and Egypt, automobiles and other pertinences, and on purely British collective bargaining matters until publicity exposed such practices.[195]

With unemployment rife in the early 1980s, the pressure to replace the Asian and other non-domiciled seamen on European ships became intense. This coincided with publicity about the "Asian levy" and the utilization of it by the NUS. The result has been a drive by the NUS, other European unions, and the ITF to equalize wages of Asians and Europeans. The NUS at-

---

[193] Barnes, "LDC Seamen . . .," p. 11, refers to the payment to the NUS as £15 per non-domiciled seamen, but all other references put it as £30. It was originally set at £15, but has been increased to £30.

[194] Barnes, "LDC Seamen . . .," p. 11, also refers to this Greek figure of $30.

[195] Neither the General Council of British Shipping nor the NUS ever publicized their "Asian levy" arrangement. An article by Peter Paterson, "Seamen in trouble over employers' payment," was published in the (London) *Sunday Times*, July 18, 1976, p. 47, and a letter to the (London) *Daily Telegraph* by Oliver G. Sims, September 13, 1982, brought it to light again. See Mr. Sims' letter o *Lloyd's List*, November 5, 1982, "Likely aftermath to the Asian levy"; see also the following stories in *Lloyd's List*: Victor Smart, "Special fund is set up for NUS Asian levy," December 3, 1982; Victor Smart, "Moral dilemmas beset NUS over Asian levy," December 6, 1982; *ibid.*, "Indian seamen's union receives Asian level plea," January 13, 1983; "Saga of Asian levy that cannot be given away," January 18, 1983; "Character of Asian levy justifies union reform"; letter from David Martin, *Lloyd's List*, February 1, 1983.

tempted, but failed, to induce the Indian NUSI and the Indian government either to agree to pay the Asian seamen wages more equal to the Europeans or to pay the £30 levy directly to the seamen or to the NUSI. Most observers believe that if wages are equalized, the NUS will be the big loser, for it may well force British flag owners to transfer many of their ships to FOC registry in order to be competitive. This would cause the loss of jobs not only for non-domiciled seamen but also for thousands of British officers and seamen. Nevertheless, upon urging of the NUS the Labour Party, prior to its overwhelming defeat in the 1983 British general elections, promised that if it were returned to power it would amend the British Race Relations Act to make payment of lower wages to non-domiciled seamen illegal on British ships.[196] Equalization would, of course, also drastically reduce the income of the NUS by ending its lucrative "Asian levy."

Finally, it should be noted that the use by unions of funds such as the Asian levy has become fairly widespread. We have already noted that the Seamen's Union of Australia and other Australian maritime unions have found it convenient to supplement their incomes in this manner. In Sweden, two-thirds of the funds collected from shipowners by boycotts or threats thereof have been spent by the Swedish Seamen's Union for its own purposes, including such matters as a $2,500 dinner in Miami during the 1980 ITF congress and a visit by a Russian delegation.[197] In the following chapter, we shall examine how the ITF spends the huge sums which it collects and show that the Third World seamen reap few benefits from the welfare fund purportedly established for them. These fiscal facts, plus the record described above, emphasize once more that the seafarers' unions of the developed world have in the ITF a tool for protecting their jobs against the encroachments of seamen from the Third World. We shall discuss this further in the concluding chapter where this aspect of ITF policy is balanced against its services to all seamen.

------

[196] Victor Smart, "ITF seeks full rate for Third World seamen," *Lloyd's List*, March 1, 1983, p. 1; and *ibid.*; "ITF leaders to urge campaign on ratings' pay," *Lloyd's List*, March 21, 1983, p. 1.

[197] "Seamen's Union in New Scandal," *Swedish Shipping Gazette*, No. 33-34, 1982; and "Seamen's Unions—Again," *Halland Nyheter*, August 14, 1982 (translated from Swedish).

The Seamen Supply Explosion

The Third World supplies thousands of seamen to the shipping world. One estimate is that 1.5 to 2 million such nationals serve on FOC ships.[198] Here we examine the policies of four countries— the Philippines, South Korea, Hong Kong and Singapore—and the impact of the ITF thereon.

Philippines. Some 130,772 Filipino seamen are registered with the Philippine Overseas Employment Association, but the downturn in the industry had about one-half unemployed in early 1983. Nevertheless, the Philippines is the biggest supplier of seamen in the world, providing crews for over thirty maritime nations. These seamen are required to remit 70 percent of their basic monthly wages back to the Philippines, and these remittances represent one of the country's most important sources of foreign exchange, totaling over $150 million in 1981.[199]

Only about 15,000 of the seamen from the Philippines working at any given time are members of the Associated Marine Officers' and Seamen's Union, an ITF affiliate, and receive the ITF AB minimum ($499 per month at the beginning of 1983).[200] Because there are so many Filipino seamen, and perhaps because the majority either do not receive the ITF minimum or are considered unlikely to be receiving it, any FOC ship with a Filipino crew will probably be a target for an ITF inspection. This has caused a series of protests against ITF activity by Filipino interests.[201] Moreover, many ship operators believe that Filipino crews are likely either to be easily swayed by ITF inspectors or anxious to use those inspectors to gain more income; hence such crews are unpopular with shipowners in Southeast Asia and Hong Kong.[202] Nevertheless, crews from the Philippines serve on vessels throughout the world and are frequently found on those owned by U.S. and Japanese interests. In addition, Philippine shipowners are increasing in number and, of course, when they employ seamen from their own country they may pay sub-minimum rates, but such ships are not classified as FOC.

---

198 Barnes, "LDC Seamen . . .," p. 8.

199 "The Philippines," *Lloyd's List*, Special Report, p. 7-10.

200 *Ibid.*

201 See, e.g., Filipino Association for Mariners' Employment, Inc., Board Resolution No. 2, Series 1981. Copy in authors' possession.

202 Interviews with shipping companies, Singapore and Hong Kong, July 1982.

South Korea. Already a significant factor in shipbuilding, South Korea also has expansive maritime aspirations. It is creating a merchant fleet and training seamen for jobs on other flag ships.[203]

The South Korean's Seamen's Union is an ITF affiliate, but it has come under fire for signing contracts and granting blue certificates on behalf of the ITF. Hong Kong and Greek unions are among the several that claim these contracts—the number in December 1982 stood at 670 and in March 1983, 712—permit substandard conditions and are not enforced.[204] The Greek Panhellenic Seamen's Union (PNO) in particular has endeavored to have the South Korean union suspended from the ITF, and has been supported by the British NUS, but the ITF has managed to avoid such drastic action.[205]

It is indeed most likely that South Korean—and several other Third World unions—have in fact made deals at sub-ITF wages. Moreover, the oversupply of seamen, the artificially high ITF wage rates for Third World standards, the fact that much lower seafaring wages are still higher than other employment opportunities in such countries, and the desire of their governments for sources of hard currency, all insure that off-ITF contract deals will continue to be made.

Singapore. This island country, by carefully managed policies, has developed remarkably. Once a major open registry, Singapore now requires quite stringent conditions before it will permit its flag to be used. No ships are registered unless a majority of the company is Singapore-owned or unless the company is registered on the Singapore stock exchange. A ship older than 7 years is denied registry, and all ships must meet seaworthy and safety conditions.

---

203 See "S. Korea Maritime Industries," *Lloyd's List,* Special Report, March 14, 1983, pp. 5-10; and Bridget Hogan, "South Koreans plan major fleet expansion," *Lloyd's List,* March 19, 1983, p. 1.

204 "S. Koreans accused of crew treachery," *Lloyd's List,* December 1, 1982; Victor Smart, "Ban on S. Korean Seamen's Union," *Lloyd's List,* December 8, 1982; and *ibid.,* "S. Koreans call halt to Greek free flag deals," *Lloyd's List,* March 3, 1983, p. 1; and *ibid.,* "NUS seeks to expel S. Korea from the ITF," *Lloyd's List,* March 26, 1983, p. 1.

205 "Seamen's unions set to clash on free flags issue," *Lloyd's List,* March 19, 1983, p. 1; Victor Smart, "Greeks under S. Korean flag face blacking," *Lloyd's List,* March 23, 1983, p. 1; and "Union row is patched up," *Lloyd's List,* March 24, 1983, p. 1; and Victor Smart, "NUS seeks to expel S. Korea from the ITF," *Lloyd's List,* March 26, 1983, p. 1. See also *ITF Newsletter,* No. 3 (March 1983), pp. 22-24.

Singapore does not insist on a Singapore crew with its flag.
Only about 9,000-10,000 Singapore seamen are registered with its
National Maritime Board. It is a country of almost full employment; with jobs available on land, the supply of seamen is limited.
Ship managers obtain their labor supply from the National Maritime Board, a tripartite agency, and/or from a permanent staff
of their own trainees. Shipowners must put 22 percent of the
wages paid to seamen in a government fund, which is credited to
the account of the individual seamen and is available for their
buying or building houses. In addition, the shipping employer
must contribute a stipulated amount per month for all seafarers
earning below a prescribed minimum. This is used for training
and development and to encourage employers to have training
plans.[206]

Like their Indian counterparts, union, company, and government officials in Singapore are firmly against paying European
or American wages on their flag vessels. The Singapore wages
are high for Southeast Asia, especially so when the savings and
training benefits are included. Singapore leaders point out, however, that shipboard wages must be related to those paid on
shore and that to do otherwise would seriously disrupt their
economic situation. They therefore maintain that the ITF's concern should be job availability and fair and equal treatment, not
who owns a ship. They bitterly resent any charge that their
wages are not fair; they especialy resent the Australian situation
where the Seamen's Union of Australia, among other ITF affiliates, as described above, has harassed Singapore-flag ships
and the ITF has been unable or unwilling to be of assistance.

Hong Kong. This British crown colony's economy has always
been heavily based upon the maritime industries and remains so
today, despite the strong development of industry within its
borders. Hong Kong has its own flag and is also a heavy user
of FOC registries, especially Liberian, but also Panamanian,
Taiwanese, and others. Many of the large shipowners are
Chinese who fled communist rule, arrived in Hong Kong penni-
less, and have developed huge fortunes. Such companies trade
all over the world. In addition, there are many small operators
who trade lesser distances or concentrate on trading in a
particular area or with certain countries.

---

[206] These and the following paragraphs are based upon interviews with
Singapore union, management, and government officials, July 11-12, 1982.

Hong Kong has a reasonably strong marine officers' union, affiliated with the ITF and headed by an Australian. Its members include Hong Kong Chinese, British, Australian, and Indian nationals, all qualified under British or equivalent standards. Two seamen's unions exist, one politically oriented toward Taiwan, which is an ITF affiliate, and one toward mainland China. Both are politicized and not strong as unions. Crews are heavily Chinese, both Hong Kong and Taiwan, but Filipino, Burmese, and many other nationalities are found on the Hong Kong-owned vessels.[207]

Hong Kong does not intervene for the ITF to enforce its standards on FOC ships. As one union official put it, "We have to work at these things slowly, keep friendly, and help the company make a profit." [208] Hong Kong-flag ships are generally recognized as meeting ITF standards, but everyone agrees that there are many instances of double bookkeeping, dual contract agreements, etc., which permit operators to provide evidence that they meet ITF standards when actually they do not. Large operators, often at the insistence of charterers, place a few of their ships under the Hong Kong flag and obtain an ITF blue certificate for these vessels, especially when the vessel is trading to Australia or another country where there is strong ITF support. One large shipowner who owns fifty ships, has thirty-seven under the Liberian flag and thirteen under the Hong Kong one. Shifts are made as trading routes alter. The Chinese in Hong Kong have come from the mainland in order to improve their economic and political conditions. As one observer remarked:

> They stick together, whether millionaire owner or lowest grade of seaman. Most shipowners keep two sets of books. Workers sign for ITF wages but do not get them. They rarely blow the gun against the company. It is not considered strange here. The people have the best possible jobs that they can get when they are at sea and wages miles ahead of what they can get elsewhere.[209]

ITF's Evasion Problem

The above analysis has pointed out some problems of evasion which the ITF faces, such as the granting of blue certificates by South Korean unions on terms probably below ITF standards and

---

[207] This section is primarily based upon interviews with Hong Kong maritime union, management, and government officials, July 13-15, 1982.

[208] Interview, July 15, 1982.

[209] Interview, July 14, 1982.

the double booking featured on the Hong Kong scene. Observers on three continents—whether union, management, or government—all agreed, when contacted by the authors, that evasion was widespread and that it was a calculated response by owners, seamen, and governments to the threat to their shipping industry and jobs which they perceive in ITF actions and policies. Double accounting is common to areas other than just Hong Kong, according to the general secretary of the National Union of Seamen of India (NUSI).[210] He also tells of this case:

> There is a classic case where a vessel on its way to Australia, took off the regular crew from low wage area at Singapore, kept them in a hotel, engaged a fresh crew on ITF wage rates from Singapore and proceeded to Australia. After the vessel's return to Singapore in a few weeks time, the crew on ITF Agreement was discharged and the regular crew taken back on board, thus avoiding payment of back wages.[211]

Moreover, if back pay is obtained, there is no guarantee that the crew members will actually receive it. The questions involving the use of such payments in Sweden and Australia have already been noted. The managing director of a major Hong Kong shipping company wrote in July 1982 in regard to an ITF boycott in Australia:

> This matter . . . happened in April 1981 and crew's back pay in amount of US $184,666.36 had been remitted to the Waterside Workers' Federation in Australia. But over 15 months elapsed and as we know not even one of the crew received his share of the back pay. . . .[212]

An Asian labor union official told one of the authors:

> On the welfare fund, you collect it and send it to the ITF when you sign an agreement—$200 per man—you do not get anything directly out of the welfare fund except money for trips to regional conferences or the Fair Practices Committee meetings. You gain more members because companies want agreements to get a blue certificate, so in that way it can be worthwhile.[213]

If backpay is given to Third World seamen, it may cause problems with their governments. Such countries as India or the Philippines either tax away the backpay or bar the seamen

---

[210] Barnes, "LDC Seamen . . .," p. 9.

[211] *Ibid.*

[212] Communication in authors' possession.

[213] Interview, July 1982.

who receive it from obtaining employment in the shipping industry unless the money is returned. Informal ways of blacklisting are allegedly in existence in other Third World countries to make it difficult for seamen to accept the benefits of successful ITF boycotts.[214] Consequently, Third World seamen are often likely to eschew ITF proffered assistance and to cooperate with ship operators who are avoiding ITF standards.

ITF'S CAMPAIGN THROUGH OTHER AGENCIES

Besides its direct campaign against FOC shipping, the ITF continues to utilize other organizations and agencies to achieve its purposes. For example, as already noted in this chapter, the ITF has been both very active and extraordinarily successful in obtaining support for ILO conventions and recommendations which improve standards on ships and provide a basis for it to demand high wages on FOC vessels. Appendix C amplifies the story of the ITF's successful role in the ILO.

Two other thrusts need to be noted. The first is the ITF's support of the "scrap and build" proposal of the European Metalworkers' Federation (EMF); the second is the continuing support which the ITF gives to the drive of the United Nations Conference on Trade and Development (UNCTAD) to have Third World countries literally take over a large portion of shipping from developed countries and thus phase out FOC shipping.

The EMF's "Scrap and Build" Proposal

The European Metalworkers' Federation (EMF) operates as a coordinating body for Western European national unions in the metals and electrical industries.[215] As such, it is vitally interested in shipbuilding, which in Europe and the United States has been on a serious decline for at least the last decade. In March 1979, the EMF Executive Committee "examined and approved the outline of a 'scrap and build' programme for ships." [216] It proposed

---

[214] Barnes, "LDC Seamen . . .," pp. 15-16; interviews, various Asian ports, June-July 1982.

[215] The EMF is a committee of the European Trade Union Confederation (ETUC), and as such is not affiliated with the International Metalworkers' Federation (IMF), although the two organizations have many common affiliates. See Northrup and Rowan, *Multinational Collective Bargaining,* Chapters III-V, for analyses both of IMF and EMF activities in relation to the metal and electrical industries.

[216] "Shipbuilding and Protection Against the Pollution of the Seas," EMF Press Release, March 21, 1979, p. 2.

1. A 2 scrap for 1 build ratio as a basis, modified in accordance with a formula to be devised for ships over 50,000 compensated grt.

2. Shipowners scrapping and building on this basis to be eligible for special credit terms or a scrap premium or a combination of the two.

3. The premium or credit to be provided by the country in which the new ships are built. Flexibility could be allowed to each member country in the exact form of support to be given within an agreed ceiling and common guidelines.

4. Community funds to be provided to assist in the cost of these national payments as part of the overall policy of supporting and developing national shipping and shipbuilding industries. This would avoid excessive concentration of new orders in any one country.

5. The scheme to be introduced by the Commission for shipowners and shipbuilders in member states. But Japan and other shipping and shipbuilding countries be invited to operate similar schemes, with safeguards against low cost competition damaging European shipyards.

6. The scheme to be limited to 60 million dwt of ships scrapped over the 3 year period 1979-1981.

7. Owners to be allowed to scrap approved ships where it is most advantageous to them, but consideration to be given to a separate support scheme for the European shipbreaking industry in order to enable it to offer prices comparable to those in the Far East.[217]

Interestingly enough, the European Community's Economic and Social Committee issued an "Opinion . . . on Problems Currently Facing Community Shipping Policy, Particularly Maritime Safety, the Growing Importance of the New Shipping Nations, the Development of Flags of Convenience and the Discrimination against Certain Flags" on April 4, 1979, which appears to have been influenced in large measure by the work of the EMF.[218]

---

[217] "Scrap and Build," EMF Executive Committee Report, February 11, 1979, p. 7.

[218] European Economic Community, Economic and Social Committee, "Opinion . . . on Problems Currently Facing Community Shipping Policy, Par-

The committee's proposals included much of what the EMF demanded and the harmonization of pay and working conditions on board ships with the right of European Community inspectors (perhaps supporting ITF demands) to uphold established standards. Acting in concert, the EMF and the European Community, of course, have both been interested in protecting European jobs and furthering restrictions on FOC shipping.

The EMF's shipbuilding demands were meant to harmonize with those of the ITF, and the EMF worked closely with the Transport Committee of the European Trade Union Confederation in developing them. The proposals' fourfold aim: 1) to create shipbuilding needs by scrapping existing ships; 2) to bring the resultant work to European shipyards; 3) to create jobs for European maritime employees by eliminating use of less-developed country personnel now working on FOC ships; and 4) to establish, through the European Community, a tripartite directing body in which the EMF is the accredited representative for employees

The scrap and build proposal was abandoned because member countries of the European Community found it too expensive to be feasible. The EMF's executive, however, believes that considerable progress toward its goals can be achieved as a result of the agreements reached at the European Conference on Shipping Safety, held in Paris, January 26, 1982. European countries agreed to inspect one-fourth of all foreign vessels in their ports and rigidly hold them to International Maritime Organisation and International Labour Organisation standards. Obviously the purpose is to pressure FOC vessels and to curtail FOC shipping in favor of vessels flying European flags.[219] We have, however, heard of no impact of this policy, but the ITF has alerted its inspectors to ensure its enforcement.[220]

UNCTAD and the ITF

The ITF has found a sympathetic forum in the United Nations Conference on Trade and Development (UNCTAD), where surprisingly, in view of its difficulties with Third World unions

ticularly Maritime Safety, the Growing Importance of the New Shipping Nations, the Development of Flags of Convenience and the Discrimination Against Certain Flags," Brussels, April 4, 1979.

[219] European Metalworkers' Federation, *Secretariat's Report on Activities 1980-83* (Brussels, 1983), pp. 61-64.

[220] *ITF Newsletter*, No. 3 (March 1983), p. 23.

and governments as already described, it is allied with the
"Group of 77," the Third World countries who with Communist
bloc support and a radical secretariat control this organization.
UNCTAD is concerned with shipping as a matter of course,
but its current primary objective is the transfer of wealth from
developed countries, known as "Group B," to the Group of 77.
One way to do this is to phase out FOC shipping and to transfer
the vessels to the Group of 77. The target is to transfer 20
percent of the world's shipping by 1990.[221]

The three major shipping proposals being advocated by
UNCTAD are: 1) a code of conduct for liner conferences (rate
setting organizations of shippers) so that equal flat shares in
the liner trades for bilateral partners are guaranteed; 2) similar
arrangements for bulk trades; and 3) the ending of open registries for FOC shipping. The first is somewhat noncontroversial
because it conforms generally to the status quo for regular trade
of general cargo between two countries. It will go into effect in
October 1983 because it has been ratified by West Germany and
enough other countries representing over 25 percent of the world
merchant fleet. Other European countries have promised to do so
also, and meanwhile are pledged to observe the code in dealing
with Third World but not in dealing with developed countries.
Insofar as the second point is concerned, the Group B countries,
and apparently the USSR, are opposed to any cargo sharing code
being implemented for bulk cargoes. Group B countries are
refusing to compromise on point three, and the United States has
refused to participate in working meetings because it believes
that the UNCTAD secretariat has arrogated power to itself by
abolishing the rule of consensus in favor of majority rule—one
vote per country regardless of size or wealth. Panama and
Liberia have joined the United States in this position.

All evidence is that the ITF works closely with the UNCTAD
secretariat. UNCTAD headquarters is in Geneva, as is that of
the ILO, and is visited by a large labor observer delegation. The
ITF is given the floor frequently on the open registry question
and has been permitted to have the final word at a number of
key UNCTAD meetings. The ITF has made it clear that it
regards the UNCTAD's secretariat and its policy on open registry
as a key ally of great promise. How UNCTAD can be successful, however, in view of the opposition of developed countries,

---

[221] A more detailed analysis of UNCTAD's shipping policies is found in
Appendix C, with appropriate citations.

and how Third World countries can acquire the capital to become major maritime operators are, of course, major problems which must be solved before UNCTAD's objectives can come to fruition. The ITF believes that if FOC shipping is phased out, the ships will go to the developed countries' flags; the UNCTAD secretariat believes that they will go to the flags of the under-developed ones—completely diverse reasons for supporting phase out! Nevertheless, the role of UNCTAD must be considered in evaluating the ITF's FOC campaign, which is the subject of the next chapter.

CHAPTER IV

Procedure, Coverage, and Evaluation of ITFs' FOC Campaign

Having examined the cases and some legal aspects of the ITF-FOC campaign in principal maritime countries, we now focus upon the extent of the campaign in terms of the number of ships covered and evaluate the results in terms of different parties and criteria. Before doing so, the ITF procedure to secure compliance to its demands is reviewed.

ITF REQUIREMENTS FOR FOC VESSELS

As was repeatedly pointed out in Chapter III, the key to the ITF's ability to force FOC ships to agree to its demands is its ability through affiliates to hold ships in port at great cost to their owners or charterers until they succumb. Thus even in countries such as Germany, the Netherlands, or even the United States, payments to and agreements with the ITF are made because legal action requires costly delays. Therefore, when an ITF inspector boards a ship, and an FOC vessel without a blue certificate wants above all to avoid difficulties and delay, the following procedure takes place.[1]

1. An agreement is signed either with the ITF or an ITF affiliated union (see Figure IV-1).

2. Each seaman is provided with an employment contract (Figure IV-2).

3. All seamen on board, regardless of their wishes, must either be members of an ITF-affiliated union, or if not eligible therefor, must be enrolled in the ITF's Special

---

[1] Our work in this section was made easier by the excellent summary of information found in B.L. Williamson's unpublished, private study, "The International Transport Workers' Federation" (1982).

FIGURE IV-1
ITF Special Agreement

This special agreement is made the .... day of ....

one thousand nine hundred and .... **and effective from**

....

BETWEEN:

(i) The INTERNATIONAL TRANSPORT WORKERS' FEDERATION (hereinafter called 'the ITF') whose headquarters are at 133-135 Great Suffolk Street, London SE1 1PD in the United Kingdom (telephone: 01-403 2733, telegrams: INTRANSFE LONDON SE1); and

(ii)   ....

(hereinafter called 'the Company') whose address is

....

....

(telephone: telex: telegrams:)

in respect of the ....flag ship ....
hereinafter called 'the Ship';

WHEREAS:

1   the ITF is an independent trade union organisation comprising fully autonomous trade union organisations in transport and allied services throughout the world and members of the Special Seafarers' Section of the ITF;

2   the Company is the registered owner/manager of the Ship; described in Schedule 1 hereto;

3   the ITF and the Company desire to regulate the conditions of employment of all seafarers (hereinafter individually called a 'Seafarer') serving from time to time aboard the Ship;

NOW IT IS AGREED:

Article 1: The Company undertakes as follows:

a   to employ each Seafarer in accordance with the terms of the current ITF Collective Agreement for World Wide trading (hereinafter called the ITF Collective Agreement) as amended from time to time in accordance with Article 5 below;

b   to incorporate the terms and conditions of the ITF Collective Agreement into the individual contract of employment of each seafarer and into the Ship's Articles and furnish copies of these documents to the ITF. Any seafarer, enjoying terms and conditions which are, taken as a whole, recognised by the ITF as more favourable to the seafarer, shall continue to enjoy such terms and conditions;

FIGURE IV-1 (continued)

c   to pay on behalf of each Seafarer contributions and fees at the rates shown in Schedule 2 hereto to the Seafarers' International Welfare Protection and Assistance Fund and to the Special Seafarers' Section of the ITF. The contributions and fees shall be paid to the ITF annually and in advance;

d   to display aboard the Ship copies of the Special Agreement, the ITF Collective Agreement and the ITF Blue Certificate to be issued under Article 2 hereof in a prominent place to which each Seafarer shall have access at all times; and

e   to grant to representatives of the ITF and of trade union organisations affiliated to the ITF free access to each Seafarer at all reasonable times whether or not aboard the Ship, whether the Ship is in berth or not.

Article 2: the ITF undertakes, having received and approved the copies of the documents referred to in Article 1(b) above, and received the fees and contributions payable under Article 1(c) above, to issue and each year to renew an ITF Blue Certificate (hereinafter called the 'ITF Blue Certificate') certifying that the Ship is covered by a Collective Agreement acceptable to the ITF, provided that the property in the ITF Blue Certificate shall at all times remain in the ITF.

Article 3: in the event of default by the Company of any of its undertakings herein, the ITF may determine this Special Agreement immediately upon notification to the Company. Upon such termination, the Company shall forthwith return the ITF Blue Certificate to or to the order of the ITF.

Article 4: this Special Agreement shall remain in force for a period of twelve months from the date hereof and thereafter from year to year, provided that either party may give notice of termination to the other no later than one month before any anniversary of this Special Agreement whereupon the same shall determine upon such anniversary.

Article 5: the ITF shall be entitled to change the rates in the ITF Collective Agreement and the rates shown in Schedule 2 hereto upon 2 months' notice to the Company whereupon the changed rates shall come into force from the date specified.

Article 6: all notices given by the Company and the ITF hereunder shall be given in writing addressed to the ITF at its address hereinbefore described and to the Company at the address described in Schedule 1 hereto.

Article 7: this Special Agreement exists in quadruplicate of which two shall be kept by each party.

Date and place ....

Signed on behalf of the Company: Signed on behalf of the ITF:

....

FIGURE IV-1 (continued)

Schedule 1

NAME OF VESSEL ....

OFFICIAL NUMBER ....

PORT OF REGISTRY ....

DATE OF REGISTRY ....

REGISTERED TONNAGE (gross/net) ....

ENGINE HORSEPOWER (NHP/IHP/BHP) ....

NUMBER OF SEAMEN AND APPRENTICES
FOR WHICH ACCOMMODATION IS CERTIFIED ....

REGISTERED MANAGING OWNER OR MANAGER ....

whose address is at:

....

....
(telephone: telex: telegrams:)

Schedule 2

ITF SPECIAL SEAFARERS' SECTION

Entrance fees	At US$20 per man	US$..............
Membership fees	At US$40 per man per year	US$..............
SEAFARERS' INTERNATIONAL WELFARE PROTECTION AND ASSISTANCE FUND	At US$200 per man per year	US$..............
TOTAL		US$..............

The sum of US$........................is equivalent to ....

Received with thanks:

....
                        On behalf of the ITF

Source: ITF.

FIGURE IV-2
Seaman's Employment Contract

Date   **and agreed to be effective from**

This Employment Contract is entered into between the Seaman and the Owner of the Vessel (hereinafter called the Employer.)

THE SEAMAN

Surname:	Given names:
Full home address:	
Position:	Medical certificate issued on:
Estimated time of taking up position:	Port where position is taken up:
Nationality:	Passport no.: Seaman's book no.:

THE EMPLOYER

Name:
Address:

THE VESSEL

Name:	Official no.:
Flag:	Port of registry:

TERMS OF THE CONTRACT

Period of employment:	Wages from and including:	Hours of work: 8 per day Monday to Friday
Basic monthly wage:	Weekday overtime rate: per hour:	Saturday, Sunday and Public Holiday overtime rate: per hour:
Leave:	Daily leave pay:	Daily subsistence allowance on leave:

1. The current ITF Collective Agreement shall be considered to be incorporated into and to form part of this contract.

2. The Ship's Articles shall be deemed for all purposes to include the terms of this Contract (including the ITF Collective Agreement) and it shall be the duty of the Employer to ensure that the Ship's Articles reflect these terms. These terms shall take precedence over all other terms.

3. The ITF may vary the terms and conditions of the ITF Collective Agreement from time to time. Terms and Conditions as so varied shall form part of this Contract with effect from the date of the Variation in place of the Terms and Conditions current immediately preceding the Variation.

CONFIRMATION OF THE CONTRACT

Signature of Employer:	Signature of Seaman:

Source: ITF.

Seafarers Department at a joining fee of $20 and a
membership fee of $40 per annum, both per seaman paid
in advance.[2]

4. The shipowner must contribute $200 per seafarer per
   annum to the ITF welfare fund which is examined below.

5. Back pay is demanded from the date of each seaman's
   signing on shipboard to the date of the ITF contract
   signing for the difference between the wages paid and the
   ITF agreement wages. This amount can be negotiated
   but as shown in Table IV-15 below, it amounted to over
   $55,154.12 per ship boycott in 1981.

6. The owner must agree to maintain stipulated conditions,
   despite any waivers by the crew, to allow ITF inspectors
   access to all records and each crew member, and to advise
   the ITF of all crew changes and contract changes. The
   blue certificate and contract must always be available for
   inspection by crew members.

Table IV-1 sets forth the basic rate worldwide and Far East
for the key able seamen, 1972-1983, demanded by the ITF, together with the percentage increases. In each case there was no
negotiation. The increases in rates were decided upon by the ITF
and its affiliates and put into effect. Tables IV-2 and IV-3 show
the rates and other cash benefits for world wide and Far East
wages as demanded by the ITF since January 1, 1983, for all
key shipboard classifications.

The ITF also establishes ship manning schedules which are
based upon British standards, as set forth in the United Kingdom
Shipping Notice M.798. Such standards vary by ship according
to design, use, and degree of automation. Most observers, including the shipping minister in the current British government,[3]
believe that the British standards provide for overmanning, an
opinion clearly supported by the recent decisions of the Norwegian and Greek governments to reduce their ship manning requirements, as noted in Chapter III. The extent to which re-

---

[2] Such a requirement, without the necessary consent or under duress, of
course, would seem to contravene employee free choice in the selection of a
bargaining agent and therefore violate the U.S. National Labor Relations
(Taft-Hartley) Act.

[3] "Sproat urges more cuts to halt fleet decline," *Lloyd's List*, March 22, 1983,
p. 3.

TABLE IV-1
ITF Basic Minimum Monthly Rate
Able Bodied Seaman
(1972-1983)

Effective Date	Worldwide US$	Far East US$
1972	288 [a]	205 [a]
9/1/74	396 [a]	280 [a]
9/1/75	483	343
3/1/77	531	373
9/1/77	579	411
9/1/78	621	441
9/1/79	674	478
9/1/81	703	499
4/1/82	785	557
1/1/83	821	698

Source: Published ITF "Agreements."
[a] The 1972 and 1974 rates were published in pound sterling. They were converted to U.S. dollars at the average annual rates of $2.5018 for 1972 and $2.3160 for 1974 and rounded to the nearest dollar.

duced manning can cut costs is illustrated in Tables IV-4 through IV-9 which estimate the total monthly costs for the ITF's manning scale at 1982 and 1983 ITF rates worldwide for ships of different gross registered tons (grt). Looking at Table IV-4, for example, it can be seen that a reduction of four or five crewmen can easily reduce monthly manning costs $4-6 thousand per month, with up to an additional 20-40 percent of this figure being saved as a result of reduced fringe benefit costs. Clearly, FOC ships which do not conform to such rigid manning requirements can effectuate considerable savings. This is not to suggest, however, that reasonable manning standards can be ignored: as insurers often point out, under manning can be dangerous.[4]

Exceptions

Not all ITF-approved vessels meet these specifications. There are several categories of ships which escape its attention, or are not troubled by ITF inspectors. These include the following:

Communist bloc vessels. The ITF takes the position that these ships are not FOC vessels, and therefore they do not come within

---

[4] Lee Coppack, "ILU warns shipowners on manning economies," *Lloyd's List*, March 25, 1983, p. 3.

TABLE IV-2
ITF Collective Agreement World Wide Wage Scale and
Other Cash Benefits
Effective as of January 1, 1983

	Para 3	Para 9		Para 12
		Hourly O/T Rate		
Rank or Rating	Basic monthly pay (US$)	Para 5 Weekdays 1/135th of monthly	Para 6 Sats. Sundays and Public Hols. 1/75th of monthly	Cash Compensation for unclaimed annual leave (per day) 1/25th of monthly
1. Master	2766	20.50	36.90	110.60
2. Chief Eng. Officer	2514	18.60	33.50	100.60
3. Chief Navigating Officer	1786	13.20	23.80	71.40
4. 2nd " "	1430	10.60	19.10	57.20
5. 3rd " "	1378	10.20	18.40	55.10
6. 1st Engineer Officer	1786	13.20	23.80	71.40
7. 2nd " "	1430	10.60	19.10	57.20
8. 3rd " "	1378	10.20	18.40	55.10
9. Radio Officer)				
10. Electrical Engineer Off.)	1430	10.60	19.10	57.20
11. Chief Steward)				
12. Electrician	1203	8.90	16.00	48.10
13. Boatswain)				
14. Carpenter)				
15. Fitter/Repairer)				
16. Chief Cook)	917	6.80	12.20	36.70
17. Donkeyman)				
18. Engineroom Storekeeper)				
19. Pumpman)				
20. Boatswain's Mate)				
21. Quartermaster)	851	6.30	11.30	34.00
22. Assistant Electrician)				
23. Able Seaman)				
24. Fireman/Motorman)				
25. Oiler/Greaser)	821	6.10	11.00	32.80
26. 2nd Steward)				
27. 2nd Cook)	699	5.20	9.30	28.00
28. Messroom Steward)				
29. Ordinary Seaman)	611	4.50	8.10	24.40
30. Wiper)				
31. Deck Boy (1))	350	2.60	4.70	14.00
32. Catering Boy (1))				

(1) In no case shall a person over the age of 18 (eighteen) years be engaged as a boy or be paid at a boy's rate.

NB: A seafarer who is over the age of 18 and who is not listed among the categories of ratings shall be paid at least the equivalent of the rate of an Able Seaman.

TABLE IV-2 (continued)

Cash Benefits	
Paragraph 17	
Compensation for Loss of Life	i) to immediate next of kin— US$ 24,844.00
	ii) to each dependent child under the age of 18— US$ 7,118.00
Paragraph 21	
Subsistence Allowance	daily subsistence allowance whilst on paid leave— US$ 17.60
Paragraph 22	
Crew's Effects, Loss or Damage by Marine Peril	Maximum—US$ 2,842.00

Source: ITF release, January 1983.

the orbit of its campaign. It is universally agreed, however, that the terms and conditions of employment aboard these ships are considerably below many FOC vessels. This, of course, is a source of great irritation to FOC operators and a point of contention among ITF Asian affiliates who have referred to the anomaly with bitterness.[5]

National agreements. The ITF accepts national agreements of affiliated unions as a substitute for its agreement if it is assured that the national agreement is equivalent or superior to its agreement. As the South Korean case suggests, however, this can cause problems if the national agreements are not enforced. On the other hand, the ITF arrogates to itself the right to determine whether to accept national agreements. In Chapter III we noted cases when ships with Spanish, Singapore, Indian, and other national agreements were boycotted even though the national unions were ITF affiliates.

Cruise ships. The ITF has established a special agreement for cruise ships which differs from its standard ones in terms of lower wages and less onerous hours and overtime provisions.

---

[5] At the two conferences of the Asian Maritime Unions in Singapore in April and August 1979, C.V. Devan Nair, then head of the Singapore National Trade Union Congress and now president of this island country, bitterly assailed the ITF and its western officials as being either under the influence of, or soft on communism.

Table IV-3
*ITF Collective Agreement Far East Wage Scale and
Other Cash Benefits*
Effective as of January 1, 1983

Rank or Rating	Para 3	Para 9		Para 12
		Hourly O/T Rate		
	Basic monthly pay (US$)	Para 5 Weekdays 1/135th of monthly	Para 6 Sats. Sundays and Public Hols. 1/75th of monthly	Cash Compensation for unclaimed annual leave (per day) 1/25th of monthly
1. Master	2351	17.40	31.30	94.00
2. Chief Eng. Officer	2137	15.80	28.50	85.50
3. Chief Navigating Officer	1518	11.20	20.20	60.70
4. 2nd " "	1216	9.00	16.20	48.60
5. 3rd " "	1171	8.70	15.60	46.80
6. 1st Engineer Officer	1518	11.20	20.20	60.70
7. 2nd " "	1216	9.00	16.20	48.60
8. 3rd " "	1171	8.70	15.60	46.80
9. Radio Officer)				
10. Electrical Engineer Off.)	1216	9.00	16.20	48.60
11. Chief Steward)				
12. Electrician	1023	7.60	13.60	40.90
13. Boatswain)				
14. Carpenter)				
15. Fitter/Repairer)				
16. Chief Cook)	779	5.80	10.40	31.20
17. Donkeyman)				
18. Engineroom Storekeeper)				
19. Pumpman)				
20. Boatswain's Mate)				
21. Quartermaster)	723	5.40	9.60	28.90
22. Assistant Electrician)				
23. Able Seaman)				
24. Fireman/Motorman)				
25. Oiler/Greaser)	698	5.20	9.30	27.90
26. 2nd Steward)				
27. 2nd Cook)	594	4.40	7.90	23.80
28. Messroom Steward)				
29. Ordinary Seaman)	519	3.80	6.90	20.80
30. Wiper)				
31. Deck Boy (1))	298	2.20	4.00	11.90
32. Catering Boy (1))				

(1) In no case shall a person over the age of 18 (eighteen) years be engaged as a boy or be paid at a boy's rate.

NB: A seafarer who is over the age of 18 and who is not listed among the categories of ratings shall be paid at least the equivalent of the rate of an Able Seaman.

TABLE IV-3 (continued)

Cash Benefits

Paragraph 17

Compensation for Loss of Life   i) to immediate next of kin—
US$ 21,117.00

ii) to each dependent child
under the age of 18—
US$ 6,050.00

Paragraph 21

Subsistence Allowance   daily subsistence allowance
whilst on paid leave—
US$ 15.00

Paragraph 22

Crew's Effects, Loss or Damage
by Marine Peril   Maximum—US$2,416.00

Source: ITF release, January 1983.

TABLE IV-4
ITF Manning Standards 15,000 GRT and Over
Estimated monthly crew cost (worldwide)—rates effective
as of April 1, 1982

Rank or Rating	Basic Pay US$	40 Hours Normal US$	60 Hours Sat/Sun US$	3 Days Leave Pay US$	Total Pay Per Month US$
Master	2,675	792.00	2,142.00	321.00	5,930.00
C/Off	1,727	512.00	1,380.00	207.30	3,826.30
2/Off	1,383	408.00	1,104.00	165.90	3,060.90
3/Off	1,333	396.00	1,068.00	159.90	2,956.90
R/Off	1,383	408.00	1,104.00	165.90	3,060.90
C/Eng	2,431	720.00	1,944.00	291.60	5,386.60
1/Eng	1,727	512.00	1,380.00	207.30	3,826.30
2/Eng	1,383	408.00	1,104.00	165.90	3,060.90
3/Eng	1,333	396.00	1,068.00	159.90	2,956.90
Bosun	877	260.00	702.00	105.30	1,944.30
9 AB's	7,065	2,088.00	5,670.00	847.80	15,670.80
Donkeyman	877	260.00	702.00	105.30	1,944.30
C/Stwd	1,383	408.00	1,104.00	165.90	3,060.90
2/Stwd	785	232.00	630.00	94.20	1,741.20
A/Stwd	668	196.00	534.00	80.10	1,478.10
Cook	877	260.00	702.00	105.30	1,944.30
2/Cook	668	196.00	534.00	80.10	1,478.10
A/Cook	668	196.00	534.00	80.10	1,478.10
2 Messmen	1,336	392.00	1,068.00	160.20	2,956.20

TOTAL CREW 28   TOTAL MONTHLY CREW COST   US$ 67,762.00*

Source: ITF schedules adapted and compiled by B. L. Williamson, "The International Transport Workers Federation," (unpublished study, 1982).
* Total monthly crew costs under ITF "agreements" effective January 1, 1983,
worldwide rates, (4.6 percent increases)=US$70,879.05.

TABLE IV-5

ITF Manning Standards 5,500-15,000 GRT

Estimated monthly crew cost (worldwide)—rates effective
as of April 1, 1982

Rank or Rating	Basic Pay US$	40 Hours Normal US$	60 Hours Sat/Sun US$	3 Days Leave Pay US$	Total Pay Per Month US$
Master	2,675	792.00	2,142.00	321.00	5,930.00
C/Off	1,727	512.00	1,380.00	207.30	3,826.30
2/Off	1,383	408.00	1,104.00	165.90	3,060.90
3/Off	1,333	396.00	1,068.00	159.90	2,956.90
R/Off	1,383	408.00	1,104.00	165.90	3,060.90
C/Eng	2,431	720.00	1,944.00	291.60	5,386.60
1/Eng	1,727	512.00	1,380.00	207.30	3,826.30
2/Eng	1,383	408.00	1,104.00	165.90	3,060.90
3/Eng	1,333	396.00	1,068.00	159.90	2,956.90
Bosun	877	260.00	702.00	105.30	1,944.30
7 AB's	5,495	1,624.00	4,410.00	659.40	12,188.40
Donkeyman	877	260.00	702.00	105.30	1,944.30
C/Stwd	1,383	408.00	1,104.00	165.90	3,060.90
2/Stwd	785	232.00	630.00	94.20	1,741.20
A/Stwd	668	196.00	534.00	80.10	1,478.10
Cook	877	260.00	702.00	105.30	1,944.30
2/Cook	668	196.00	534.00	80.10	1,478.10
A/Cook	668	196.00	534.00	80.10	1,478.10
2 Messmen	1,336	392.00	1,068.00	160.20	2,956.20

TOTAL CREW 26   TOTAL MONTHLY CREW COST   US$ 64,279.60*

Source: ITF schedules adapted and compiled by B. L. Williamson, "The International Transport Workers Federation," (unpublished study, 1982).
* Total monthly crew costs under ITF "agreements" effective January 1, 1983, worldwide rates, (4.6 percent increases)=US$67,236.46.

Total crew costs. Since 1981, the ITF has agreed to accept "total crew costs" and funding arrangements as a bonafide basis for acceptable national agreements. Total crew costs are calculated from all wage, fringe benefit, manning and other quantifiable labor charges. Then, if these are below ITF standards, the difference is to be given to a national seafarers fund. This arrangement is permissible under ITF standards only if the crew and officers of a ship are of the same nationality and the affected union, government, and employers agree on the funding arrangement.[6]

Deals. One hears repeatedly both from national union officials and maritime employers that "deals" are cut with the ITF permitting substandard wages and exemption from boycotts. Just

---

[6] Leo Barnes, "LDC Seamen Have to Be Competitive," in *Is the ITF Right?* (London: *Lloyd's of London Press*, 1981), pp. 17-20.

TABLE IV-6
ITF Manning Standards 2,550-5,500 GRT
Estimated monthly crew cost (worldwide)—rates effective
as of April 1, 1982

Rank or Rating	Basic Pay US$	40 Hours Normal US$	60 Hours Sat/Sun US$	3 Days Leave Pay US$	Total Pay Per Month US$
Master	2,675	792.00	2,142.00	321.00	5,930.00
C/Off	1,727	512.00	1,380.00	207.30	3,826.30
2/Off	1,383	408.00	1,104.00	165.90	3,060.90
3/Off	1,333	396.00	1,068.00	159.90	2,956.90
R/Off	1,383	408.00	1,104.00	165.90	3,060.90
C/Eng	2,431	720.00	1,944.00	291.60	5,386.60
1/Eng	1,727	512.00	1,380.00	207.30	3,826.30
2/Eng	1,383	408.00	1,104.00	165.90	3,060.90
3/Eng	1,333	396.00	1,068.00	159.90	2,956.90
Bosun	877	260.00	702.00	105.30	1,944.30
6 AB's	4,710	1,392.00	3,780.00	565.20	10,447.20
Donkeyman	877	260.00	702.00	105.30	1,944.30
C/Stwd	1,383	408.00	1,104.00	165.90	3,060.90
Cook	877	260.00	702.00	105.30	1,944.30
A/Cook	668	196.00	534.00	80.10	1,478.10
2 Messmen	1,336	392.00	1,068.00	160.20	2,956.20

TOTAL CREW 22   TOTAL MONTHLY CREW COST   US$ 57,956.20*

Source: ITF schedules adapted and compiled by B. L. Williamson, "The International Transport Workers Federation," (unpublished study, 1982).
* Total monthly crew costs under ITF "agreements" effective January 1, 1983, worldwide rates, (4.6 percent increases)=US$60,622.19.

what shipowners offer in return for such arrangements is not clear, but some ships without blue certificates apparently are not boycotted.

BLUE CERTIFICATE COVERAGE

Table IV-10 shows the number of vessels which the ITF has designated "approved" since 1970. The decline between 1982 and 1983 is probably the result of the depressed state of the industry rather than of a decline in successful ITF activity. It is also likely, however, that the changed character of the legal situation in the British Isles, described at length in the previous chapter, has affected the ITF's ability to compel conformance to its contract.

It is not possible to gauge accurately what percent of the ocean transport FOC ships have blue certificates because the number of ships varies almost daily. The Institute of Shipping Economics (Bremen, West Germany) lists, as of October 1982, a total of

TABLE IV-7
ITF Manning Standards 1,600-2,550 GRT
Estimated monthly crew cost (worldwide)—rates effective
as of April 1, 1982

Rank or Rating	Basic Pay US$	40 Hours Normal US$	60 Hours Sat/Sun US$	3 Days Leave Pay US$	Total Pay Per Month US$
Master	2,675	792.00	2,142.00	321.00	5,930.00
C/Off	1,727	512.00	1,380.00	207.30	3,826.30
2/Off	1,383	408.00	1,104.00	165.90	3,060.90
3/Off	1,333	396.00	1,068.00	159.90	2,956.90
R/Off	1,383	408.00	1,104.00	165.90	3,060.90
C/Eng	2,431	720.00	1,944.00	291.60	5,386.60
1/Eng	1,727	512.00	1,380.00	207.30	3,826.30
2/Eng	1,383	408.00	1,104.00	165.90	3,060.90
3/Eng	1,333	396.00	1,068.00	159.90	2,956.90
Bosun	877	260.00	702.00	105.30	1,944.30
5 AB's	3,925	1,160.00	3,150.00	471.00	8,706.00
Donkeyman	877	260.00	702.00	105.30	1,944.30
C/Stwd	1,383	408.00	1,104.00	165.90	3,060.90
Cook	877	260.00	702.00	105.30	1,944.30
2 Messmen	1,336	392.00	1,068.00	100.20	2,956.20

TOTAL CREW 20   TOTAL MONTHLY CREW COST   US$ 54,621.70*

Source: ITF schedules adapted and compiled by B. L. Williamson, "The International Transport Workers Federation," (unpublished study, 1982).
* Total monthly crew costs under ITF "agreements" effective January 1, 1983, wordwide rates, (4.6 percent increases)=US$57,134.30.

7,458 vessels of 300 gross registered tons (grt) or over for fourteen countries which either now have, or have been, open registries.[7] If the ITF has approved 1,722 of these (its March 1983 figure, Table IV-10) that would mean that its contracts, or contracts approved by it, cover 23 percent of FOC shipping. Since the larger FOC ships are most likely to attract the ITF's attention, it is difficult to dispute the general claim of the ITF leadership that at least 25 percent of FOC shipping, of 300 grt, or more, is covered by its agreements.

How many of these FOC ships which carry blue certificates are actually paying the ITF wage rates or better is another matter. As noted in Chapter III, as of March 1983, 712 of the blue cer-

---

[7] "Total World Merchant Fleet As of October 1st, 1982," *Shipping Statistics* (Institute of Shipping Economics, Bremen, West Germany), Vol. 26, No. 12 (December 1982), Table 1, pp. xii/11-12. The countries listed which are included in our FOC total are Liberia, Panama, Singapore, Cyprus, Bermuda, Malta, Cayman Islands, Sri Lanka, St. Vincent, Costa Rica, Vanuta, and St. Lucia. (No listing was found for the Netherlands Antilles.)

TABLE IV-8
ITF Manning Standards 700-1,600 GRT
Estimated monthly crew cost (worldwide)—rates effective
as of April 1, 1982

Rank or Rating	Basic Pay US$	40 Hours Normal US$	60 Hours Sat/Sun US$	3 Days Leave Pay US$	Total Pay Per Month US$
Master	2,675	792.00	2,142.00	321.00	5,930.00
C/Off	1,727	512.00	1,380.00	207.30	3,826.30
2/Off	1,383	408.00	1,104.00	165.90	3,060.90
C/Eng	2,431	720.00	1,944.00	291.60	5,386.60
1/Eng	1,727	512.00	1,380.00	207.30	3,826.30
2/Eng	1,383	408.00	1,104.00	165.90	3,060.90
Bosun	877	260.00	702.00	105.30	1,944.30
3 AB's	2,355	696.00	1,890.00	282.60	5,223.60
Donkeyman	877	260.00	702.00	105.30	1,944.30
Cook/Stwd	877	260.00	702.00	105.30	1,944.30
1 Messman	668	196.00	534.00	80.10	1,478.10

TOTAL CREW 13   TOTAL MONTHLY CREW COST   US$ 37,625.60*

Source: ITF schedules adapted and compiled by B. L. Williamson, "The International Transport Workers Federation," (an unpublished study, 1982).
* Total monthly crew costs under ITF "agreements" effective January 1, 1983 worldwide rates, (4.6 percent increases)=US$39,356.38.

TABLE IV-9
ITF Manning Standards 0-700 GRT
Estimated monthly crew cost (worldwide)—rates effective
as of April 1, 1982

Rank or Rating	Basic Pay US$	40 Hours Normal US$	60 Hours Sat/Sun US$	3 Days Leave Pay US$	Total Pay Per Month US$
Master	2,675	792.00	2,142.00	321.00	5,930.00
C/Off	1,727	512.00	1,380.00	207.30	3,826.30
2/Off	1,383	408.00	1,104.00	165.90	3,060.90
C/Eng	2,431	720.00	1,944.00	291.60	5,386.60
1/Eng	1,727	512.00	1,380.00	207.30	3,826.30
3 AB's	2,355	696.00	1,890.00	282.60	5,223.60
Donkeyman	877	260.00	702.00	105.30	1,944.30
Cook/Stwd	877	260.00	702.00	105.30	1,944.30

TOTAL CREW 10   TOTAL MONTHLY CREW COST   US$ 31,142.30*

Source: ITF schedules adapted and compiled by B. L. Williamson, "The International Transport Workers Federation," (an unpublished study, 1982).
* Total monthly crew costs under ITF "agreements" effective January 1, 1983, worldwide rates, (4.6 percent increases)=US$32,574.85.

TABLE IV-10
ITF Approved Ships, 1970-1983

Date of Count	No. of Approved Ships
1/1/70	95
1/1/71	149
6/1/72	207
12/31/73	420
12/31/74	637
3/1/75	640
1/1/76	800
12/31/76	950
2/7/77	990
3/8/78	1,136
1/1/79	1,520
3/1/79	1,232
1/1/80	1,307
1/1/81	1,920
1/1/82	2,091
3/1/83	1,722

Source: 1970-1981, various ITF reports; 1983, *Lloyd's List,* March 26, 1983, p. 1.

tificate carrying vessels have received their approvals from the Korean Seamen's Union (KSU)—an astounding 41 percent of the total.[8] The rush of FOC ship operators to sign with the South Koreans is a clear indication that it is a good deal for them and lends credence to the charge by the British National Union of Seamen (NUS), the Greek Panhellenic Seamen's Federation (PNO), and other ITF affiliates that the KSU is handing out certificates without maintaining ITF standards.[9] This has forced both the KSU and the South Korean government to review their procedures.[10]

---

[8] Victor Smart, "NUS seeks to expel S. Korea from the ITF," *Lloyd's List,* March 26, 1983, p. 1.

[9] See "S. Koreans accused of crew 'treachery'," *Lloyd's List,* December 1, 1982, p. 1; and Victor Smart, "NUS seeks to expel S. Korea . . . ."

[10] In addition to the promises of the Korean Seamen's Union and the government of South Korea to reexamine and revise their procedures for granting blue certificates, the ITF has attemped to devise a program, short of expelling the KSU to see that this is done. See Victor Smart, "S. Koreans call halt to Greek free flag deals," *Lloyd's List,* March 3, 1983, p. 1; and Bridget Hogan, "S. Korea to review licensing of ships," *Lloyd's List,* April 6, 1982, p. 4; and *ITF Newsletter,* No. 3, (March 1983), pp. 22-24.

It is likely that other Third World countries are also engaged to a much lesser degree than the South Koreans in undercutting the ITF standards and that the ITF itself does make deals. Moreover, the extent of double bookkeeping and operator-crew connivance to maintain good standing in the eyes of the ITF while paying sub-ITF wages is undoubtedly widespread. It would, therefore, not be surprising if at least one-half of the ships carrying blue certificates do not meet ITF standards. As long as the shipping industry continues in a depressed state, such evasion is likely to grow. Laid up ships and out-of-work seafarers are increasingly willing to cut prices and wages in order to gain work in such periods of stress.

Charterers' and Owners' Attitudes

A fundamental reason why many shipowners carry a blue certificate is that charterers insist upon it. The cost of a boycott can be substantially greater than payment of ITF wages and a contribution to the welfare fund. Moreover, to the owner of a large ship, especially a new one costing $20-50 million, the payment of $10,000 more per month in wages is insignificant when interest could cost $300-500 thousand per year. On the other hand, the owners of smaller, second hand vessels, which could cost as little as $3-6 million, find that $10,000 more in wages per month can eliminate profit. It is, therefore not surprising that Greek owners, who are often relatively small entrepreneurs operating small fleets of older ships, have gravitated to the South Korean union and its easy-to-obtain blue certificates, particularly during the current depressed period in the industry.

Blue Certificates and National Conditions

The ITF leadership has long admitted that FOC ships include some vessels that meet all standards for safety and pay wages well above its minima. The tankers fleet of the United States oil companies are usually cited as being in this category, but many other vessels fit this description also. Yet, as described in Chapter III, vessels of such companies are harassed and boycotted just like ships that pay substandard wages. The ITF focuses narrowly on the flag, regardless of the rates of pay, the conditions of work, or the desires of the affected employees. It is this aspect of the ITF's policy which subjects it to the most criticism.

The ITF's early career, particularly its use of the International Labour Organisation (ILO), was devoted to improving the condition of seafarers. It makes a similar claim for its FOC campaign. In part this can be supported. There is no question that the threat of ITF action and its marshalling of public opinion have forced FOC countries to raise their standards, to devote more attention and legislation to safety practices, and to have greater concern with the rights, training, and well-being of seafarers. The absence of unions, and/or their weaknesses in such countries, has created a void that the ITF in part has filled.

On the other hand, the ITF has from the inception of its campaign equated FOC shipping with substandard conditions. This both ignores the actual situation and disregards the tremendous economic differences between the developed and the underdeveloped countries and the needs of their respective maritime labor forces.

By equating FOC shipping with substandard wages and labor conditions, the ITF not only inaccurately categorizes those who, like the United States petroleum companies, provide above standard conditions on FOC vessels, but it ignores the national flags that pay wages that are reportedly among the lowest in the world shipping industry. We refer, of course, to the growing fleets of the Soviet Union and its East European satellites. There are no reliable data as to wages aboard these vessels, but no shipping union or management person has been encountered who seriously believes that these countries do not pay substantially less than ILO minima, however much they may claim to the contrary.

Of course, the Soviets and their allies could, like the countries of the Indian subcontinent, point out that their maritime wages cannot be out of line with the wage system in their land-based industries. The ITF, however, has rejected this justification. It now demands the equalization of Asian maritime wages with those of Europe and North America. As was pointed out in Chapter III, this policy seems designed to eliminate Asian worker competition for the benefit of their developed world counterparts. Obviously, such a policy will strengthen the propensity for evasion, double bookkeeping, and meaningless blue certificates. It could also transfer maritime work to the Soviet bloc, which is already undercutting world prices in shipping.

The ITF's policies continue to tilt heavily toward its key European and North American affiliates. The fact that the developed country unions dominated the ITF's staff, officers, and executive board (see Chapter II) may make this tilt inevitable, but it may still be commented upon. By equating FOC shipping with substandard conditions and at the same time refusing to tolerate differential wages for economies that are vastly different, the ITF is in danger of becoming ever more a tool that unions in developed countries can use to ward off job competition from underdeveloped countries rather than being an international coordinating body for the purpose of improving and safeguarding seafarers' work and wages worldwide.

THE FINANCES OF THE ITF FOC CAMPAIGN

As was made clear in Chapter III, a key part of the ITF's campaign against FOC shipping is the requirement that blue certificate holders and those boycotted contribute to the ITF "welfare fund." What this involves for the ITF and what the ITF does with the funds received are the subjects of this section.

Seafarers' International Assistance, Welfare and Protection Fund and the Seafarers' Trust

The ITF Seafarers' International Assistance, Welfare and Protection Fund (the Fund) operates with money received from payments made by flag or crew of convenience operators as a result of agreements connected with the FOC campaign. The Fund, which was separated from the general fund in 1965, was founded to make assistance and welfare payments on behalf of seafarers for such purposes as seamen's homes. Those attending the ITF's 1980 congress adopted an amendment to their organization's constitution specifically authorizing the ITF to provide help to individual transport workers, including seamen.[11] In addition to this, the ITF Seafarers' Trust (the Trust) was subsequently created with money from the Fund. The Trust serves as a disbursing account to which money from the Fund is transferred for disbursement to various projects. These clarifications obviously came in response to recent court action against the ITF by shippers opposed to its drive to force contributions to the Fund. These court challenges have imposed increasing costs in time and money on the ITF. As Table IV-11 makes clear, legal and professional expenses to the Fund have risen sharply in recent years, from £38,514 (US $73,408) in 1977 to £91,557 (US $203,623) only two years later. Considering these legal costs as well as the very sizeable allocation to the ITF general fund to cover the secretariat's administrative work, the overhead charged

---

[11] *ITF Newsletter*, No. 8, (August 1980), p. 69.

TABLE IV-11
*ITF Seafarers' International Assistance, Welfare and
Protection Fund
Income and Expenditure Accounts*
(1977-1979—in pounds sterling, £)

	1977 a	1978 b	1979 c
Income			
Welfare Contributions and Seafarers' Membership Fees d	2,075,971	3,254,178	3,788,529
Interest and Dividends (less Corporation Tax)	180,274	324,571	404,996
Rent Receivable, H.Q. Offices	—	8,688	36,086
Total Income	2,256,245	3,587,437	4,229,611
Expenditure			
Welfare Grants	437,554	733,095	457,397
Assistance to Seamen	7,363	30,432	5,527
Interests on Crew Back Pay Settlements	—	9,385	33,488
Allocation to General Fund for Administration, Services, etc.	163,841	207,597	325,418
Head Office Expenditure on Meetings, Travel and Representation	66,968	60,377	91,686
Grants to Seafarers' Unions	1,000	3,316	2,242
Reimbursements to Seafarers' Unions in Respect of Representation	126,584	292,167	292,151
Legal and Professional Expenses	38,514	54,517	91,557
Exchange Difference	—	—	94,265
Total Expenditure	841,824	1,390,886	1,393,728
Surplus/Deficit			
Operating Surplus	1,414,421	2,196,551	2,835,883
Surplus (+)/Loss (−) on Sales of Investments after Deduction of Tax	+13,204	−2,273	+49,681
Total Surplus	1,427,625	2,194,278	2,885,564
Balance			
Balance at Beginning of Year	3,153,595	4,581,220	7,655,400
Net Contributions for 1977 not previously brought into Account e	—	879,902	—
Balance at End of Year	4,581.220	7,655,400	10,540,964

Source: ITF, *Financial Statements and Auditors' Reports 1977 to 1979*, presented to ITF 33d Congress, Miami, July 17-25, 1980, p. 8.
a £ = US$1.9060.
b £ = US$2.0345.
c £ = US$2.2240.
d remitted by shipowners and collecting unions.
e funds held by Korean and Taiwan unions.

to the Fund is quite considerable. By way of contrast, the expenditures for the objectives of the Fund—welfare grants and assistance to seamen—accounted for only one-third of total expenditures in 1979. In addition, the size of the Fund is growing at an impressive rate while the percentage of funds spent on welfare and assistance is declining.

Even more remarkable has been the growth of the Fund's income and overall surplus (Table IV-12). Between 1971 and 1979, for example, total Fund income increased almost ten-fold to £ 4,229,611 (US $9,406,655). During the same period, the Fund went from showing a small operating deficit of £ 2,107 (US $5,378) to posting an operating surplus of almost three million pounds. Because of the increasing number of successful port actions conducted since the early 1970s, particularly in Australia and in certain European countries, and because of the desires of many charterers and shipowners to pay rather than to risk boycotts, the Fund was able by the end of 1979 to show a total accumulated surplus of £ 10,540,964 (US $23,443,103).

TABLE IV-12
ITF Welfare Funds, Income, Expenditures and Surplus
(Pounds Sterling—£)

Year	Income £	Expenditure £	Surplus £	Adjustment for Exceptional Income/ (Expenditure) £	Balance at Year End £
1971	43,293				
1972	196,142				
1973	323,397				659,404
1974	670,973	187,958	483,015	(8,212)	1,134,207
1975	1,038,336	288,237	750,009	25,549	1,909,855
1976	1,739,237	499,741	1,239,496	4,244	3,153,595
1977	2,256,245	841,824	1,414,421	13,204	4,581,220
1978	3,587,437	1,390,886	2,196,551	877,629	7,655,400
1979	4,229,611	1,393,728	2,835,883	49,681	10,540,964
1980	3,860,010	895,439	2,964,571		13,505,535
1981	6,243,159	1,010,677	5,232,482	(34,688)	18,703,329*

Source: ITF reports including meeting of the Fair Practices Committee, London 1982. £18,703,329 @ 1981 exchange rate of $2.079 equaled $37,928,480.
* Includes funds transferred to trust in 1981.

This is an extraordinary situation for an international trade union secretariat. Most ITSs regularly have difficulty simply covering their yearly operating expenses and often end fiscal years with deficits. The ITF's general fund (Table II-5, Chapter II) has a 1979 surplus of £ 37,028, less than 5 percent of that of the welfare fund. Moreover, the general fund's surplus was clearly attributable to payment of regular expenses and overhead from the welfare fund. There can be little doubt that, with such enormous financial resources at its disposal, the ITF has the potential to act forcefully to promote the interests of its constituents. The accumulation of such riches, however, involves problems for the ITF, not only from the organized shippers who are compelled to provide the money for the fund, but from government authorities and from the Third World seamen on whose behalf the ITF claims the funds are supposedly collected. A look at how the Fund was managed in 1981 is instructive in understanding how the Fund is utilized. At the ITF Fair Practices Committee meeting in London, June 2-3, 1982, the 1981 accounts of the Fund were presented along with the 1981 accounts of the Trust. These unaudited accounts, as set forth in Table IV-13, are most revealing.

TABLE IV-13

Seafarers' International Assistance Welfare & Protection Fund
Provisional Accounts Year Ending December 31, 1981*
(Pounds Sterling—£)

Income	£
Remitted by Shipowners & Collecting Unions	
Welfare Contributions	4,700,653
Crew Membership Fees	330,321
Subtotal	*5,030,974*
Interest & Dividends	1,562,120
Less Corporation Tax	388,289
Subtotal	*1,173,831*
Rent Receivable-HQ Office	38,354
TOTAL FUND INCOME 1981	6,243,159
Expenditure	
Welfare Grants	78,343
Assistance to Seamen	10,154
Interest to Crew Back Pay Settlements	19,500
Subtotal	*107,997*

TABLE IV-13 (continued)

Allocation to General Fund-Staff Services Rendered, and Indirect Expenses Incurred on behalf of the Fund	386,001
Head Office Expenditures for Meetings, Travel Administration & Representation—Direct Expenses	124,230
Grants to Seafarers Unions	3,538
Direct Reimbursements to Unions and/or Their Officers in respect of Representation	321,929
Legal & Professional Expenses	66,982
Subtotal	*902,680*
TOTAL FUND EXPENDITURE 1981	1,010,677
Operating Surplus for 1981	5,232,482
Loss on Sale of Investments (Net)	34,688
TOTAL SURPLUS 1981	5,197,794
Balance of Fund at beginning of Year	13,505,535
Less Funds transferred to Charitable Trust	4,178,351
Subtotal	*9,327,184*
BALANCE OF FUND AT END OF YEAR	14,524,978
Provision	
Foreign Currency Stabilization	1,325,645
Receipts Awaiting Allocation	428,959
TOTAL FUND RESOURCES	16,279,582
Assets	
Cash at Banks (London & Abroad)	9,188,618
Investments (Including Property)	5,510,788
Interest Receivable	95,504
Current Accounts—Affiliated Unions	4,018,097
Current Account—General Fund	17,358
Recoverable Expenses	960
TOTAL ASSETS	18,831,325
Less Liabilities	
Sundry Creditors & Advances	1,976
Crew Back Pay & Compensation Awaiting Distribution	2,320,166
Taxation 1981	229,601
TOTAL LIABILITIES	2,551,743
TOTAL NET ASSETS	16,279,582

Source: A Brief Report on attending the ITF Fair Practices Committee Meeting, London, 2nd to 3rd June, 1982.
* Subject to audit.

In 1981 the Fund collected £ 5,030,974 (US $10,202,312) in welfare contributions and membership fees, a large proportion of which was subsequently transferred to the Trust. The Fund's total 1981 income, including interest, dividends and rent was £ 6,243,159 (US $12,660,502). Rent was listed as income because the Fund financed and owns the ITF headquarters building and rents space to the ITF. At the beginning of 1981 there was already £ 13,505,535 (US $27,387,874) in the Fund to which this income was added.

Excluding £ 4,178,351 (US $8,473,278) in funds transferred to the Trust (which will be dealt with below), the Fund had £ 1,010,677 (US $2,049,552) in expenditures. Eighty-nine percent of these expenditures were for overhead, whereas only 11 percent was spent on welfare grants, assistance to seamen and interest on crews' back pay for settlements. Included in overhead was £ 386,001 (US $782,771) for allocation to the general fund for staff services rendered and indirect expenses incurred on behalf of the Fund. This again emphasizes that the ITF general fund is subsidized by transfers from the welfare fund.

Of the £ 4,178,351 (US $8,473.278) transferred to the Trust in February 1981, £ 378,277.18 or 9 percent was expended in 1981. Table IV-14 shows grants made as of May 1982. Of the thirty-two grants made from the Trust, twenty-eight were to unions in developed nations. The other four grants were for American or European facilities in port cities in the Philippines, Indonesia, Oman, and South Africa. Thirty-two percent of the grants were to British affiliated union projects. Some of the more interesting grants made from this money—collected from the operators of FOC ships whose crews are made up overwhelmingly of Third World seamen—include: £ 17,000 (US $34,474) to the Rosenhill Seafarers' Centre, Gothenburg, Sweden for floodlights for a running track (Swedish Seamen's Union); £ 18,800 (US $38,164) to the Merchant Seamen's War Memorial Society, Great Britain, for purchase of equipment (British National Union of Seamen); £ 3,267.45 (US $6,651) for provision of video casettes on certain Japanese ships (All Japan Seamen's Union—KAIIN); £ 30,231.55 (US $61,370.64) to United Seamen's Service, USA (U.S. National Maritime Union); and £ 20,000 (US $40,600) to expenses of "Sports Week" (Norwegian Seamen's Union).

This large accumulation of funds, the meager expenditures therefrom, and the concentration of expenditures on activities in behalf of unions in developed countries emphasize the character

TABLE IV-14
ITF Seafarers' Trust: Grants Made (As At 7 May 1982)

Grantee	£
Anchor House, Hull, England —improvements (British NUS)	11,000.00
Durban Bayhead Club —building extension (British MNAOA)	3,800.00
Liverpool Personal Service Society —re late Claes Hoberg (British NUS)	50.00
Missions to Seamen, Halifax, Canada —extension to accommodation (Canadian CBRT&GW)	4,000.00
International Sports Committee for Seafarers —towards expenses of "Sports Week" (Norwegian Seamen's Union)	20,000.00
Seafarers' Hotel, Copenhagen —renewal of furniture (Danish Metal Søfart)	12,000.00
Stella Maris Club, Sydney —purchase of bus (Australian WWF)	7,385.00
Bay of Plenty Seafarers' Centre, New Zealand —purchase of bus (New Zealand WWF)	7,685.00
Missions to Seamen, Vancouver —improvements to canteen (Canadian CBRT&GW)	3,050.00
Seamen's Welfare Foundation, Rotterdam —printing of brochure (Dutch FWZ)	2,000.00
United Seamen's Service, USA —towards activities in 1981 (American NMU)	30,231.55
Merchant Seamen's War Memorial Society, Great Britain —purchase of equipment (British NUS)	18,800.00
German Seamen's Mission, Djakarta —purchase of minibus (German OeTV)	5,000.00

Source: A Brief Report on attending the ITF Fair Practices Committee
Meeting, London, 2nd to 3rd June, 1982.

of the ITF as an organization that is primarily concerned with promoting the interests of seamen who are members of unions in the developed world. The examination of the money collected for the welfare fund also supports the point made to the authors by members of Asian seafarers' unions. These union members made it clear that, while on the one hand ITF activities did bolster their unions by gaining them members from shippers who felt that they required a blue certificate in order to trade in certain ports, on the other hand their organizations received little from the money collected for the welfare fund except for trips to meetings.[12]

In addition, the size of the Fund and its growth add to the temptation of the ITF inspectors, who are mainly officers and agents of national unions, to "pocket some of the take." We have already noted the questionable practices that have been found in Sweden, Australia, and Great Britain, and they have been alleged elsewhere. Some shipowners admitted payoffs in several countries in interviews with the authors. The extent, or even the truthfulness of some of these charges, are not known, but it would be surprising, given such availability of easy money, if some irregularities were not occurring.

There are two main explanations for the fact that the Fund and Trust are growing in size to such an extent rather than being expended on welfare activities. One is that the ITF leadership apparently believes that eventually the legal activities of the shipowners or government officials may require the return of the Fund to those who were forced to contribute to it. The other is that the Fund may be regarded as a potential war chest for the continuing FOC campaign. Whatever the ITF's motivations in building such a large fund, it will be most interesting to watch the pattern of expenditure in the future to see whether more is spent in the developing nations where the members of the Special Seafarers' Department overwhelmingly reside and also to see whether the Fund and Trust continue to grow.

One reason why funds are spent more in developed than in underdeveloped countries is, of course, the domination of the ITF and its governmental structure by members from the developed countries. In addition to the officers and executive board, as shown by its composition in 1979 (Table IV-15), the Fair Practices Committee historically was almost entirely drawn from unions of the developed world. As a result of the difficulties with the Asian unions and the temporary suspension of the National Union of Seafarers of India, Bombay (NUSI), the committee was expanded to include a number of Third World unions. The attendance at the June 1982 meeting of the committee, set forth in Table IV-16, shows a slightly wider representation and the presence of a number of Third World union observers. The committee is, however, co-chaired by executives of the Australian Waterside Workers' Federation and the Danish Seafarers and is

---

[12] Interviews, various Asian ports, June-July 1982.

TABLE IV-15
International Transport Workers' Federation
Fair Practices Committee
(December 31, 1979)

Country	Seafarers	Dockers
Argentina	A. Giovenco	
Australia		T.I. Bull
Belgium	R. van Cant	A. Vervliet
Canada	R. Gralewicz	D. Nicholson
Finland	R. Herdin	P. Teikari
France		J. Duniau
Germany	D. Benze	M. Rosenberg
Israel	A.A. Chisik	
Italy	F. Giorgi	L. Betti
Japan	K. Kihata	
Netherlands	W. Ch. van Zuylen	B.J. Van Eldik
New Zealand	J. Woods	E.G. Thompson
Norway	E. Tollerud	
Sweden	G. Karlsson	H. Ericson
Switzerland	K. Rebsamen	
United Kingdom	E. Nevin J. Slater	J.L. Jones
United States	J. Fay S.J. Wall	T.W. Gleason Sr.

Co-Chairmen: K. Mols Sørensen (Chairman, Seafarers' Section)
C.H. Fitzgibbon (Chairman, Dockers' Section)

Source: ITF, *Report on Activities 1977-1978-1979*, p. 111.

clearly controlled by the developed country representatives and the ITF staff.

Therefore, it remains to be determined, as the existence of this Fund becomes widely known, whether shipowners will continue their contributions or whether they will move more aggressively to oppose it. As was noted in Chapter III, there have been no cases brought in the United Kingdom to recover monies paid to the ITF for its welfare fund despite a clear notice that such suits are actionable. As long as it remains less costly and easier to pay than to fight, the welfare fund will continue to grow.

Back Pay

Besides collecting entrance (initiation) fees, dues, and contributions to its welfare fund, the ITF, as already noted, assesses boycotted shipowners backpay, allegedly to be paid to seamen for

TABLE IV-16
International Transport Workers' Federation
Fair Practices Committee Meeting
London, 2-3 June 1982—Provisional Attendance List

Country and Union	Members	Advisers
Australia		
Waterside Workers' Federation	C.H. Fitzgibbon (Co-Chairman) T.I. Bull	L.J. Symes
Merchant Service Guild	F. Ross	
Belgium		
Belgische Transportarbeidersbond	R. van Cant A. Vervliet	E. Baudet M. de Volder R. Dielis A. Lambregts
Brazil		
Confederaçao Nacional dos Trabal- hadores em Transportes Marítimos, Fluviais e Aéreos	M. Sant'anna	
Canada		
Canadian Brotherhood of Railway, Transport & General Workers	J. Levia *	G. McCullough
Denmark		
Dansk Styrmandsforening	K. Mols Sørensen (Co-Chairman)	
Specialarbejderforbundet i Danmark (SiD)	A. Kruse	J. Rask H. Hansen
Finland		
Suomen Merimies Unioni ry	L. Heinonen	K. Sadeluoto
Suomen Auto-Ja Kuljetusalan Työtekijäliitto ry	L. Roppola	K. Kehikoinen
France		
Fédération Générale des Transports et de l'Equipment—CFDT	A. Barbero	
Fédération F.O. des Travaux Publics et Portuaires de la Marine et des Transports	C. Costagnier *	
Germany		
Gewerkschaft öffentliche Dienste, Transport u. Verkehr	D. Benze M. Rosenberg	G. Wille H. Schmeling I. Logemann H. Wohlleben

TABLE IV-16 (continued)

Country and Union	Members	Advisers
Ghana		
Ghana Merchant Navy Officers' Association	N. Ashietey	
India		
National Union of Seafarers of India	L. Barnes	
Israel		
Israeli Sea Officers' Union	Y. Groman *	
Italy		
Federazione Italiana Lavoratori del Mare	M. Guidi	R. Nesciobelli B. del Bonis
Japan		
All Japan Seamen's Union	K. Kihata	
Korea		
Korean Seamen's Union	H.C. Bang	K.J. Ko
Netherlands		
Federatie van Werknemersorganisaties in de Zeevaart	C. Roodenburg	J. Putter R. Touwen
Vervoersbond FNV	K. Marges *	
Norway		
Norsk Sjømannsforbund	Ø. Ringvold	H. Aasarød S. Nilsen
Panama		
Federación Industrial de Trabajadores del Transporte Terrestre, Aéreos, Maritimos Portuarios y Similares	C. Villareal	
Portugal		
Federacao Naçional dos Sindicatos de Trabalhadores Portuarios	C. Duarte Sousa	A. Laureano
Philippines		
Associated Marine Officers' and Seamen's Union of the Philippines	G. Oca	
Singapore		
Singapore Organisation of Seamen	Choo Eng Khoon *	Leow Ching Chuan

TABLE IV-16 (continued)

Country and Union	Members	Advisers
Spain		
Federación del Transporte de ELA-STV	Juan Bengoetxea *	José Ibarguren
Federación de Trabajadores del Transporte del Estado Español—UGT	L. Amor	A. Aguirre
Sweden		
Svenska Sjöfolksförbundet	A. Lindström *	L. Jansson
Svenska Transportarbetareförbundet	H. Wahlström	B. Gustavsson
Switzerland		
VHTL Sekretariat Rhein- and See-schiffahrt	K. Rebsamen	
Taiwan (Rp. of China)		
National Chinese Seamen's Union	Yang Shin Chen	Lie Ching-Chee
Trinidad		
Seamen & Waterfront Workers' Trade Union	F. Mungroo	
United Kingdom		
The Merchant Navy & Airline Officers' Association	M. Bourne *	
Transport & General Workers' Union	J. Connolly *	
U.S.A.		
International Longshoremen's Assoc.	T.W. Gleason	
National Maritime Union of America		R. Lioeanjie

* Denotes substitute for member.

	Observers
Country and Union	Name
Finland	
Luotsiliitto (Lotsförbundet) ry	O. Haeyrinen
Hong Kong	
The Merchant Navy Officers' Guild	A. Griffiths
Amalgamated Union of Seafarers—HK	Au Yeung Ming Leung Tat Shing
South Africa	
General Workers' Union	D. Lewis I. Frantz
Sweden	
Svenska Maskinbefälsförbundet	F. Havik

TABLE IV-16 (continued)

Country and Union	Name
U.K. (ITF)	
National Union of Railwaymen	Peter King
	Harry Shaw
	Harry Windsor
	John Ross
U.S.A.	
International Organization of Masters,	Alan Scott
Mates & Pilots	Patrick King

ITF Regional Representatives	
Latin American & the Caribbean	M. Gomez, E. Costilla & F. Maricato
Asia	M.S. Hoda

ITF Secretariat

Harold Lewis, A. Selander & Brian Laughton

Source: A Brief Report on Attending the ITF Fair Practices Committee Meeting, London, 2nd to 3rd June, 1982.

Note: This list contains the names of all participants who had notified the secretariat of their attendance as at 28 May 1982.

the difference between their wages on the ship prior to the signing of the ITF agreement and what they would have received if the ITF agreement had been in force from the inception of their employment. As was discussed in Chapter III, the extent to which these monies find their way into the seamen's pockets in whose name they are collected is certainly limited. Moreover, seamen who do receive back pay can find themselves in considerable difficulties with their countries, again as noted in Chapter III, or they might be discriminated against by their employer.

Yet the amounts of money involved are impressive. Table IV-17 shows the backpay paid by owners for the years 1974-1981, with estimated data for 1980. Nearly £ 8 million (US $16,223,-200) was paid out in 1981 alone, and an estimated total of £ 45,088,714 (US $88,600,565) was collected by the end of 1982. (The decline in the annual receipts since 1979 is undoubtedly caused both by a drop in world trade and by greater shipper resistance.)

The temptation to use parts of this huge sum for other purposes has already been noted and its diversion may be fairly widespread. Moreover, the ITF does indeed find it difficult to disperse it to Third World seamen because of the problems already noted. Finally, there are recurring rumors that additional sums are given directly to ITF inspectors, national union functionaries, and others who might impede ship movements. Such rumors can neither be authenticated nor quantified.

TABLE IV-17
Back Pay Won by the ITF
1974-1981

| | No. of Ships | | Total | Avg/Ship |
Year	Total	Monthly Average	£	£
1974	101	8.4	800,000	7,920
1975	120	10	1,300,000	10,833
1976	152	12.7	2,960,000	19,474
1977	175	14.6	3,740,959	21,377
1978	200	16.7	4,937,432	24,687
1979	338	28.2	8,567,323	25,347
1980	240 [a]	20.0 [a]	8,000,000 [a]	33,333 [a]
1981	224	18.7	7,958,000	35,526
1982	NA	NA	6,625,000	NA

Source: See Table IV-4 for 1974-1981. For 1982, *ITF Newsletter*, No. 3, (March 1983), p. 23. 1981 total equals $16,138,028 and average $72,043.
1982 total equals $10,600.00.
NA=Not Available.
[a] estimate.

Table IV-18 shows the back pay sums collected in each country in 1981. It comes as no surprise to see that Australia leads all countries in this regard by a considerable amount, even though the nearly $3.6 million collected there does not include whatever the Seamen's Union of Australia is obtaining in its own campaign, a campaign which is not part of the ITF. Next comes ITF direct collection—back pay sent to ITF headquarters rather than to an ITF affiliate. The more than one million dollars each collected by Germany and the Netherlands is, however, startling in view of the fact that legal redress can be secured there. It emphasizes that charterers and shipowners would rather pay than fight, even when legal redress is available, in order to avoid costly delays.

TABLE IV-18
Back Pay Collected by the ITF, 1981

Country	1981 12 months US$	Monthly average US$
Australia	3,593,742	299,478
Belgium	569,884	47,490
Canada	789,171	65,764
Denmark	—	—
Finland	300,667	25,055
France	40,000	3,333
Germany	1,256,351	104,696
Greece	36,043	3,004
Ireland	523,269	43,606
Israel	272,238	22,687
Italy	828,658	69,055
Netherlands	1,340,143	111,679
New Zealand	464,304	38,629
Norway	45,009	3,750
Portugal	111,000	9,250
Spain	69,121	5,760
Sweden	544,411	45,368
United Kingdom	683,685	56,974
United States	65,000	5,417
Direct collection/ITF London	2,561,092	213,424
Total	14,324,295	1,174,482

Source: A Brief Report on Attending the ITF Fair Practices Committee Meeting, London, 2nd to 3rd June, 1982.

CONCLUDING REMARKS

The International Transport Workers' Federation (ITF) is a unique organization. Like other international trade union secretariats (ITSs), it is a coordinating body for national unions. As such it supplies information, represents and coordinates national transport unions' interests before international governmental bodies, and performs other similar functions. It has handled these duties very successfully over the years; no other ITS can boast of a record at the International Labour Organisation (ILO) that approaches that of the ITF in terms of conventions adopted or recommendations agreed to. The ITF's accomplishments at the ILO have won it recognition as a spokesman for seamen's rights and welfare and also as an opponent of unsafe practices in all transportation industries, but especially in ocean transport.

There is also no doubt, as has already been pointed out, that the ITF's campaign against flag-of-convenience (FOC) shipping has forced shipowners to upgrade the conditions on board these ships and to improve the wages and working conditions of seafarers who work on these vessels. It has also induced the open registry countries to improve the laws governing these matters and to move their standards toward, or equal to, those recommended by the ILO.

On the other hand, the attempt of the ITF to equate FOC vessels with substandard ones—wherein the words of its former general secretary, "some [FOC] owners are among the best employers in the world, e.g., the U.S. oil companies, while others are certainly the worst" [13]—would appear to make the ITF an agent of European and North American trade unions attempting to hold or to gain work at the expense of seamen in less developed countries. In its FOC campaign, the ITF has collected millions of dollars and spent little on the welfare of seafarers. Moreover, only a tiny fraction of its small welfare expenditures have been given for the benefit of Third World seamen serving on FOC ships, seamen whose welfare is the alleged reason for collecting the funds.

The wage policy of the ITF is clearly skewed toward the need of European and North American seamen. As Dr. Leo Barnes, general secretary, National Union of Seafarers of India, Bombay, (NUSI), has pointed out, the ITF is the only ITS which advocates a uniform international wage schedule regardless of different national economic and social conditions.[14] Third World maritime countries and their unions see in this policy a clear attempt to drive their seafarers out of jobs. Moreover, the policy of the ITF in assigning to itself and to its affiliates the right to determine whether a martime union is legitimate and, if not, to arrogate to itself the right to supplant that union without necessarily consulting the affected employees raises serious questions of national law and freedom to choose. According to Dr. Barnes, ITF's seafarer affiliates from the Third World are deeply concerned about "the rigid and inflexible implementation of ITF

---

[13] Charles H. Blyth, address to Company of Master Mariners, London, December 8, 1975.

[14] Barnes, "LDC Seamen . . .," pp. 7-8.

wage policy which has jeopardized the interests of their members serving on non-national flag vessels." [15] Meanwhile, the low wages on ships of the Soviet bloc remain unaffected by boycotts.

The Future?

What will happen to the FOC campaign in the future? We see no great change as long as charterers and shipowners find it cheaper to pay rather than to litigate or fight and as long as national legislation in key countries tolerates the boycotts. With a newly elected Labour government in Australia, boycotts there are likely to be protected even more than they have been; the Social Democrat government in Sweden and any government in Finland are most unlikely to restrict ITF activities. Thus there remains only the possibility of more restrictions on ITF boycotts in the United Kingdom, and perhaps the possibility of attempts to restrict, or even to confiscate the welfare fund. The ITF could presumably thwart such action by moving its headquarters or the location of its funds.

We thus conclude that the ITF is likely to remain as a unique organization, which serves on the one hand as a typical, but very successful ITS, but which also:

1. Once negotiated a multinational labor agreement with an international employers' association;

2. engages in direct boycotts against vessels from a variety of countries;

3. signs agreements with shipowners even in disregard of national agreements;

4. collects millions of dollars which it utilizes with minimum regulation or regard to the alleged purposes for which the funds are collected;

5. maintains wage policies which seem designed to limit the competition of Third World seamen with those from the developed world.

Finally, the ITF is an organization that has vowed to eliminate all FOC ships from commerce. It has failed to do so, but has grown wealthy in the process. It now faces an interesting dilemma. In the unlikely event that it would succeed in its avowed purpose, the ITF would eliminate the source of its wealth.

---

[15] *Ibid.*, p. 21.

APPENDIXES

Appendix A

The ITF campaign in Australia prior to mid-1977 is set forth in the accompanying article written under Wharton Industrial Research Unit aegis and reproduced by permission from the *Journal of Industrial Relations* (Australia).

AUSTRALIAN MARITIME UNIONS AND THE INTERNATIONAL TRANSPORT WORKERS' FEDERATION

KINGSLEY LAFFER*

One of the more interesting developments in recent times has been the emergence of international trade unions. This paper considers the participation of Australian maritime unions in the International Transport Workers' Federation. The Federation's campaign against "flags of convenience" and "crews of convenience" is discussed and its success is highlighted. None the less, problems were encountered during the course of the campaign and these are discussed in detail. Of particular interest is the apparent hostility to the campaign of overseas shipowners and governments compared to the indifference displayed by Australian shipowners. In fact, Australian employers and government seem to believe that the campaign is a normal and reasonable trade union activity. (Ed.)

* Visiting Research Professor, Industrial Research Unit, The Wharton School, University of Pennsylvania. This study is part of an extensive study of multinational industrial relations being conducted by the Industrial Research Unit, The Wharton School, University of Pennsylvania, under the leadership of the Director, Professor Herbert R. Northrup, and the Co-Director, Professor Richard L. Rowan. A previous article in this series by Professors Rowan and Northrup appeared in this *Journal* in March 1975. The author wishes to thank the many people who have assisted, especially Less Symes, ITF Inspector, Sydney; Ailsa Dawes, WWF Librarian; and Norman Docker, Assistant Federal Secretary, WWF; also Phillip O'Toole, NSW Secretary, Federated Clerks Union and Barry Goldstiver, Senior Industrial Officer, CSR Ltd. Responsibility for the use made of information provided must, of course, rest with the author.

Reprinted from the *Journal of Industrial Relations* (Australia), June 1977.

BACKGROUND

AUSTRALIAN MARITIME unions have long given considerable attention to international matters. The unions have long been willing to detain ships in furtherance of their policies. They have often sought to redress complaints of poor wages and conditions of foreign seamen in ships calling at Australian ports. They were ready to protest the export of pig iron to Japan before World War II, government policies in South Africa and Chile, and the Vietnam War. It is proposed to consider here an important recent development, the strong participation by Australian maritime unions in the work of the International Transport Workers' Federation (ITF).

The ITF was founded in 1896; among its founders were the celebrated British Trade Union Leaders, Tom Mann and Ben Tillett. The ITF is one of the fifteen International Trade Secretariats, international unions organized on an industry basis to which national unions are affiliated. These Secretariats in turn maintain a loose affiliation to the International Confederation of Free Trade Unions (ICFTU) headquartered in Brussels.[1] The ITF now has eight sections, two of which are the Dockers' Section and the Seafarers' Section. The Head Office is in London. C. H. Blyth is ITF's General Secretary and Chief Administrative Officer. In the course of its rather chequered history,[2] it developed among its many activities a campaign against "flags of convenience" (FOCs) and "crews of convenience" (COCs).[3] The 30th Congress of the ITF in Vienna, July-August 1971:

---

[1] For additional information see John P. Windmuller, *Labour Internationals*, Bulletin 61, New York State School of Industrial and Labour Relations, Cornell University, 1969; "International Trade Union Organizations" in Solomon Barkin *et al.* (eds.), *International Labour*, Industrial Relations Research Association, Wisconsin, 1967.

[2] For a history of the ITF campaign, see the forthcoming study by Richard L. Rowan, *International Standards in Ocean Transport*, to be published by the Industrial Research Unit of the Wharton School. See also K. A. Golding, "In the Forefront of Trade Union History 1896-1971", *ITF Journal*, Vol. 31, No. 2, Summer 1971.

[3] The following definitions have been adopted by the ITF: When the beneficial ownership and control of a vessel is found to lie elsewhere than in the country of the flag the vessel is flying, the vessel is considered as sailing under a flag of convenience. (ITF Fair Practices Committee, London, January 1974.) Any shipowner who, without prior consultation and agreement with the bona fide seafarers' trade union(s) recognized as such by the ITF, in the country of the flag of the vessel(s), departs from the practice of manning his vessel(s) with the seafarers of that country, shall be deemed

"decided to take more vigorous action to protect seafarers serving on "flag of convenience" ships and recommended the appointment of persons specifically for the purpose of keeping a close watch over the interests of such seafarers in some of the world's major ports . . . It also decided to carry out an investigation of the impact of the growth of multinational companies on the work and life of persons engaged in transport." [4]

Organized Australian trade union participation in the ITF flags of convenience compaign stemmed from the attendance of Mr. C. H. Fitzgibbon, General Secretary of the Waterside Workers' Federation (WWF), at this Congress.

THE GROWTH OF THE CAMPAIGN

When he returned to Australia, Fitzgibbon spoke enthusiastically of the possibilities of international trade union action:

The experience . . . already indicated that the only effective answer in the sense of protecting dockworkers against technological changes in the stevedoring industry lies in an international approach . . . It is essential to have policies not just consistent with the needs of the industrialized countries but also consistent with the needs of the newly developed countries . . . .

[The conference, he said] disclosed the value of international affiliation, if only for one reason—contacts that could be made and understanding that could be developed of the problems of other countries.[5]

With the development of containerization in the 1960s Fitzgibbon gave much attention to the significance of technological change. Regarding containerization, Fitzgibbon wanted to protect waterside workers' jobs from its impact and, conversely, exploit it to their advantage. He also became interested in the significance of multinational corporations. He began to see maritime unions' problems in terms of the impact of multinational corporations on workers' standards. In some notes prepared for an ITF Fair Practices Committee in London in January 1972 he said:

International transport workers were forced to suffer from multinational corporations.

---

to have engaged a crew of convenience. (ITF 31st Congress, Stockholm, August 1974, *Report on Activities*, p. 161.) The shipowners use the term "flags of necessity" but it is the union usage that has been generally adopted. See Rowan, *op. cit.*, for fuller discussion.

[4] *International Labour Review*, December 1971, pp. 561-562.

[5] *Maritime Worker*, Sydney, 19/8/71.

Shipowners were the originators of the first significant multi-national or trans-national system.[6]

However, in all the justified alarm expressed by trade unionists at the growth of multi-national corporations, which use exploited labour of underdeveloped countries, not enough attention has been paid to multi-national marine stratagems.

Unionists will, we hope, come to see the struggle against flags of convenience as internationally indivisible. The poorer nations whose names are tarnished by the system, whose cheaper labour is exploited, are in danger of being kept poor to sustain the flags of convenience fleets, now of mammoth proportions. Trade unionists of the advanced countries are threatened by the substandard conditions of those countries, more so in the age of the multi-national corporations and cheap-flag fleets.[7]

With these interests and with a background of long WWF tradition of international involvement behind him, Fitzgibbon has spearheaded the ITF campaign in Australia and has been its main architect.

He duly attended the ITF Fair Practices Committee, London, January 1972. Soon after his return he obtained an endorsement from an Executive Meeting of the Australian Council of Trade Unions (ACTU), the central trade union co-ordinating body. On March 20, at a meeting of seagoing and waterfront unions held under the auspices of the ACTU, it was agreed that they would combine in a campaign of action against FOC and COC vessels. The following unions either attended or were consulted: WWF, Seamen's union, Merchant Service Guild, Professional Radio and Electricians Institute, Federated Marine Stewards and Pantrymen's Association, Federated Shipwrights and Ship Constructors Association. It was decided that:

> The Maritime Unions and the Waterside Workers' Federation under the auspices of the ACTU agree to combine in a campaign of action against Flags of Convenience and Crew of Convenience vessels.

> The intention of the campaign will be to ensure that: The owners of "Flag of Convenience" or "Crew of Convenience" vessels who are not parties to agreements with bona fide trade unions covering the wages and conditions of the crew sign ITF agreements which will provide for wages and conditions of employment and repatriation provisions acceptable to the International Trade Union Movement . . .

---

[6] Shipowners are not in fact, multinational companies, since they traditionally operate solely from home country bases.

[7] Material prepared by C. H. Fitzgibbon for ITF Fair Trade Practices Committee, London, January, 1972.

In order to give effect to the campaign the Unions determine:

That where a 'Flag of Convenience' or 'Crew of Convenience' vessel ... enters an Australian port all unions to refuse services or labours to such a vessel until it is covered by an ITF Agreement and the other above-mentioned requirements of the Trade Unions are met.

The assistance of International Seafarers will be sought in such actions...[8]

About this time, Fitzgibbon wrote a letter (undated) to Australian shippers which, after explaining the FOC and COC issue and stating the union approach to this, said:

Our advice to Australian exporters and importers would be that they should ensure their protection in relation to any future charters entered into involving vessels which could be described as "Flags of Convenience" or "Crew of Convenience." These protections could be sought in one of two ways:

(1) By first determining that the vessel was not a "Flag of Convenience" or "Crew of Convenience" vessel, or if it was that it was already covered by an international transport workers' federation (ITF) agreement or a bona fide trade union agreement,

(2) If (1) above was not the position a clause be inserted in the charter arrangements to provide that, if the vessel was the subject of any industrial dispute arising from the fact that it was a "Flag of Convenience" or "Crew of Convenience" vessel, the cost of any delays arising therefrom be borne by the owners of the vessel and not by the charterer.[9]

On April 6, 1972, history was made when Fitzgibbon signed, on behalf of the ITF, a special contract covering the Korean crew of the Liberian flag NADINE owned by Global Bulk Carriers of New York. Sydney waterside workers refused labour in order to force the signing of the agreement, which was to remain in force for a year. The wage of an able seaman (AB) was raised from $US135 a month to approximately $US207 a month. The Koreans became members of the Special Seafarers' Section of the ITF, and the owners agreed to pay a membership fee of £UK8 per man per year and a welfare fund payment of $US107.[10] The NADINE was the first of many ships encountered in the Australian ITF campaign. The latter was largely organized and co-ordinated by Mr. T. I. Bull, a WWF official who was given this responsibility in addition

---

[8] *Maritime Worker*, 24/3/72. *Seamen's Journal*, Sydney, April 1972.

[9] Information supplied by an Australian employer. See also statement by T. Bull, *Australian*, 27/3/72.

[10] *Maritime Worker*, 12/4/72.

to his other duties. In the course of time, however, he found it increasingly difficult to carry out both the ITF and his normal duties. On September 22, 1974, he was replaced by a full-time ITF inspector, Mr. Les Symes.

THE CARRYING OUT OF THE CAMPAIGN

When a FOC or COC ship enters an Australian port, the captain is asked if the ship has the ITF Blue Certificate. Its possession indicates that either an ITF Collective Agreement or some other agreement acceptable to the ITF had been signed. Usually this interview is carried out by an official of the WWF or the Seamen's Union. In Sydney, the local ITF Inspector will interview the captain. The interview may also be conducted by an official of another maritime union or even by one from a non-maritime union, and possibly even by a rank and file member of a union. A new standard ITF Agreement was introduced on August 1, 1972. In its present form, it covers such matters as wages, hours of duty, overtime rates, manning, leave on pay, sick pay, compensation for loss of life, compensation for disability, repatriation, food, accommodation and bedding, subsistence allowance, loss or damage to crew's effects by marine peril, termination of employment, and membership fees and representation.[11]

The ITF Collective Agreement Wage Scale establishes basic monthly pay applicable to various occupational groups from Master to Catering Boy, as well as rates for overtime, Saturdays, Sundays and public holidays, and for cash compensation for unclaimed annual leave. On this scale, the current rate for an Able Seaman, effective from September 1, 1975, is $US483 per month with an hourly overtime rate of $US3.60, an hourly holiday rate of $US6.40 and a rate for unclaimed annual leave of $US19.30 per day. There is also a special Collective Agreement Far Eastern Rate for an AB of $US343 per month, overtime $US2.50 per hour, holiday pay $US4.60 per hour, annual leave compensation $US13.70 per day. These may be compared with the current ILO recommended minimum (December 1975) of $US125 per month.

If neither an ITF agreement nor an acceptable alternative has been signed, the ship is banned until this has been done and the

---

11 The information in this and the succeeding three paragraphs was made available by Les Symes, ITF Inspector, Sydney.

appropriate wages paid to the crew. Sometimes the payment of substantial back pay is insisted upon, depending on the particular circumstances. When it is considered that there has been excessive exploitation of the crew, when conditions are bad, when the company is unscrupulous and unco-operative and there are no extenuating circumstances, the amount of back pay will tend to be relatively high. The ITF representative usually insists that the required payments to the crew be made in his presence. Any arrangements for transmitting some of the money to a home country must be approved by him.

When the crew are not members of a bona fide trade union, the owners must provide a crew list and enrol the members of the crew in the Special Seafarers' Section of the ITF. This involves payment by the owner of an enrolment fee of £UK4 per man and an annual contribution fee of £UK8 per month at present (December 1975). An amount of $US12 per man per month welfare contribution, i.e., $US144 per year, must also be paid by the owner to the ITF Seafarers' International Assistance, Welfare and Protection Fund. An important use of this fund is to provide seamen's amenities throughout the world.

In the year ending December 31, 1974, the ITF collected through its affiliates around the world Seafarers' Section fees and welfare contributions totalling £UK623,147.98 and of this sum spent £UK128,283.30 on welfare grants. In a press statement on April 10, 1975, Fitzgibbon announced that the ITF Fair Practices Committee had allocated $A35,000 to upgrade facilities provided for the use of all nations by Seamen's Missions in Australian ports. These figures may be compared with collections of Welfare Contributions and Seafarers' Membership Fees of £UK43,293 in 1971, £UK196,142 in 1972 and £UK323,397 in 1973. At December 31, 1973, the Net Total Assets in the Seafarers' International Assistance, Welfare and Protection Fund stood at £UK659,404. Taking into account the large collections in 1974, the total assets at the end of that year could well have been of the order of £UK1,100,000.[12] It would appear that only a relatively small part of the collections is being spent and that a substantial fund is being built up for possible eventual use in a manner yet to be determined.

---

[12] See ITF 31st Congress Stockholm, August 1974, Financial Statements and Auditors' Reports. Unfortunately, an up-to-date Financial Statement was not available.

THE WWF AND THE SEAMEN'S UNION

As a result of the close association of Fitzgibbon with the ITF and the former's keen interest and drive, the leadership of the campaign in Australia was undertaken by the WWF. The Seamen's Union, however, has also played an important part, invariably co-operating with the campaign to the extent required and sometimes undertaking most of the initiative and action. The tugs and their crews, moreover, which often play a key role, belong to the Seamen's Union in most states. This participation of the seamen is very important because both the Seamen's Union and the WWF have very good opportunities for communicating with captains and crews and exercising leadership among the various unions when action is required.

This occurs notwithstanding significant ideological and other differences between the WWF and the Seamen's Union. Whereas, as noted above, the ITF is associated with the ICFTU, the Seamen's Union has links with the Trade Secretariat of the Communist World Federation of Trade Unions (WFTU) headquartered in Prague. Mr. Elliott, the Seamen's Union Secretary, is himself a pro-Moscow Communist. The WFTU has, however, had a much less significant impact in the international shipping field than the ITF and the *Seamen's Journal* has made many references to the ITF but few to the WFTU Trade Secretariat.

Relations between the WWF and the Seamen's Union have, however, been uneasy, to say the least, because of the Seamen's Union's involvement in the imposition of levies on foreign ships which had participated casually in the Australian coastal trade on a special "permit" basis. These became the subject of investigation by a Royal Commission (the Sweeney Commission) which reported adversely concerning them. Elliott of the Seamen's Union had sought to have his levies regarded as similar in character to those of the ITF, a view which was rejected not only by Fitzgibbon but also by the Commission.[13]

In other respects the approaches of the WWF and the Seamen's Union are also not identical. Although the Seamen's Union certainly is interested both in curbing the multinationals and aiding the welfare of the crews of foreign ships, it always tends to stress possible effects on the employment of Australian seamen.

---

[13] See Royal Commission into Alleged Payments to Maritime Unions, *Interim Report* Australian Government Publishing Service, 1975; *Final Report, ibid.*, April 1976; *Maritime Worker*, 22/10/74.

"The Runaway Ships are Running Away with our Jobs" was a headline in its *Journal*. Commenting on the specific matter then being reported it said, "This move by another runaway flag should worry us because the flag of Singapore carries most of the bauxite out of Weipa and a large amount of coal from Queensland ports".[14] The Seamen's Union wants to increase the employment of Australian seamen in Australia's export and import trade and sees poor wages and conditions in overseas ships as an obstacle to this. Although it is aware of and supports these aspects, the WWF is much more involved in the ITF as an important development in international trade union organization. "Never in the history of trade unionism has an international labour organization lifted the standard of so many workers of so many nationalities as has the ITF", it claims.[15] It sees the ITF as playing an increasing role in international industrial relations especially in relation to controlling the multinationals in a world of technological change.

The WWF and other Australian maritime unions have been praised by the ITF Secretariat and received a whole paragraph in the 1974 Stockholm Conference Report. "The whole-hearted participation of the Waterside Workers' Federation and the other maritime unions has greatly boosted the ITF Campaign", it reported, giving some details. Fitzgibbon, a member of the ITF General Council since early in the Campaign, was co-opted to the Fair Practices Committee of the Special Seafarers' Section in January 1973. He was unanimously elected Chairman of the Dockers' Section, Joint Chairman of the Seafarers' and Dockers' Section, and Joint Chairman of the Fair Practices Committee in August 1974.[16]

Although the WWF and the Seamen's Union provide leadership in the placing of bans on ships, other unions may play an important and even essential part. "Pilots refuse to take her out, linesmen won't handle her lines, seamen won't work tugs for her and watersiders won't work cargo" was said of the SAFEOCEAN ADELAIDE, a ship "with Dutch officers, and a South African black crew on apartheid system wages".[17] Mari-

[14] *Seamen's Journal,* June 1972.

[15] *Marittime Worker,* 30/7/74.

[16] *Seamen's Journal,* September 1973; ITF 31st Congress, Stockholm, *Report on Activities,* August 1974, pp. 15, 105, 111; *Maritime Worker,* 10/9/74.

[17] *Maritime Worker,* 27/6/72.

time unions co-operate closely. They meet under the auspices of the ACTU and in the separate states.

Fitzgibbon does not expect the ability of the ITF to apply these pressures to diminish. He recently said:

> "Mechanization and capital intensive work areas invariably mean that union members are involved in more important key functions in the overall operation and control of transport systems . . .
>
> "Therefore to a question posed 'Will the organization of unions grow weaker in the future'? I believe the answer must be 'No'. Its position is ensured by modern technology and capital intensive undertakings."

He does, however, see a need for improved union organization, particularly in the direction of becoming more intermodal rather than remaining merely intramodal:

> "If not intermodal unions at least co-operation between unions in the various modes will have to develop or conversely a greater number of self-destructive jurisdictional dispute areas."

Trade union action, he thought, must also become more international:

> "The future of the trade unions must lead them towards a developing international role rather than a narrow industry or narrow national role . . . the growth of transport undertaking to a supranational and multi-national basis makes these approaches essential for progressive organizations." [18]

RESISTANCE OF FOREIGN-FLAG SHIPOWNERS

The methods referred to above seem to have been very effective. Sometimes, however, a ship signs an ITF agreement only to repudiate it after leaving Australia. It may require that ITF wages, which the owner has been forced to pay, be deducted from future wages. The sanction in these cases is that if the ship appears subsequently in an Australian port, or in any port in which active ITF affiliates operate without legal restraint, it is likely to find itself in trouble. Although, however, the model ITF Collective Agreement of September 1974 lists 112 representatives and affiliated Dockers' and Seafarers' Unions in fifty countries, which appears to cast the ITF net fairly widely, relatively few affiliates and countries are in fact, effective in implementing the ITF program.

---

[18] C. H. Fitzgibbon, "Future Union Influences on Transport", paper delivered to International Transport Conference, Sydney, 9/9/75.

To evade ITF standards, a ship may sometimes leave a port without benefit of linesmen, pilot, or tugs. Much publicity was given in Sydney recently to the Greek-owned ship, Cypriot flag, LAMANT, which left Sydney Harbour at dawn.[19] Such a ship is, of course, in danger of being subject to ITF attention in other ports.

Another approach was that of the FAYLENNE which had a Panamanian flag and a Filipino crew. An employing agency in Manila had induced the crew to sign an affidavit agreeing not to align with the ITF, not to affiliate with or join any union, and to repay any wages gained by any organization in excess of the wages under the agreed contract. At about the same time as this ship appeared in Australia, the ITF in Canada reported a similar case. This kind of affidavit was found unacceptable. An agreement was reached with the owner's representatives to apply the ITF scale to the crew. The Philippines Department of Labour, with an adjunct National Seamen's Board that controls all seagoing labour, was persuaded to suspend those agencies using the affidavit. The tactics employed by the ITF to achieve this result are of considerable interest: "The ITF posed to the Philippines principals the possibility of strong counter-measures against their interests not only in Australia but on a world-wide basis." [20] This case indicates the possibility of future development of ITF techniques from application to particular ships to international action against all of a company's ships and interests if it is considered appropriate in the circumstances, and where the legal situation in the various countries permits.

Such cases are, however, now becoming very much the exception rather than the rule. Most ships coming to Australia know

---

[19] Les Symes, ITF Inspector in Sydney, reported: The morning LAMANT sailed an inspection of the crew's quarters was scheduled.

Undertakings were given that the toilets would be repaired, so that they would flush and not regurgitate up the floor drain hole to swill about the feet.

Also the broken pipe in another toilet would be repaired, so that it could be used without need for wet weather gear to avoid the shower provided by the perforated lagging over the broken joint, and for boots to protect crewmen's feet when the battered standing board submerged in the permanent pool of water.

Fire extinguishers were to be inspected for serviceability. Those previously seen were empty. One was ticketed for inspection in 1971.

Other issues were lines, blankets, washing machines beyond repair (agreed replacement) and the heating system to be made functional.

Last but not least, wages.
Maritime Worker, 12/8/75.

[20] *Maritime Worker*, 2/9/75.

of the ITF requirements and arrive either armed with the ITF blue certificate or prepared to obtain one. The writer had the opportunity to visit two ships with the ITF Inspector, Les Symes, and was impressed with the cool and easy way he asked his ITF questions and the readiness with which they were answered. It was very much a routine operation in these particular cases.

SITUATIONS AND PROBLEMS

Apart from such episodes as those mentioned, the ITF has had to cope with a number of different types of situation. The many problems that have arisen have forced the ITF to develop an increasing flexibility and sophistication in its policies.

Mr. T. I. Bull of the WWF, in the light of almost a year's experience, provided in February 1973 a fivefold classification of ships. This was:

1. Ships belonging to maritime companies employing their own crews and with 'acceptable' wages and conditions negotiated by bona fide unions in their own country, i.e. British, Scandinavian, Dutch, German, etc. flag vessels.

2. Ships flying flags of convenience or using crews of convenience which have either finalized an international ITF agreement or have reached an acceptable (to the ITF) agreement with a bona fide union in the country from which the crew is drawn, such as for Panamanian, Liberian, Hondurasian flag vessels.

3. Ships using flags or crews of convenience which have not concluded agreements with the ITF or its affiliates or bona fide union, and which are therefore subject to the ITF campaign when apprehended—such as Panamanian, Hondurasian or any other flags using crews from non-organized areas.

4. Ships which are crewed from countries where the bona fide union is for some reason (organizational, political) not capable of forcing satisfactory agreement, such as Singapore, Hong Kong, Philippines, Indonesia, India, Pakistan or Bangladesh seamen.

5. Ships from the Pacific area or using crews drawn from the Pacific area where the union movements, if they exist, are only in the embryo stage and need—and deserve—assistance from the Australian movement. These include ships flying British, French, German and other flags using crews from Papua-New Guinea, Solomon Islands, Fiji, Gilbert Islands.[21]

This classification provides a useful basis for discussion of the problems that have arisen. Although not logically watertight, it

---

[21] *Maritime Worker,* 6/2/73.

has the great advantage of being based on the WWF's own experience.

National Agreements with Bona Fide Unions

The ITF policy in relation to the first type, ships operating under acceptable national agreements with bona fide unions, is as stated by Charles Blyth, General Secretary of the ITF. At the ITF Second Asian Regional Seafarers' Conference in October 1974, he said:

> [C]oncerning national flag vessels with national crews, the ITF once again stated that this was a matter of concern for the particular country and the particular union and that the ITF affiliated unions in other countries had no right to interfere in such national agreements.[22]

A first point to be made is that such ships often operate with wages and conditions below ITF standards, or even below the levels in some FOC and COC vessels, yet in many cases the former will escape ITF action to which the latter are subject. It may be noted also that the ITF has never acted against ships of the Eastern bloc (Russia, Poland, etc.). Blyth has, however, pointed out that "it is another matter if an affiliate decides to call in a fellow ITF affiliate for assistance". "Instances of this abound in the seventy-six years of the ITF's existence to the extent that they amount to a tradition", he claims.[23] A further aspect is also brought out by Charles Blyth, "[T]he ITF's interest is limited to one qualification only, namely that the rate of pay should be no less than the minimum standard established by the International Labour Organisation".[24] What all this amounts to is that the ITF respects bona fide national agreements but is willing to intervene if asked or if the rates of pay are not up to ILO standards, at present (December 1975) $US125 per month for an AB.

There is thus room under this first heading for a very broad range of rates between the current ILO minimum of $US125 per month and the ITF World Rate of $US483 or above and the ITF Asian/Far Eastern Rate of $US343, for an AB. Early reports on the ITF campaign complained, however, that in many instances agreements finalized by ITF affiliates did not even come

---

[22] *Maritime Worker*, 12/11/74.

[23] *Maritime Worker*, 6/2/73.

[24] *Ibid.*

up to the minimum levels recommended by the ILO.[25] Moreover the ITF, as noted, does not necessarily intervene if a national flag and crew are involved and the rates are substandard.

ITF or Other Acceptable Agreements

Bull's second category is FOC and COC ships which have acceptable ITF or other agreements with bona fide unions. The category of acceptable agreement with a bona fide union again indicates the possibility of a range of acceptable rates between the ILO and the ITF rates.

Ships Which Have Not Concluded Acceptable Agreements

Bull's third group consists of FOC and COC ships which have not concluded ITF or other acceptable agreements. These are, of course, at the heart of the ITF campaign because of the very bad reputation many have as regards wages, conditions and safety. A recent OECD Maritime Transport Report, 1974, found, indeed, after a two-year study, that losses of convenience ships were four times as high as those of the rest of the world.[26]

C. H. Blyth, nevertheless, has warned, "Among extremes associated with Flags of Convenience, making generalisation hazardous, is that some owners are among the best employers in the world, e.g., the US oil companies, while others are certainly the worst." [27] As Rowan has pointed out,[28] the ITF campaign has frequently found itself out on a limb and had to pull back as a result of action taken against such ships, especially by its Finnish and Swedish affiliates. It is ITF policy that ships with good wages and conditions are still liable for contributions to the ITF Welfare Fund and may also be required to enrol crew members not belonging to a bona fide union into the Special Seafarers' Section of the ITF. Rowan gives examples of strong and sometimes successful employer resistance to such demands. In such cases, the issue has swung away from emphasis on wages and conditions towards emphasis on recognition of the ITF and its status as an international bargaining agent.

---

[25] *Report on ACTU Endorsed FOC-COC Campaign to May 23, 1972.*

[26] OECD, *Maritime Transport 1974*, OECD, Paris, 1975, pp. 88-94.

[27] Address to Company of Master Mariners, London, 12/3/75.

[28] Rowan, *op. cit.*

Countries with Weak Unions

The fourth group, ships crewed from countries with weak unions, has been the source of many problems for the ITF. The unions have sometimes been ambivalent about the amount of help they wanted from the ITF and have sometimes sought lower than ITF standards. Strong opposition to the ITF has at times come from the governments of these countries. To meet these problems, a special Asian/Far Eastern scale, about 71 per cent of the World scale, was introduced in July 1972, but some countries found these rates still well above what seemed appropriate to their particular situations. India and Singapore may be given as examples of the problems that have arisen and how they have been tackled. A Philippines example has already been given.

Concern was expressed early that the Indian Seamen's Union, an ITF affiliate, had reached agreement with British shipowners on a wage scale for Indian seamen not only below the ITF standard but also below the ILO standard.[29] In June 1972 it was reported that a very sharp letter had been received from the Seamen's Union of India protesting at the ITF's interest in Indian seamen.[30] At an ACTU meeting of maritime unions in September 1972, it was agreed that in relation to Asian matters the ITF affiliated unions may adopt a flexible approach to wages and conditions on FOC and COC ships, but that in no case should any agreement be reached in which wages, hours and manning were inferior to ILO standards. The ITF point of view has been expressed by Charles Blyth:

> We see a vicious downward spiral where the shipowner can play off the Singaporean against the Indonesian, the Filipino against the Korean, or the Papuan against any.
>
> There is no dignity and ultimately no future for the Asian seafarer in selling himself more cheaply than his Asian brother for the betterment of the foreign shareholders thousands of miles away. It is only in this context that the ITF policies can be properly judged.[31]

Flexibility can, of course, bring its own problems. For example, it was reported in May 1972 that the Greek owner of the Liberian registered SYRIE had complained that his Indian crew

---

[29] *Maritime Worker*, 27/6/72.

[30] Report on ACTU Endorsed Maritime Unions Campaign re Flags of Convenience and Crews of Convenience to June 15, 1972.

[31] *Maritime Worker*, 6/2/73.

was being paid much more than the Indian crew of a British registered vessel moored nearby working under an agreement negotiated with an Indian ITF affiliate. The Indian Welfare officer from the Indian High Commissioner's Office strongly objected to an improvement in wages and conditions for the Indian crew aboard the SYRIE, with the result that the Indian crew was reluctant to accept the ITF agreement.[32]

The Indian situation continued to be discussed at various conferences. For example, the ITF Asian Seafarers' Conference in May 1973 declared its concern at the great disparity between rates paid to Asian and other seamen and stressed the "danger of the multinational shipping companies holding down the level of wages in Asian countries through exploitation of the competition for employment among Asian seamen." However, the delegates from India and Pakistan were somewhat apprehensive in that they expressed fear that if the cost of Asian crews to the shipowners was raised to too high a figure the existing employment of their members might be in danger.[33]

The Indians were also concerned at the distortion of Indian wage relativities that would arise from payment of ITF imposed wage levels. At a Joint Seafarers' and Dockers' Conference held in London in March 1975 it was reported:

> The National Union of Seafarers of India (Bombay) has informed us that, in co-operation with the Indian government, they have instructed their members to refuse to accept any pay increases over and above the National Maritime Board Rate . . . and warned them that if they do they will be removed from the register of seamen and the shipping master at Bombay will ensure that they are paid off only at Indian NMB rates.[34]

A solution has, however, apparently been found. Agreement has been reached that the difference between the Indian rate and the ILO rate shall be paid into a special welfare fund. The federal officers of the WWF reported to their Federal Council in November 1974:

> One of the greatest achievements was the lifting of all Indian, Bangladesh and Pakistan seafarers' rates to the ILO minimum of £UK48 or $US115 or which about £UK32 per month is paid to the crew and about £UK16 per month paid into a Special Fund for the benefit of all Indian, Bangladesh and Pakistan seamen in relieving

[32] Report on ACTU Endorsed FOC-COC Campaign to May 23, 1972.

[33] *Maritime Worker*, 8/5/73.

[34] *Report of ITF Fair Practices Committee Meeting*, London, March 19, 20, 1973.

unemployment and providing industry pensions. That Fund is operated in India and Pakistan and not by the ITF although it is proposed that an ITF nominee be on the Board of Trustees.[35]

Indian and ITF wage policies were thus to some extent reconciled. Questions, however, remain as to what happens to the moneys deposited in the welfare fund, who is to control it, and how it is to be utilized.

Singapore provides another example of a case where problems arose. Bull reported in February 1973 that the WWF and the ITF, together with the Singapore Organization of Seamen (SOS), were still in battle with a number of owners concerning the wages and conditions of Singapore seamen.[36] The WWF, however, was then able to report some success in that it had lifted rates for seamen on some Blue Star ships by more than 100 per cent.[37] Shortly after this the Singapore Organization of Seamen asked the WWF to lift the ban on Singapore-manned vessels. A government inquiry was to take place to examine the wages and conditions of work of Singapore seamen. Meanwhile, agreement had been reached with Singapore employers to grant interim increases in wages and overtime of 30 per cent. The SOS thanked the WWF for its assistance.[38] It had been reported at a Joint Seafarers' and Dockers' Conference held in London in March 1973:

> The National Maritime or Seamen's Boards of India, Pakistan, Singapore and Philippines have been supporting owners in their efforts to avoid meeting their obligations to their crews arising from ITF agreements. This has led to considerable hardship for a number of crews as well as threatening their future employment prospects.

The above-mentioned Singapore Board of Inquiry was appointed on February 12, 1973, but for various reasons did not report until July 15, 1974. It was very critical of the ITF campaign:

> Towards the end, prior to the breaking up of the negotiations, the situation and the relationship existing between the Singapore Maritime Employer's Federation and the Singapore Organization of Seamen was doubly aggravated by the clearly discernible atti-

---

[35] *Maritime Worker*, 12/11/74; ITF 31st Congress, Stockholm, August 1974, *Report on Activities*, p. 102.

[36] *Maritime Worker*, 6/2/73.

[37] *Ibid.*, 27/2/73.

[38] *Ibid.*, 20/3/73.

tude taken by the Australian Waterside Workers' Federation. Matters came to a head with the Australian Waterside Workers' Federation black-listing Singapore registered ships, employing Singapore crews in Australian ports, by withdrawal of labour or services pending the acceptance by the owners of the recommendations of the International Transport Workers' Federation. Evidence disclosed at our Inquiry indicated that the Singapore Organization of Seamen was quick to desire this new move on the part of the Australian Waterside Workers' Federation. We hold the view and would recommend that no trade union in Singapore, whether of employers or employees, should surrender the right to advance its members cause and welfare to foreign organizations—either of employer or employees.[39]

The Board, however, determined a rate of $Sing.397 per month for those employed on foreign-going vessels and $Sing.252 for those employed on vessels operating locally. These rates were provisionally accepted by the ITF. Trouble, however, still arises from time to time.[40]

Pacific Island Crews

This fifth group consists of ships employing Pacific Island crews whose countries either have no unions or have them only very much in an embryo stage. Many cases in which very low rates were being paid to Pacific Island crews had come to the notice of the WWF, e.g. Solomon Islanders on the GOLDEN SWAN, $A26 per month,[41] and Papua-New Guineans on the JETTE BUE, $A36 per month for a six-day forty-eight-hour week.[42]

The Gilbert and Ellice Islands' crew situation may be considered as an example of the problems that can arise. Action was taken against German and British ships employing Gilbert and Ellice Island crews. The ITF, with the personal assistance of Charles Blyth, gave support to the newly formed Gilbert and Ellice Islands Overseas Seamen's Union, and sponsored an agreement between the German shipping representatives and the Seamen's Union providing for a 9 per cent wage increase immedi-

---

[39] *Report of Board of Inquiry into Dispute Between Maritime Employers and the Singapore Seamen's Organization*, July 1974.

[40] See *ITF Newsletter*, No. 7, July 1976, regarding action against the Singapore-Flag Coaster DIVINA. I am indebted to Mrs. Mary Immediata for bringing this case to my attention.

[41] *Daily Commercial News*, Sydney, 20/3/72.

[42] *Maritime Worker*, 12/4/72.

ately, with further increases of 8 per cent for each of the remaining two years of the three-year agreement.[43] Over a year later it was reported that of fifty-six ships employing Gilbertian seamen, twelve were under flags of convenience. The latter owners had said they would dismiss the crews of these ships if they were forced to pay ITF rates.[44]

The upshot was that the ITF, in co-operation with the WWF, decided that it had to give considerable weight to the possible economic and employment effects of the wages determined. The Gilbert and Ellice Islands have a very poor and underdeveloped economy and the seamen's earnings are a vital source of foreign exchange. An essential seamen's training school was provided by Shipping Company subsidies. The ITF took these special circumstances into account in settling for a rate of $A132 per month for an AB.[45]

AUSTRALIAN SHIPOWNERS POLICIES AND ATTITUDES

Enough examples have been given to show that some overseas shipowners and governments are very hostile to the ITF Campaign. Many of those who do co-operate with the ITF and accept its standards do so under duress. Australian shipowners, however, do not appear to be greatly concerned. They see no great advantage and possibly much disadvantage in antagonizing the powerful maritime unions by opposing the campaign and spreading disputes beyond ships directly affected. Any adverse effects are felt by overseas shipowners rather than by Australian shipowners as their employment is mainly of Australian seamen in Australia's coastal trade. Moreover, they have aspirations, which have been encouraged to some extent both by the former Labor Government and by the Liberal-Country Party Government which came to power in December 1975, to participate more fully in the shipping of Australia's exports. If these latter hopes materialize, the higher wages on foreign ships gained by the ITF will marginally reduce the latter's competitiveness and thus operate to the advantage of Australian shipowners.

Another aspect is that recognition of trade unions, through the working of arbitration, has been a broadly accepted feature of

---

[43] *Maritime Worker*, 6/2/73.

[44] *Report of Joint Seafarers' and Dockers' Section Conference*, ITF 31st Congress, Stockholm, August 1974.

[45] Information provided by Les Symes.

the Australian industrial relations system from early in the century. Thus, Australian shipowners, even if they did not always approve of the ITF campaign, would in the Australian culture have some built-in readiness to accept it and regard it as a reasonable trade union activity. One might perhaps expect broader considerations such as the potential of the ITF as an international trade union organization or of the large Seafarers' Industrial Assistance, Welfare and Protection Fund to be reflected in Australian shipowners attitudes, but there is no indication that this is the case.

The most useful statement is simply that most Australian shipping employers are just indifferent to the ITF Campaign.

Because of the higher freight rates they have to pay as a result of foreign shipowners' higher costs, exporters are no doubt adversely affected. But although this group is always complaining about freight rates, it does not appear to have given the ITF any attention. Another group affected would be consumers, who ultimately have to pay the higher costs of importing. Although the consumer movement is quite lively in Australia, it appears to have taken no interest in the ITF.

AUSTRALIAN GOVERNMENT ATTITUDES

The recent Labor Government clearly supported the ITF campaign. When a question of special payments to maritime unions arose in 1974 and the Royal Commission was appointed to inquire into these, attempts were made to have the ITF campaign included in the Commission's terms of reference. This was refused by the government. Mr. Clyde Cameron, then Minister for Labour, said:

> I believe it is legitimate for a union to take action which forces huge foreign corporations to recognize that they have not paid a fair day's wages to their employees for the work they do.[46]

Mr. C. K. Jones, then Minister for Transport, held a similar point of view:

> I agree that International Transport Federation rates should be paid to all crews of international ships. It is part of the Policy of the Labor Party and the trade union movement. It is true that I told Charlie Fitzgibbon, who is a personal friend of mine that there is no risk of any interference by me or any action being taken

---

[46] *Sydney Morning Herald*, 4/9/74.

against his union while it was insisting on the crews of foreign
ships being paid ITF rates of pay.[47]

The Royal Commission itself commented:

> I formed the opinion that these payments were payments under
> industrial agreements and probably by now could be termed pay-
> ments of a normal commercial nature and I regard these as outside
> the terms of reference.[48]

This statement sums up a significant aspect of informed Australian attitudes. The ITF campaign is largely regarded as a
normal and reasonable trade union activity.

So far there has been no statement on the matter from the
present Liberal-Country Party government. It is not impossible,
however, that foreign policy issues may some time have some
impact on the situation. Asian governments are said to have
made frequent protests to the Australian government about the
campaign. Concerning these also, neither the Labor nor the
succeeding Liberal-Country Party government has as yet taken
any significant action in response.

Legal Aspects

Rowan has shown the great importance of a country's legal
system for the success or otherwise of the ITF campaign there.
Thus, while the Swedish unions are able to operate with great
freedom, adverse legal decisions have virtually destroyed the
participation of United States trade unions in ITF activity.[49]
In Australia, the legal situation is rather complex and uncertain.
Firstly, the ITF banning of ships could be dealt with by the
Australian Conciliation and Arbitration Commission, with the
possibility that after an appropriate procedure had been followed,
fines might be imposed by the Australian Industrial Court. In
practice, it is extremely unlikely that in the Australian industrial
climate, the Court would be willing to impose such fines. It is,
however, a legal possibility and could probably be initiated by
an employer referring an "industrial dispute" to the Commission.
Such a dispute, however, would have to be between an employer
and his own employees. For example, stevedoring employers
could take the WWF to the Commission for refusing to load and
unload cargo, or a tug operator could take his crews to the Commission for refusing to operate the tugs.[50] The foreign ship-

---

[47] *Hansard*, 19/9/74, p. 1533.

[48] *Royal Commission into Alleged Payment to Maritime Unions, op. cit.*, p. 4.

[49] Rowan, *op. cit.*

[50] See Royal Commission, *Interim Report, op. cit.*, pp. 62-63.

owners could not take any such action because the waterside
workers and tug crews, in this example, would not be his
employees.

Secondly, the governmental Stevedoring Industry Authority
could bring a ban on a ship before the Industrial Commission as
an "industrial matter" if the WWF were involved.

Thirdly, the foreign shipowner might initiate a civil action for
damages in tort. This, however, is a difficult and uncertain area.

Fourthly, the Australian government could proclaim the Crimes
Act and take action under it. Section 30K provides that:

> Whoever, by violence to the person or property of an other person,
> or by spoken threat or intimidation of any kind to whomsoever
> directed, or, without reasonable cause or excuse, by boycott or
> threat of boycott of person or property . . .
>
> (d) obstructs or hinders the transport of goods or the conveyance
> of passengers in trade or commerce with other countries or among
> the states; . . . shall be guilty of an offence.

The critical phrase is, "without reasonable cause or excuse".
It is likely that the ITF actions would be considered reasonable.[51]

Political Obstacles to Government Action

The real obstacles to action against the ITF campaign would,
however, be industrial and political rather than legal. The Australian trade union movement supports the ITF campaign, and
its strong opposition to arbitration penalties against strikes has
succeeded in bringing about their disuse. It also is opposed to
the Crimes Act. It is probable, therefore, that attempts by
employers or government to take strong action against the ITF
campaign would involve a major confrontation with the trade
union movement with tremendous industrial and political upheaval.

It is not easy to envisage the new Liberal-Country Party government engaging in a major confrontation with the trade union
movement to destroy an ITF campaign strongly opposed by only
a few Australians. Two qualifications may, however, be made.
Firstly, the Liberal-Country Party government does lean towards
a "law and order" approach to industrial relations. Its policy
says, "To achieve a more reasoned industrial relations climate,
the Liberal and National Country Parties believe that rules must
be established that carry consequences." It also spells out policies

---

[51] See Royal Commission, *Final Report, op. cit.,* pp. 169-174 for an analysis
of legal possibilities that has some relevance to the present discussion.

of deregistration, requisition of funds, fines, and so on. So by accident or design it might get itself involved in a confrontation which included the ITF campaign. Secondly, it is opposed to political strikes, saying, "The exercise of the power of industrial organizations for non-industrial purposes is not legitimate." [52] It might therefore wish to take action against political bans in which the ITF participated. In such a case it is possible that it might find the trade union movement divided to some extent.

RESULTS OF THE CAMPAIGN

One indication of ITF success is demonstrated in the collection in Australia from ninety-nine FOC-COC ships of $US301,400.54 (to February 21, 1975) in payments to the ITF Seafarers' International Assistance, Welfare and Protection Fund. Unfortunately, later figures were not available.[53]

The annual breakdown of the figures is as follows:

Year	Number of Ships	Amount Collected ($US)
1972	22	70,819.44
1973	5	13,771.52
1974	66	198,168.77
		(includes crew donations of $US469.20)
1975 (to Feb. 21)	6	18,640.81
	99	301,400.54

These Australian collections for the ITF Assistance, Welfare and Protection Fund may be compared with total world contributions to the Fund of £UK196,142 in 1972, £UK323,397 in 1973,[54] and £UK623,147.98 in 1974. The exact Australian proportion of total collections would depend on the exchange rate applicable between the English pound and the Australian dollar, but it is clear that the Australian contribution was very substantial in 1972 and 1974.

More spectacular than the above figures, although of more short-run significance, are the amounts of back pay collected and handed to crews. Precise figures were available only for the period September 29, 1974, to February 19, 1975, during which

---

[52] Liberal and National Country Parties, *Employment and Industrial Relations Policy*, 1975.

[53] Except where otherwise stated, the discussion in this section is based on material made available by Les Symes.

[54] Stockholm Conference, Financial Statements 1971-1973.

$US445,074.04 was collected in Australia for back pay. Symes estimates that the total back pay collected in Australia from the beginning of the campaign to October 1975 at about $US2,000,000, which is reasonably consistent with the precise figures given for the shorter period [sic]. This suggests that with Seafarers' Section and welfare payments at something over $US300,000 and back pay collections about $US2,000,000, the back pay collections would be about six times the amount of union and welfare payments. It is perhaps unnecessary to warn that such calculations are very rough indeed.

The collection of back pay for the crews has been an important feature of the Australian ITF campaign. Figures reported to an ITF Fair Practices Committee Meeting in March 1975 indicate that from July 1974 to mid-March 1975 Australia collected $US247,676.60 out of a total of $US439,363.43 collected by eight countries. Other countries contributing in descending order were Great Britain (where the ITF head office is situated), Sweden, Canada, New Zealand, Finland, Netherlands, and Belgium. The above figures for Australia are incomplete and greatly understate the Australian contribution. The figures as a whole are nevertheless of value in indicating the limited number of countries active in collecting back pay for crews. They also show Australia's relatively high contribution in this area.

Far more important in the long run than either the Seafarers' Section and welfare payments or back pay is the continuing gain to crews arising from the higher wages and standards obtained for them. Against this, one must of course put the loss of employment that will undoubtedly have been experienced in some cases.

CONCLUSION

It may be concluded that Australian maritime unions' participation in the ITF campaign has met with a considerable measure of success in terms of its objectives. As a development in internatioal trade union organization many problems no doubt remain to be solved. These include the different interests of different countries as regards wage and employment levels, legal difficulties in some countries, the continued opposition of many employers and governments, and possible foreign policy repercussions. As a contribution to the structuring of an international industrial relations system in the shipping industry, the ITF campaign is still very much at an early stage. A start has, however, clearly been made.

Appendix B

SURVEY OF FLAG OF CONVENIENCE BOYCOTT POTENTIAL

The attached survey of flag of convenience boycott potential was prepared by B.L. Williamson & Co., Marine Consultants, London, October 1982, as part of an unpublished report on the International Transport Workers' Federation. It is reproduced here by permission.

The author notes that he has not consulted with attorneys "to check the accuracy of details concerning the law of each jurisdiction. The information concerning boycott and strike law in the various jurisdictions must therefore be viewed in a general manner and reference made to local lawyers when accuracy is vital. Despite the necessity for generalization on this point, an account of the legal alternative is an essential factor in being able to encapsulate the workings of the ITF on an international scale."

AUSTRALIA

High risk ports:

Adelaide	Freemantle	Perth
Botany Bay	Melbourne	Port Headland
Brisbane	Newcastle	Sydney

Active ITF Inspectors:

Les Symes   Charles Fitzgibbon

Active Affiliated Seafarers and Dockers Unions:

*Waterside Workers' Federation of Australia
P.O. Box 344, Haymarket, Sydney 2000 Tel: 61 9134

Federated Marine Stewards' and Pantrymen's Association of Australasia
Trades Hall, Room 84, Goulburne Street, Sydney

Merchant Service Guild of Australia
5th Floor, 377 Sussex Street, Sydney 2000

---

*Indicates that representatives have been appointed to deal with flag of convenience matters.

Other Affiliated Seafarers and Dockers Unions:

Federated Clerks' Union of Australia

Professional Radio and Electronics' Institute of Australasia

Merchant Service Guild of Australia

Australian Institute of Marine and Power Engineers

ITF inspectors/affiliates in Australia keep a close watch on the shipping press to detect all FOC vessels scheduled to enter Australian waters. Should such a vessel not appear on the list of ITF approved vessels an enquiry will be made at the vessel's port agents as to whether the vessel is in possession of an ITF blue certificate. As the agent will not normally be given such information prior to his appointment, he will no doubt have to refer to the vessels' owners/managers or the master direct to find out. The reply would be relayed to the ITF inspector/affiliate by the agent.

If the reply is in the negative the agent will be informed that the vessel will not berth until such time as she is in possession of a blue certificate, or in some cases until such time as the vessel is given clearance by ITF headquarters in London. In such circumstances the vessel will have no alternative but to remain outside the port area until ITF demands are met, as a berth will not be allocated to a vessel which has been effectively blacked.

It quite often happens that an FOC vessel slips through the ITF screen put up to prevent such vessels entering Australian ports, only to be caught within a port area whereupon they will be visited by an ITF inspector who will carry out a spot check on the vessel. If the vessel does not have a blue certificate, the master will be given the opportunity of entering into a special agreement with the usual sanctions being threatened in default.

Generally, ITF boycott methods only involve stevedores who are members of the militant WWF. If called upon to do so by the ITF inspector the stevedores will promptly declare that they will not handle the vessel. It is not usual for stevedores to resort to such tactics as starting a vessel's cargo operations only to abandon them when partially completed.

Neither is it usual for the ITF to try to induce a strike among crew members although the standard attempts at trade union indoctrination will be made.

Should it transpire that a non-approved FOC vessel has not been detected by an ITF inspector until her cargo operations are complete, or if the vessel has been allowed to continue loading/discharging because of the nature of the cargo, or for some other reason, tugs and linemen will be asked to withhold their services. Tugmen and line-handlers can also be relied upon by the ITF to impose an effective boycott.

One further point should be mentioned concerning local conditions which prevent vessels from sailing without tugs, etc., namely that when a vessel enters an Australian port the vessel's agent is required to take the ship's register ashore and deposit it with the port authorities. The register is only returned to the vessel when she has clearance to sail. In the event of a boycott or other industrial dispute the port authorities will not give the ship clearance and the register will not be returned until such time as the dispute is resolved.

In the event of a boycott, negotiations are carried out with Les Symes in the Sydney office of the WWF. Provided an owner/manager is prepared to concede to ITF demands a boycott can be called off just as quickly as ITF demands can be fulfilled.

In 1981 Australian ITF affiliates collected a total of US$3,593,742 in back pay as a result of boycott or threatened boycott action. They have collected US$1,165,055 in the first three months of 1982 in respect of back pay.

In considering whether legal action should be commenced against the unions imposing the boycott, certain considerations must be taken into account. On the legal front the first problem encountered is which court has jurisdiction to hear an owner's application.

Labour disputes in Australia are usually brought before the Australian Conciliation and Arbitration Commission and each of the maritime unions normally involved in ITF boycotts is registered with the Commission. Where there is no direct connection with Australia, such as Australian ownership or crew members, etc., the Commisison is reluctant to exercise its jurisdiction and cannot therefore be relied upon to provide a potential solution.

An alternative is to seek an injunction under the Trade Practices Act for a restraining order. Under the Act, a union is prevented from engaging in conduct, e.g., a boycott, which hinders or prevents the supply of services of other parties to a vessel, having the purpose and likely effect of :—

1. Causing substantial loss or damage to the business of corporate owners or charterers, or

2. Substantially lessening competition in the market for shipping services in which the corporate owners or charterers are participating, or

3. Preventing or substantially hindering corporate owners or charterers from engaging in trade or commerce between Australia and places outside Australia, among the States, or within a Territory, between a State and a Territory, or between two Territories.

This remedy is only available to *corporations* and is in reality the only effective legal course of action available in Australia. There is, however, no certainty of success since each case is considered with regard to its particular facts. Local lawyers, experienced in ITF disputes, should be consulted in weighing up the likelihood of success. Given a favourable set of facts such proceedings may produce positive results very quckly, for example, a restraining order has been obtained within three days of the institution of proceedings under the Trade Practices Act.

Enforcement of an Injunction can be obtained by the imposition of a fine on the defendant union. It should be appreciated that although an owner may be able to obtain an Injunction against a union as a corporate body, the union is not itself answerable for individual members who may ignore the court directive to terminate the boycott. In this respect Australian courts are reluctant to impose effective sanctions against a union or its members if the members choose to ignore an Injunction. An owner may in such circumstances have to rely on public opinion through the media and its adverse affect on the union and its members should they choose to ignore an Injunction.

One favourable aspect of commencing legal proceedings in Australia is that they have in the past had the effect of bringing ITF affiliates to the negotiating table where they have previously stood firm in their demands.

Where a boycott is resolved by negotiations, the Sydney office of the WWF will instruct local ITF affiliates to terminate boycott activities. This is usually instantaneous.

BELGIUM

High risk ports:

Antwerp

Zeebrugge

Ghent

Active ITF Inspectors:

R. van Cant

R. Dielis

Mr. Roland van der Linden

Active Affiliated Seafarers and Dockers Unions:

*Belgische Transportarbeidersbond

Paardenmarkt 66, 2000 Antwerp

Tel: 31 18 40

FOC vessels are less frequently boycotted in Belgium than in most other European countries. The transport workers union (ITF affiliated), which represents both seamen and port workers in Belgium, is sensitive to the adverse effect that boycotts have on the attractiveness of a port to the shipping world. In this respect, the greater proportion of tonnage visiting Belgium ports—especially Antwerp—flies flags of convenience and local ITF affiliates are anxious not to drive reputable FOC vessels from the ports.

As a general rule, the ITF in Belgium do not call for boycott action unless it is at the specific request of ITF London or the result of a crew complaint requesting ITF assistance. In the latter case, the complaint will be investigated carefully to ensure it is not groundless, and in the case of a genuine complaint ITF action will be taken despite their otherwise cautious aproach.

The usual form of ITF action in, for example, Antwerp is a boycott by stevedores, tugs and lock keepers, who will each refuse to handle the vessel. The boycott will generally be accompanied by a strike on board by at least some of the crew.

It is noticeable that the ITF in Belgium are usually willing to negotiate a settlement on realistic terms. In this respect they do not always insist on full ITF standards being imposed but are prepared to restrict negotiations to rectifying the 'genuine' crew grievance. Where, for example, only part of the crew demand ITF wages the dispute will be restricted to those crew members, who are usually simultaneously discharged as part of the terms of settlement.

---

* Indicates that representatives have been appointed to deal with flag of convenience matters.

In 1981 Belgian ITF affiliates collected a total of US$569,884 in back pay as a result of boycott or threatened boycott action. They have collected US$73,941 in the first three months of 1982 in respect to back pay.

Should an owner/manager fail to reach an acceptable settlement with the ITF, Belgium courts can usually be relied upon to provide a limited form of relief. An application will be in the form of a request for a court order giving the vessel free access to the sea.

Despite the fact that boycotts are legal in Belgium the District Court of Antwerp has stated that the City of Antwerp is duly bound to guarantee free access to the exit locks at Antwerp and take all necessary steps to allow a vessel to leave port without hindrance. As the Antwerp port authority (which controls the exit locks) and the pilot and tug companies have a monopoly, their employees are bound by special contract to the government and local authority, such contract requiring them to assist in the free passage of vessels.

In the event of legal proceedings the Belgian government and port authority should be joined as parties to the proceedings and the court asked to make an appropriate order ensuring the vessel's free access to the sea. Such an injunction can usually be obtained within 1 to 3 days, but an appeal may delay matters for a further 7 days.

Injunction proceedings are also available with respect to crew, stevedores, ITF inspectors, etc., but are of limited value. According to Belgian law, the concept of a strike is considered wrong in principle. However, there also exists a basic human right which allows an individual freedom to choose whether or not to work. The result is that although a court may be willing to grant an injunction ordering the termination of a strike or boycott, it will not enforce any sanctions against the strikers. A ship may therefore be able to get in and out of a port but be unable to load or discharge.

A special situation exists at the port of Zeebrugge with respect to tankers. Because of the dangerous nature of some tankers (which are not gas free) and the harbour obstruction which a boycott would create (resulting in a disruption of energy supplies to Belgium), the Harbour authorities, including police, backed by the government are willing to assist a boycotted vessel by way of requisition if necessary.

In view of the rather particular circumstances pertaining to ITF boycotts in Belgium, not least of which is the slightly obscure form of legal relief, owners/managers of boycotted vessels should not hesitate to contact LSC Lawyers in Antwerp. They are best equipped to assess the situation quickly and suggest action appropriate to the circumstances.

CANADA

High risk ports:

Vancouver

Montreal

Halifax

Active ITF Inspectors:

Tom McGrath

Gerry McCullough

Active Affiliated Seafarers and Dockers Unions:

*Canadian Brotherhood of Railway, Transport and General Workers

Seamen's Section, Local 400, 138 East Cordova
Street, Vancouver V6A 1K9 Tel. 687 1881

*Seafarers' International Union (SIU) of Canada
634 St. James Street West, Montreal 101 P.Q.
Tel: (514) 842 8161

Canadian Merchant Service Guild
904 Lady Ellen Place, Ottawa 3, Ontario

International Longshoremen's and Warehousemen's Union
2681 East Hastings Street, Vancouver 132, B.C.

Other Affiliated Seafarers and Dockers Unions:

B.C. Ferry and Marine Workers' Union

ITF boycott activity, which is gradually increasing in Canada, is almost invariably associated with a dispute concerning crew members.

The usual procedure, at least on the West Coast, is for the ITF to induce the crew to set up a picket line and request stevedores not to cross it. Canadian trade union members—whether af-

---

* Indicates that representatives have been appointed to deal with flag of convenience matters.

filiated to the ITF or not—will not usually cross any picket line which is in accordance with their contracts of employment.

Faced with this situation, an owner must usually either resolve the dispute with the crew or discharge them, although if he is unable to resolve the dispute he may be able to obtain some form of relief from the courts. It should be noted, however, that Canadian courts are reluctant to provide interlocutory relief and on no occasion will they order crew members to return to work against their will. However, if the crew are properly discharged in accordance with their contract of employment the courts may order the crew to leave the ship.

Whenever court proceedings seem inevitable the ITF are generally more favourably disposed to reaching some form of amicable settlement. However, Canadian affiliates of the ITF collected a total of US$789,171 in 1981 in respect of back pay as a result of boycott or threatened boycott action. In the first three months of 1982 they collected a further US$478,353.

As a matter of Canadian law, the right to strike and engage in picketing and boycotting is restricted to trade unions duly certified by the Labour Relations Board, and who must conform to the provisions in the Labour Code with regard to notice. If any unions engage in boycotts or picketing which are not certified, or outside of the periods specified, the court will provide an injunction restraining them.

Two further points are of general interest to the situation in Canada. Firstly, owners/manager should be warned that it is understood that the ITF affiliate in Vancouver has a Filipino employee who makes contact with Filipino crews on FOC vessels, with a view to taking immediate advantage of any dissatisfaction or unrest among them.

Secondly, it may be of assistance to owners/managers to bear in mind that the ITF inspectors on the West Coast tend to take their weekends off without making appropriate contingency plans for a 'boycotted' vessel. If a striking crew are in any way vulnerable a weekend may thus be the appropriate time to take advantage of this.

DENMARK

High risk ports:

Helsingor	Aarhus
Holbaek	Randers

Active ITF Inspectors:

Svend Fonsskov

Knud Mols Sorensen

Active Affiliated Seafarers and Dockers Unions:

*Dansk Maskinbesaetningsforbund Tel: (01) 14 84 36
Store Strandstraede 8, 1255 Copenhagen K

Specialarbejderforbundet i Danmark (SiD)
Nyropsgade 30, Copenhagen V

Somaendenes Forbund i Danmark
Herluf Trollesgade 5, 1052 Copenhagen K

Dansk So-Restaurations Forening
Heibergsgade 14, 1056 Copenhagen K

Radiotelegrafistforeningen

Navigatorernes Hus, Havnegade 55,
1058 Copenhagen K

Dansk Styrmandsforening
Havnegade 55, 1058 Copenhagen K

Danmarks Skibsforerforening
Navigatorernes Hus, Havnegade 55,
1058 Copenhagen K

Maskinmestrenes Forening
Sankt Annae Plads 16, 1250 Copenhagen K

Other Affiliated Seafarers and Dockers Unions:

Dansk Jernbaneforbund

Handels-og Kontrorfunktionaererernes Forbund i

Danmark

Jernbaneforeningen

Dansk Metalarbejderforbund

ITF boycotts in Denmark are rare, although not altogether unknown. There were no known boycotts in 1981 but the Danish affiliates have collected US$65,694 in respect of back pay in 1982.

---

* Indicates that representatives have been appointed to deal with flag of convenience matetrs.

Details of the associated actions are not known at the time of writing.

It is not so much Danish law per se which prohibits ITF activity, but rather a contractual situation which exists between the Danish Employers Federation (DAF) and the Danish Federation of Trade Unions (LO). An agreement which regulates the employer/employee relationship is entered into every two years and under its provisions industrial action is prohibited.

Port workers in Denmark are affiliated, through their unions, to the LO and are employed by employer groups which are affiliated to the DAF. Thus if stevedores, for example, engage in ITF sympathy action they do so in violation of a provision of the two-yearly agreement, and an injunction can be obtained by the Employers' Federation from the Industrial Courts, which can also impose heavy fines on the striking stevedores.

However, there is one drawback to such court action, in that in any such attempt to have the boycott declared illegal, the court would have to hear the entire case and thus ships could well be delayed for up to one or two weeks before judgment could be obtained.

FINLAND

High risk ports:

All ports in Finland are high risk

Active ITF Inspectors:

Lavri Heinon
Seppo Soikeli

Active Affiliated Seafarers and Dockers Unions:

*Suomen Merimies-Unioni r.y.,
Iso Roobertinkatu 30, Helsinki 14 Tel: 13404

Suomen Konepaallystoliitto
Merikatu 1B, 00140, Helsinki 14

Luotsi liito
Iso Roobertinkatu 30, Helsinki 12

Suomen Laivanpaallystoliito r.y.
Hietalahdenranta 15 A Helsinki 18

---

* Indicates that representatives have been appointed to deal with flag of convenience matters.

Suomen Radiosahkottajaliito,
Sepankatu 13, Helsinki 15

Soumen Satamatyonpjohtajien Litto r.y.,
Vuorikatu 1 C 34, Kotka

Suomen Auto-Ja Kuljetusalan Tyontekijaliitto r.y.
Haapaniemenkatu 7-9 talo B 00530 Helsinki 53

The ITF affiliated Finnish Seamen's Union (FSU) keep a close check on the shipping press and note all FOC vessels scheduled to enter Finnish waters. On arrival of such a vessel alongside a berth, whether or not she is listed as an 'approved' ship and in possession of a blue certificate, an inspector will go aboard and carry out a spot check.

Unless the vessel has a blue certificate which is being properly administered the master will be advised that his ship will not be handled by the port workers until a special agreement is signed, with the usual provisions for back payment to the crew. It should be stressed that possession of a blue certificate does not automatically render a vessel immune from ITF boycotts in Finland as the FSU have been known on more than one occasion to impose boycotts on vessels with 'Korean' blue certificates.

Owners/managers should bear in mind that the chance of boycott action against non-ITF-approved FOC ships in Finland is more than just a calculated risk—it is a certainty. In addition to the usual contributions to the welfare fund, membership fees and back pay demands, the FSU also charge a 'handling fee' which usually amounts to between $1,000-$2,000. It is claimed that this is to cover their own expenses. The back pay is usually paid to the FSU who later distribute it to the crew. It will be appreciated that the crew may not necessarily have been involved in the dispute and that if they therefore refuse to take the back pay it will be remitted to the ITF in London.

ITF boycotts have proven very effective in Finland and the courts cannot be relied on to provide any form of practical relief without involving undue delay. If a vessel should find itself the subject of an ITF boycott therefore, it is usually expedient to pay up in the first instance and then take whatever legal steps are available to attempt to recover the money and perhaps obtain damages. Success will, of course, be dependent upon whether the boycott was lawful or unlawful, or alternatively was initially lawful but later became unlawful.

In 1981 Finnish ITF affiliates collected a total of US$300,667 in back pay as a result of boycott or threatened boycott action. There are no figures available for 1982.

Finnish law on the subject of boycotts is complex and uncertain and it is not proposed that it should be considered in any detail in this report. It may however be helpful to cite some examples. The following have been considered lawful in Finland:—

—boycott of ships where no ITF agreement existed;

—boycott of ships where contracted wages were not being paid-e.g., double accounts.

—boycotts of otherwise 'ITF approved' vessels where crew pay was below full ITF rates. The FSU do not approve of this ITF practice.

—boycotts of ships where masters have refused to supply information to the FSU about crew wages.

On the other hand, a lawful boycott may become unlawful if shown to be a clear misuse of the right to boycott, or if handled in an incorrect manner, e.g. by causing unreasonable delay or unreasonable losses. It appears that a boycott by the pilots federation would be unlawful.

An owner/manager who finds his vessel the subject of an ITF boycott in Finland should anticipate a 7-10 day time scale to negotiate a settlement.

FRANCE

High risk ports:

Boulogne	Le Havre	Rouen	Dunkirk
La Pallice	Marseilles	St. Malo	Sete
La Rochelle	Nantes	St. Nazaire	Port de Bouc
Bordeaux	Lorient		

Active ITF Inspectors:

Antoine Barbero	M. Deschamps
Louis Coppin	M. Cobloc
Guy Hanno	M. Adde
Jean Warmez	M. Andrien
Roland Andrieu	

Active Affiliated Seafarers and Dockers Unions:

*Federation Generale des Transports et de l'Equipment (CFDT)

Federation des Officers de la Marine Marchande F.O.
198 Avenue du Maine, Paris 14e

Other Affiliated Seafarers and Dockers Unions:

Federation Nationale des Ports et Docks et Assimiles F.O.

The ITF in France do not as a rule carry out any systematic check on FOC vessels to see whether or not they have a blue certificate. ITF inspectors do however try to encourage crew members to go on strike for ITF conditions whenever the opportunity arises. Often this opportunity occurs in a local seamen's club or through direct contact by a crew member.

If the ITF are successful in enlisting the sympathy of the crew, they will endeavour to get the members concerned to sign a mandate enlisting the support of the ITF and sometimes making allegations against the safety and sanitary standards of the vessel. The ITF will then give copies of the mandate to the tug employees and pilots who will thereupon call a boycott of the vessel.

An ITF inspector will also board the vessel and ask the master to enter into a special agreement, with the usual provisions relating to back pay. If the master refuses a crew strike will be called, occasionally accompanied by a boycott by stevedores, tugs, pilots, etc. Often ITF representatives will organise a 'sit in' on board—no doubt to maintain contact with the crew. Alternatively a van may be stationed near the gangway which is constantly manned by ITF representatives.

The ITF in France collected a total of US$40,000 from owners in respect of back pay in 1981; no figures are available for 1982.

The French courts in general look upon ITF boycotts with distaste and consider such action as taking an otherwise lawful right to strike too far. An injunction can usually be obtained against the ITF within 1-3 days, ordering them to terminate the boycott and imposing a fine for each day of non-compliance.

---

* Indicates that representatives have been appointed to deal with flag of convenience matters.

GERMANY
(FEDERAL REPUBLIC OF)

High risk ports:

Bremen   Brunsbüttel

Hamburg

Wilhelmshaven

Active ITF Inspectors:

Guntar Wille   Mr. Baars

Harald Schmelling

Active Affiliated Seafarers and Dockers Unions:

*Gewerkschaft offentliche Dienste, Transport und Verkehr
OeTV-Seeschiffahrt, Besenbinderhorf 57/11,
2 Hamburg 1 Tel: 20971

Gewerkschaft offentliche Dienste, Transport und Verkehr
Theodor-Heuss-Strasse 2, 7000 Stuttgart 1

As a general rule the ITF will not take any action against
an FOC vessel unless called on by the crew, or at the specific
request of ITF London.

Although the ITF have been known sometimes to take action
where no crew complaint existed, it is unusual for them to do
so (and illegal under German law).

The usual form of ITF action in Germany begins with an
approach to the ITF by one or more crew members. The ITF
inspector will then meet with other crew members to try to enlist
their support, and ask them all to sign a mandate requesting the
ITF to act on their behalf to better their conditions.

The ITF inspector will then approach the master asking that
he enter into a special agreement and that the crew members
be employed on ITF terms and conditions. If the master refuses
the next step will be the calling of a strike on board by the crew
members. In this respect it is a requirement of German law that
a vote be taken among crew members on whether there should be
a strike or not. If there is a majority decision in favour of strik-

---

* Indicates that representatives have been appointed to deal with
flag of convenience matters.

ing then German law is complied with and an owner has no legal remedy against the ensuing strike.

In this situation it is unnecessary for any sympathy action to be taken by other port workers such as stevedores, tugs, etc., as the crew strike by itself would have the desired effect of bringing ship operations to a standstill. Where some crew are on strike but not others, it is likely that the ITF will enlist the support of their stevedore affiliates in calling for the vessels to be boycotted. In general however there will be no boycott action by stevedores unless a strike situation exists on board, so that where a boycott by stevedores is in operation and the strike on board is resolved, (usually) all boycott action will then collapse.

Some notable exceptions to the general rule that the ITF in Germany remain within the law occurred during "action week" in May 1980. In one case concerning an FOC vessel at Hansa Port, an ITF inspector boarded the ship (without announcing who he was) and approached the radio operator in an authoritative manner demanding the portage bills. The Filipino radio operator (who kept the ship's accounts) handed the files over to him thinking he was owners' marine superintendent.

The inspector left the ship with the files under his arm only to return later and present the master with a demand for US$70,000 in back pay for the crew. When the master asked him to leave the inspector called a boycott of stevedores—which took effect immediately—notwithstanding the fact that the crew were not involved in the complaint in any way.

Although according to German law the boycott was blatantly illegal, owners were forced by charterparty commitments to accede to ITF demands, pay up and sign an ITF special agreement.

It is interesting to note that the back pay was paid to OeTV who remitted the money to ITF London. They in turn remitted it to the Philippines. When the crew returned home the local ITF representatives tried to make the back payments in the form of colour televisions, washing machines, motor cycles and the like, for fear that the crew members would return the money to owners via their crewing agency.

In 1981 German ITF affiliates collected a total of US$1,256,351 as a result of boycott or threatened boycott action. No figures are as yet available for 1982.

In considering whether to resort to the German courts for a legal remedy in a boycott situation an owner must first weigh up all the ingredients of his particular case. The most important of these is the remedy which is to be sought. This will, of course, vary depending on whether or not crew members are involved in the boycott.

In cases concerning strikes by the crew it was at one time thought that German courts would not accept jurisdiction concerning disputes on foreign flag vessels. However, it is now generally accepted that German labour courts will do so.

The labour court consists of three members, one of whom is a judge, one a union representative and one an employer's representative. In Hamburg there are special shipping chambers of the court so that it is likely that the tribunal will consist of a panel with shipping experience. However, this situation does not necessarily exist in other parts of Germany.

Two conditions must exist before an owner has any chance of success in an application to the labour court. Firstly the question of which law should be applied must be resolved, and secondly there must exist a collective bargaining agreement (CBA). Insofar as the former is concerned, there is usually no problem if, for example, the crew were recruited in the Philippines and the contract of employment specifies that Filipino law applies. The law of the vessel's flag is immaterial in such a situation, but clearly problems could arise where it is not quite so obvious which law governs the employment contract.

If these conditions exist but the court finds that the strike is legal, no remedy is available to an owner. In order to resolve whether the strike is illegal, the court will require full details of the relevant sections of the labour code governing the contracts of employment, plus a copy of the CBA. Such evidence will be put before the court in the form of affidavits with exhibits annexed. It should be appreciated that German courts require a high standard of proof before they will grant an Einstweilige Verfungung (provisional order). The reason for this is that in allowing an owner's application the court (in effect) will have conceded to his demands without the matter being heard in full.

So far as the court is concerned it does not matter that the crew are paid at a scale lower than that existing in Germany or that the terms and conditions of employment seem harsh. Provided there is no question of a contravention of basic human rights or of German public order, and provided that the crew have been paid in accordance with the terms and conditions of their contract, the owners are likely to succeed in obtaining an injunction against the striking crew members and ITF representatives. The terms of the injunction would be to the effect that each crew member should terminate his strike and the ITF inspector(s) discontinue their support of it.

It is important that in his application an owner should include a request that, in the event of an injunction being granted, a fine should be imposed if the order is disobeyed—against each person who disobeys and for each occasion that he does so. It is thought that such a fine could be as much as DM 5,000 per man per occasion. Where such an injunction has been obtained and the crew refuse to return to work, an immediate application should be made to the court to impose the fines in accordance with the order.

In certain cases it is possible for a charterer or receiver to apply for an injunction from the German County courts. Such an application would take the form of a request that the court order the crew to open the hatches etc., to allow a third party to take delivery of his property. This would be sufficient to oust the jurisdiction of the labour court and would be the preferred method of obtaining relief where such a third party existed to make the application.

Third parties, including charterers, can also seek relief from the County courts provided that the remedy sought will not have the effect of a complete resolution of the dispute. For example, they can apply for an order to the effect that the crew open the hatches, or permit a charterer or receiver to take his cargo in circumstances where it may be deteriorating, or where he has to fulfill another contract. However, it is doubtful whether an application would be successful where the applicant asks for an injunction to order the ship to sail to another port so that the charterer or receiver can take delivery of his cargo, as the effect of this would be to bring the strike to an end.

IRISH REPUBLIC

High risk ports:

Cork

Active ITF Inspectors:

Information unavailable

Active Affiliated Seafarers and Dockers Unions:

Irish Transport and General Workers' Union
Liberty Hall, Dublin 1

Seamen's Union of Ireland
149F North Strand Road, Dublin 3

N.B.   Apart from the fact that US$523,269 was collected in 1981 in respect of back pay in Ireland, no information is available about ITF activity in that country.

ISRAEL

High risk ports:

Ashdod

Haifa

Active ITF Inspectors:

Capt. Y. Groman

Active Affiliated Seafarers and Dockers Unions:

*Israeli Sea Officers' Union
Haparsim Street 22, Haifa Tel: 512231

Israeli Seamen's Union
3 Habankim Street P.O. Box 1324 Haifa

Other Affiliated Seafarers and Dockers Unions:

Transport Workers' Division of Histadrut

All FOC vessels entering Israeli ports are asked to produce a blue certificate by a representative of the Israeli sea officers unions—usually the pilot taking the vessel to berth. As pilotage is compulsory this method is effective.

If the vessel does not have a blue certificate the ITF representative will advise the master that the vessel cannot berth unless a special agreement is signed, or special instructions are received from ITF London confirming that the vessel is ITF 'approved'.

The ITF in Israel do not always insist on full back pay for the crew but do require owners' contributions to the welfare fund

---

* Indicates that representatives have been appointed to deal with flag of convenience matters.

and crew entrance and membership fees to be paid. Where, for example, the officers are members of an ITF affiliate, such as the British MNAOA, the ITF do not insist that they become members of the special seafarers department.

In 1981 ITF affiliates in Israel collected a total of US$272,238 from owners/managers in respect of back pay. No figures for 1982 are yet available.

If a negotiated settlement is not appropriate to particular circumstances, legal remedies are available and provided the boycott can be shown to be illegal an injunction can usually be obtained within 1 to 2 days. Injunctions are enforced by the imposition of fines on the unions concerned and their representatives personally.

So far as Israeli law is concerned a strike per se does not give rise to an action in tort against a union for causing a breach of contract. However strikes by public service employees such as pilots and stevedores do give rise to such an action.

In some cases, where the above remedy might not be available, third parties such as cargo receivers or charterers may well be able to successfully sue the unions involved. Once again however, advice should be taken from lawyers on the spot regarding the advisability of such action in particular circumstances.

ITALY

High risk ports:

Genoa	La Spezia
Venice	Palermo (Sicily)
Taranto	Reggio Calabria

Active ITF Inspectors:

M. Guidi	M. Berlingeri
R. Nescoibelli	F.Giorgi
B. del Bonis	M. Leoncini

Active Affiliated Seafarers and Dockers Unions:

*Federazione Italiana Lavoratori del Mare
    Settore Navi Estere, Via Milano 40
    c-14, 16126 Genoa Tel: 25-66-09

---

* Indicates that representatives have been appointed to deal with flag of convenience matters.

Unione Italiana Lavoratori Trasporti Ausiliari
Traffico e Portuali
Via Palestro 78, Rome

Federazione Italiana Lavoratori dei Porti, (FILP-CISL)
Via Piave 61, 16124 Genoa

Federazione Italiana Lavoratori del Mare (FILM-CISL)
Via Catone 15-10, CAP 0093 Rome

Unione Italiana Marittimi
Via Lucullo 6, Rome

N.B. Although not affiliated to ITF, Confederazione Generale
Italiana del Lavoro (CGIL), a left-wing political trade
union, is frequently associated with ITF induced boycotts.

There is no evidence to suggest that Italian ITF inspectors/
affiliates employ systematic methods of checking FOC vessels
entering Italian waters to ascertain whether they have blue
certificates or are otherwise considered to be approved ships.

It appears that individual inspectors in Italy are very much
a law unto themselves and ITF London exercises little or no
control over them.

Although it is generally thought that local ITF inspectors
will not cause a vessel to be the subject of a boycott unless contacted by a dissatisfied crew member, it has been confirmed by
more than one source that some left-wing activists within the
C.G.I.L. often try to induce crew members to express dissatisfaction with their employment conditions for the sole purpose of
creating the required ingredients allowing a lawful boycott to
be called.

Their usual tactic is to contact crew members ashore in the
seaman's club and/or in bars, whereupon the usual process of ITF
indoctrination is begun. Such crew members are asked to sign
a mandate to the effect that the vessel is sub-standard and that
the food is bad, usually also stating that fire and boat drills have
not been carried out for some time, and so on. The mandate will
also give the ITF power of attorney to act on behalf of the crew.
Once signed, the next step is for the ITF inspector to board the
vessel and demand that an ITF special agreement be signed,
threatening that in default of this a boycott will be called.

It is also reported that the ITF in Genoa have enlisted some
Filipinos among their staff who visit Filipino crewed vessels in
Genoa to check on conditions on board and to try to win over the

crew to demand an ITF special agreement. Such efforts have also led to the signing of mandates giving the ITF power of attorney, with the obvious consequences.

In the event that a master in the above situation refuses to enter into a special agreement a boycott by port workers will be called which may be partial or complete. It is more common for stevedores to call a partial boycott, whereby they will work during part of their shift only.

Once a boycott has been called a vessel will find it difficult to obtain any port services or assistance until such time as the dispute has been resolved. Even if the vessel is only blacked by stevedores, an owner will find that tugs, immigrations, customs, harbour authorities, and even the much trusted port agent, will be afraid to be seen assisting the vessel, although the port agents generally give as much assistance as is possible under the circumstances. However, the harbour master will usually prohibit any crew change and refuse to give the vessel clearance to sail; immigrations will not give exit visas for Asian crew members to be repatriated; and so on.

In certain cases where owners have disregarded directions of the harbour master and immigration authority, port agents have been able to smooth matters over by using a little initiative, and without any adverse repercussions for owners.

Owners and managers should be warned that companies in Italy having more than 30 or 40 employees are required by law to have a trade union representative on their premises. Not only do such representatives keep an eye on fellow workers with regard to contact with boycotted vessels, but in the case of port agencies they may also pass sensitive information back to the ITF in the form of copies of telexes, etc.

It will be appreciated that there will always be a flurry of telephone and telex communication in a boycott situation. Precautions should therefore be taken when tactics are being considered to ensure absolute confidentiality and to avoid sending and receiving telexes through agents. On the other hand such a situation may be used to an owner's advantage should he want false information to be "leaked".

Another motivating force behind some ITF boycotts in Italy revolves around the political aspirations of some union leaders who also happen to be ITF inspectors. Naturally, there is a lot of publicity through the media during a boycott and such political aspirants utilise this to full advantage.

Furthermore, a boycott can also be a potential source of revenue for an inspector or associated union in Italy. Such income may or may not be used to sponsor other political activities, e.g. rallies, etc. It has been reported that in addition to owners' contributions to the welfare fund, etc. a separate fee is charged by Italian ITF affiliates. There is also evidence which supports allegations that crew members pay a proportion of back payments received to the ITF inspector. It is believed that this 'commission' remains in Italy and is not remitted to ITF London.

One further point of general interest to ITF activities in Italy concerns a specific boycott which owners were able to frustrate. It was brought about following allegations of the vessel being sub-standard—which in this particular case, and no doubt in many others—proved to be totally untrue.

The owner's representative, by systematically visiting the offices of each union involved in the boycott (there were many), managed to prove to the satisfaction of the union leaders that the allegations in the mandate were unfounded. On receiving such proof that the vessel was in good condition and that the crew had no legitimate complaints the various union leaders suspended the boycott allowing the vessel to resume normal port operations.

Another pertinent example occurred when the ITF inspector at Taranto threatened immediate boycott action if an owner refused to enter into an ITF special agreement. The inspector did not have a signed mandate from the crew, as they did not, in fact, support the action. When challenged by owner's representative that he was not entitled by law to call a boycott, the ITF inspector withdrew gracefully. The stevedores continued working throughout.

In 1981 Italian ITF affiliates collected a total of US$828,658 as a result of boycott or threatened boycott action. No figures are as yet available for 1982.

In considering legal remedies in Italy, a distinction should be drawn between unlawful boycotts and disputes involving crew members. Even if a court order is obtained directing stevedores, etc. to terminate a boycott, it may not be enforceable because of the political strength of the trade union movement. In Italy disputes concerning terms and conditions of employment are heard by labour judges, who are known to favour employees. Furthermore, problems arise because under Italian law employment contracts in respect of crew members are governed by the law of the vessel's flag, or as specified in their employment contract. But Italian judges are at all times bound to follow Italian law and therefore cannot apply the law of another country.

The courts in Italy should not therefore be relied upon to provide relief in a boycott situation. The only exception would be a situation in which blatantly unlawful secondary action was taken. In such a case an ex-parte application (i.e. without the other party being present) could be heard on the same day and an appropriate court order should follow.

NETHERLANDS

High risk ports:

Amsterdam	Flushing
Rotterdam	

Active ITF Inspectors:

John Putter	Mr. Roodenburg
R. Touwen	Mr. van der Mayden

Active Affiliated Seafarers and Dockers Unions:

*Federatie van Werknemersorganisaties in de Zeevaart
   Heemraadssingle 323, Roterdam 6 Tel: 010 771188

Vervocrsfederatie NVV/NKV
   Goeman Borgesiuslaan 77, 2505 Utrecht

Other Affiliated Seafarers and Dockers Unions:

Vervoersbonden FNV

Vervoersbond NKV

N.B.   Former inspector Johan Altena was sacked by FWZ in September 1981 after speaking out in public about appropriation of interest earned on back payments by FWZ. He has now quietly disappeared from the ITF scene.

It is unusual for the ITF to take any boycott action against FOC vessels in Holland unless the crew have enlisted their support, either directly or through the ITF in London.

Once a local ITF inspector has a foothold on the vessel he will endeavour to obtain a general power of attorney from the crew

---

* Indicates that representatives have been appointed to deal with flag of convenience matters.

and encourage them to go on strike. This will be followed by an approach to the master with the usual ITF demands under threat of an immediate crew strike followed by a stevedore boycott.

On the basis that crew members are involved, should the master refuse to concede to ITF demands, a crew strike will inevitably be called and the crew instructed by the inspector to keep the gangway in the raised position and only allow selected people on board. The thinking behind this tactic is to prevent representatives from owners/managers from boarding to negotiate directly with the crew, thus bypassing the ITF.

Despite the usual ITF threats of immediate boycott action by stevedores they often continue to work cargo throughout. However, if only part of the crew are on strike and it is likely that the vessel may sail on completion of cargo operations, the stevedores will sometimes boycott the vessel.

Depending on the particular circumstances, and no doubt the degree of uncertainty vis-a-vis the lawfulness of the strike/ boycott, local ITF inspectors do not always demand back pay for the crew. They are often happy to sign a special agreement with the vessel and leave it at that.

In 1981 Dutch affiliates collected a total of US$1,340,143 in back pay as a result of boycott or threatened boycott action. They have collected US$72,997 in the first three months of 1982 in respect of back pay.

The legal situation in the Netherlands vis-a-vis crew strikes and boycotts is somewhat more developed than in other European countries. The Supreme Court made a ruling in 1960 following strikes in Rotterdam and Amsterdam which resulted from the 1958 ITF boycott. Since that time there has been a series of cases in the Netherlands (some in favour of the ITF), culminating in the most recent "SAUDI INDEPENDENCE" case in which the Appeal Court of the Hague on 23rd April 1982 gave a ruling in favour of owners. In their judgement the Court states that either the law of the flag or the law chosen in the employment contracts will be decisive as to the lawfulness of a crew strike. The ITF are taking the case on appeal to the Supreme Court and a final decision is expected during the first half of 1983.*

In the meantime, the ITF is maintaining a low key approach in the Netherlands and there is little evidence of boycott activity, nor of further court action—which would most likely follow the Appeal Court ruling.

---

* The Appeal Court sustained the decision (Ed.).

In summary, the legal situation is as follows:

If the ITF call a strike of their stevedore affiliates (FNV) in support of a cause which is outside the employer/employee relationship they commit a tort of inducing a breach of contract and thereby expose themselves to an action for damages. The employer—i.e. the stevedore company—will be able to seek relief from the court by way of an injunction to terminate the strike/boycott on the basis that they are not in a position to influence the fulfillment of ITF demands.

If the crew of a ship go on strike the owner/manager *may* be able to obtain an injunction from the court ordering the crew to terminate the strike. In order to do this an owner/manager must adduce sufficient evidence to show that the crew are in breach of their contract of employment by striking. In this respect the court will consider the appropriate law which governs the contract of employment as well as the terms and conditions of employment. If no evidence of the proper law is available, the court will most likely apply Dutch law—in which case the action would probably fail. (If an order is obtained and the crew refuse to obey it the court will permit the owner/manager to sack the offending crew members and replace them. Also, as regards the ITF, the court will order them to refrain from supporting the strike, in default of which a fine will be imposed, which could be of the order of Dfl.100,000 per day.)

In the present circumstances it is unlikely that the ITF will launch any major offensive in the Netherlands—at least not until the Supreme Court gives a final ruling in the "SAUDI INDEPENDENCE" case. Should a vessel meanwhile be subjected to ITF activity, an injunction can usually be obtained within 2-5 days. However, it should be remembered that—as in most other European countries—there is no binding system of precedent in the Netherlands, and a lower court need not follow a ruling of a higher court, which could result in delay.

Consequently there can never be any certainty of success at first instance and every effort should therefore be made to resolve matters amicably before resorting to court action.

NEW ZEALAND

High risk ports:

Tauranga

Active ITF Inspectors:

Mr. Lewis

Active Affiliated Seafarers and Dockers Unions:

> *New Zealand Waterside Workers' Federation
> Box 27004, 1st Floor, 220 Willis Street
> Wellington   Tel: 850 792

> New Zealand Seamen's union
> P.O. Box 27-263 Upper Willis Street
> Wellington

> New Zealand Merchant Service Guild
> 4th Floor, Central House, 26 Brandon Street
> P.O. Box 552, Wellington

Other Affiliated Seafarers and Dockers Unions:

> Federated Cooks' and Stewards' Union of New Zealand
> New Zealand Institute of Marine and Power Engineers

N.B.   The only information available at the time of writing with respect to ITF activity in New Zealand is that in 1981 US$464,303 was collected in respect of back pay, and that the courts will not order unwilling stevedores to work.

NORWAY

High risk ports:

Narvik	**Sarpsborg**
Heroya	**Stavanger**
Kristiansand	**Arendal**

Active ITF Inspectors:

O Ringvold	Steinar Garberg
A Dale	**Mr. Abraaham**
Mr. St. Stifjell	Sverre Nilsen

Active Affiliated Seafarers and Dockers Unions:

> *Norsk Sjomannsforbund Tel: 42 18 90
> Sjomennenes Hus, Grev Wedelsplass 7, Oslo

> Det Norske Maskinistforbund
> Arbiensgate 1, III Oslo

---

* Indicates that representatives have been appointed to deal with flag of convenience matters.

Norsk Styrmandsforening
Arbiensgate 11, Oslo 2

Norsk Transportarbeiderforbund
Folkets Hus, Youngsgate 11, VI Oslo

The ITF in Norway do not generally become involved in boycott action unless it is at the specific request of ITF London, or if approached by crew members. Notwithstanding this the Norwegian Seamens Union does check the official schedule of vessels in Norwegian waters and monitors the movements of FOC vessels.

The legal situation in Norway is fairly clear and requires (among other things) that in order for a boycott to be lawful the crew must be a party to the dispute. Notwithstanding this however, the ITF do occasionally call on a vessel to enter into a special agreement (normally at the request of ITF London), and threaten boycott action in default. This is not usually associated with a demand for back pay for the crew as such a demand would be contrary to Norwegian law. Furthermore, if there is already a collective agreement with a bona fide trade union in existence, the Norwegian ITF do not usually insist on a special agreement being signed.

In a case where the crew are a party to the dispute, the ITF must comply with certain requirements of Norwegian law before they can boycott a ship. The most important of these (for an owner/manager) is the giving of proper notice. Apparently 5 days is considered sufficient. There are also various other provisions of Norwegian law which prevent the ITF from demanding full ITF conditions for the crew. For example, clause 5 of the special agreement would have to be deleted; and the freedom of an individual to choose whether or not he wishes to join a trade union must at all times be respected.

In essence it is unlikely that ITF action in Norway will go beyond a crew strike situation, which can probably be settled by signature of an amended special agreement entitling the crew to ITF wages only from the date of signature. The Norwegian ITF do not insist on payment of owners' welfare fund contributions or crew membership and entrance fees.

The ITF in Norway collected a total of US$45,009 in 1981 in respect of back pay and US$76,997 in the first three months of 1982.

In the event of an ITF boycott in Norway an application can be made for an injunction at fairly short notice which will be given if the boycott is unlawful. This can be followed by an application for the boycott to be declared unlawful, coupled with an action for damages. In one example of such an action succeeding the ITF were ordered by the Narvik Municipal Court to pay damages to the owners of the "NAWALA" of US$297,561.03, plus interest (at 10%) for unlawful boycott action against the vessel in 1979. The appeal court upheld the ruling of the lower court in November 1981 and increased the rate of interest to 15% from 1st December 1980.

PORTUGAL

High risk ports:

Lisbon

Aveiro

Oporto

Active ITF Inspectors:

Antonio Laureano Baptista de Oliveira

Active Affiliated Seafarers and Dockers Unions:

*Federaçao Nacional dos Sindicatos de
   Trabalhadores Portuarios

Other Affiliated Seafarers and Dockers Unions:

Sindicato dos Fogueiros de Mar e Terra do Sul
   e Ilhas Adjacentes

Federaçao dos Sindicatos do Mar

N.B.   Apart from the fact that US$111,000 was collected in 1981 in respect of back pay no other information is presently available about ITF activity in Portugal.

SPAIN

High risk ports:

| Huelva | Aviles | Barcelona |
| Bilbao | Las Palmas | Seville |

Active ITF Inspectors:

Augustin Aguirre

---

* Indicates that representatives have been appointed to deal with flag of convenience matters.

Active Affiliated Seafarers and Dockers Unions:
*Federación de Transportes (UGT)
Alonso Cano 63, 1 Esq. Madrid 2
Tel: Madrid 6126

Other Affiliated Seafarers and Dockers Unions:
Federación del Transporte de ELA-STV

ITF activity in Spain is steadily on the increase now that Mr. Augustine Aguirre is a full time ITF inspector. Although he is primarily based in Bilbao he is eager and willing to travel to all parts of Spain in support of the anti-FOC campaign. In 1981 a total of US$69,121 was collected from owners in respect of back pay; the figure for the first three months of 1982 is $246,010. Back payments are remitted to Mr. Aquirre in person.

From the information available it appears that crew members are usually involved in an ITF dispute in Spain and that the ITF do not always demand full ITF scales to be imposed. In one case the ITF insisted that a Filipino crew should be paid in accordance with the Oca CBA, but in another (Panama flag) only that the crew be paid not less than minimum ILO rates or minimum Panamanian, whichever was greater. There is therefore no consistency and thus no pattern to ITF activity in Spain—apart from ITF involvement with FOC vessels being generally on the increase.

It should be noted that Spanish crewing agencies are not prepared to assist owners/managers of vessels which are the subject of ITF action in Spain. No doubt this stems from the close contact such agencies must maintain with the ITF to obtain blue certificates.

At the time of writing no information is available on the legal situation in Spain with regard to strikes/boycotts.

SWEDEN

High risk ports:
All ports in Sweden are high risk

Active ITF Inspectors:

A. Lindstrom	Lili-Anne Skoogh
Lars Jansson	

---

* Indicates that representatives have been appointed to deal with flag of convenience matters.

Active Affiliated Seafarers and Dockers Unions:

*Svenska Sjofolksforbundet
    Jarntorget 1, 413 04 Goteborg Tel: 17 31 30

Svenska Transportarbetareforbundet
    101 22 Stockholm, Box 158

Svenska Maskinbefalsforbundet
    103 63 Stockholm Box 3157

Sveriges Fartygsbefalsforening
    Skeppsbron 32, 3 tr, 103 63 Stockholm

Other Affiliated Seafarers and Dockers Unions:

Handelstjanstemannaforbundet

Sveriges Arbetsledareforbund

The ITF in Sweden keep a close watch on the shipping press
for movements of FOC vessels within Swedish waters, with a
view to conducting systematic spot checks. Those FOC vessels
operating without a blue certificate will be threatened with immediate boycott action unless a special agreement is signed.

In 1981 Swedish affiliates of the ITF collected a total of
US$544,411 in respect of back pay and they collected a further
US$161,968 during the first three months of 1982.

The ITF campaign enjoys a very high success rate in Sweden
as ITF boycotts as such are entirely legal, notwithstanding the
fact that the crew members on whose behalf the boycott is enforced may be completely content with their existing terms and
conditions of employment.

If an FOC vessel becomes the subject of an ITF boycott in
Sweden owners/managers cannot rely on the courts to provide
any form of relief and should therefore enter immediate negotiations with the ITF, with a view to reaching a settlement with
minimum delay.

UNITED KINGDOM

High risk ports:

All major U.K. ports are high risk

---

* Indicates that representatives have been appointed to deal with
flag of convenience matters.

Active ITF Inspectors:

John Nelson	Ken Turner
Harry Shaw	Joe Barlow
Jim Hennighan	Jim Woods
Harry Windsor	Basil Gregory
John Ross	Larry Green
Pat Guinane	J. Rouland

Active Affiliated Seafarers and Dockers Unions:

*National Union or Seamen
  Maritime House, Old Town, Clapham,
  London SW4 OJP   Tel: (01) 622 4481

*Merchant Navy & Airline Officers' Association
  750-760 High Road, Leytonstone,
  London E11 3BB Tel: (01) 989 6677

Radio & Electronic Officers' Union
  4-6 Branfill Road, Upminster, Essex RM14 2XX

Transport and General Workers' Union
  Transport House, Smith Square, London SW1

Other Affiliated Seafarers and Dockers Unions:

National Union of Railwaymen

Transport Salaried Staffs Association

Although the ITF employ no systematic method of checking FOC vessels in the United Kingdom, ITF activity is nonetheless high and ITF inspectors—usually branch secretaries of the NUS —are located in all the major ports. There are at least two full time inspectors—John Nelson and Harry Shaw—but the others are no less enthusiastic despite their part-time involvement.

In 1981 the ITF collected a total of US$683,685 in respect of back pay in the United Kingdom. In the first three months of 1982 they collected $19,576.

Apart from vessels specially selected by ITF London for boycott, the various inspectors board FOC vessels randomly to see whether they have blue certificates and/or whether they can muster some support from the crew to join the ITF. The ITF

---

* Indicates that representatives have been appointed to deal with flag of convenience matters.

also makes contact with the crews of FOC vessels in the various seamen's clubs ashore.

Despite the fact that the crew of an FOC vessel may be content with existing pay and conditions the ITF are not deterred from calling a boycott if the master refuses to enter into a special agreement.

The methods of individual ITF inspectors vary somewhat throughout the country. In Glasgow, for example, a picket line is usually formed by NUS members who will ensure that tugs and pilot are advised that a vessel has been blacked. The Harbour Master will not allow pilots to take vessels out of port without tugs.

In the event of a boycott in Glasgow a vessel is usually moved to a layby berth at the request of the Harbour Master—he will obtain a court order to move the vessel and put a shifting gang on board if master and owners do not co-operate.

In non-tidal docks the ITF usually inspire a boycott through the lock gate keepers, and stevedores will continue working cargo throughout. Vessels on river berths are usually boycotted by tugs unless the vessel will be able to sail without tug assistance, in which case a stevedore boycott will also be imposed.

Unless special circumstances apply (e.g. the vessel is on time charter) boycott activity in the United Kingdom is legal and the courts cannot be relied upon to provide relief. In such circumstances a boycott will be maintained until the owner/manager accedes to ITF demands or is otherwise able to exercise some form of self-help, e.g. sailing without tugs, etc.

However, an ITF boycott in the United Kingdom is unlawful if it amounts to what is known as secondary action. This occurs, for example, in a situation where a vessel is on time charter and it is the charterers who have contracted for port services such as lock gates to be opened or stevedores to work cargo. If the ITF were to call for a boycott of such services they would be deemed to be unlawfully interfering with a commercial contract between two parties who are not connected with the dispute in question, i.e. the terms and conditions of employment between ship owners/managers and crew. In such circumstances owners will be able to obtain injunctive relief from the court within 24-48 hours.

In one case (in Scotland) the above principle has been extended to a situation where a vessel was on a voyage charter, and the Sheriff's Court granted an injunction on the basis that it was the vessel's managers who had contracted for tug services and not owners. In this case the Sheriff drew an analogy between the position of managers and that of charterers and concluded that the ITF had engaged in unlawful secondary action. It is uncertain whether this reasoning would be followed by the High Court in England.

In view of the rather peculiar circumstances in the United Kingdom, which give trade unions immunity from prosecution, it is necessary to issue writs against named individuals of the ITF and any affiliated union representatives who are involved in any boycott.

In the event of a boycott in the United Kingdom advice should be sought on the particular facts in order to ascertain the chances of obtaining an injunction through the courts.

Should an owner/manager decide to concede to ITF demands he will not be required to make any contribution to the welfare fund as this has been declared illegal by the House of Lords (the final appeal court in the United Kingdom).

UNITED STATES

High risk ports:

New Orleans	Houston
Honolulu (Hawaii)	Baltimore
Brownsville (Texas)	

Active ITF Inspectors:

Attorneys are often used by the ITF in the U.S.A.

Active Affiliated Seafarers and Dockers Unions:

International Longshoremen's Association
17 Battery Place, Room 1530, New York,
N.Y. 10004

Seafarers' International Union of North America
675 Fourth Avenue, Brooklyn, New York 10032

The Radio Officers' Union
Room 1315, 225 West 34th Street, New York, N.Y. 10001

National Martime Union of America
346 West 17th Street, New York, N.Y. 10011

International Organization of Masters, Mates & Pilots
39 Broadway, New York, N.Y. 10006

American Radio Association
> 270 Madison Avenue (39th and 40th Street) Rooms
> 206-210, New York, N.Y.

National Marine Engineers' Beneficial Association
> 17 Battery Place, New York, N.Y. 10004

Other Affiliated Seafarers and Dockers Unions:

International Association of Machinists and
> Aerospace Workers

Very little information is available concerning ITF activity in the USA. It is believed however that the ITF do not engage in boycott activity themselves, but will encourage crew members to strike and seek support from seamen on tugs, etc. Crew are also encouraged to go ashore to prevent ships from sailing as pilots are reluctant to take undermanned vessels to sea, fearing that sanctions may then be taken against themselves.

In 1981 a total of US$65,000 was collected by the ITF in the USA in respect of back pay; US$128,000 was collected in the first three months of 1982.

Appendix C

THE ITF AND INTERNATIONAL GOVERNMENT ORGANIZATIONS *

The ITF has a long history of cooperation with and use of international intergovernmental organizations. The most important of these are three agencies of the United Nations: the International Labour Organisation (ILO), the United Nations Commission on Trade and Development (UNCTAD), and the International Maritime Organization (IMO), formerly the Intergovernmental Maritime Consultative Organization (IMCO). In addition, the ITF puts considerable effort into relations with the International Civil Aviation Organization (ICAO), the Conference of European Ministers of Transport (CEMT), and the European Economic Community (EEOC).[1]

THE INTERNATIONAL LABOUR ORGANISATION (ILO)

It is natural that an international trade union secretariat such as the ITF would seek both to influence the ILO and to gain its objectives through the ILO. For a number of reasons, including effective effort and the international nature of many of the industries represented in the ITF's sections, the ITF has wielded tremendous influence in the ILO's maritime affairs interest.

Largely through the ITF's influence, maritime issues have prompted more ILO conventions than any other single area (see Table C-2). Indeed, with the other ITF concerns, such as dock workers, more than 40 percent of ILO conventions covering specific industries or occupations have been prompted by the ITF and its affiliated unions, making the ITF the single most influential labor group in the ILO in terms of results achieved.

---

* Craig A. Leman, Research Assistant, assisted in the preparation of this Appendix.

[1] K.A. Golding, "In the Forefront of Trade Union History, 1896-1971: Looking Back on 75 Years of the ITF," *ITF Journal*, Vol. 31, No. 2 (Summer 1971), p. 50.

The Seafarers in the ILO

The ITF's Seafarers' Section was the first to take advantage of the ILO when the organization was established in 1919. ILO conventions relating to seafarers, for example, date back to 1920.[2] Subsequent seafarer success within the ILO is easily documented. Since 1926, the workers' side of the ILO Joint Maritime Commission (JMC) has consisted "almost exclusively of ITF union representatives."[3] In 1944, the ITF and the International Mercantile Marine Officer's Association (IMMOA), an organization which eventually amalgamated its membership with that of the ITF, jointly formulated the International Seafarers Charter. This document, adopted by the precedent-setting ILO Maritime Conference of 1946, was the first of a series of recommendations concerning minimum conditions of employment for seafarers.

The ITF's sea transport sections (seafarers, dockers, and fishermen) have been represented at other ILO Maritime Conferences held in 1949, 1958, 1970 and 1976. Subjects discussed at the 1976 conference included minimum standards in merchant ships, continuity of seafarer employment, holidays with pay, and the protection of young seafarers.[4] Other recent examples of ITF/ILO activity in the sea transport area are ILO meetings of experts on accident prevention on board ships at sea and in port, held in January 1977, and on safety and health problems in the offshore oil industry, held in October 1977.[5]

One of the longest and most sustained efforts of the ITF and the ILO has been centered around flag-of-convenience (FOC) shipping. In April 1933, the ITF first officially brought the FOC issue before the ILO. At the request of the ITF, the ILO raised the question of the "effect of the transfer of ships from one flag to another on the conditions of work of seamen."[6]

---

[2] *Ibid.*, p. 41.

[3] *Ibid.*

[4] International Labour Office, *Record of Proceedings of the Sixty-Second (Maritime) Session of the International Labour Conference* (Geneva: International Labour Office, 1976), pp. 163-230.

[5] *ITF Newsletter*, No. 3-4 (March-April 1977), p. 19; *ITF Newsletter*, No. 10 (October 1977), pp. 93-94.

[6] *Minutes of the Tenth Session of the Joint Maritime Commission* (Geneva, ILO, 1934), pp. 16 and 95 quoted in Enrico Argiroffo, "Flags of Convenience and Substandard Vessels," *International Labour Review*, Vol. 110 (November 1974), p. 439. The latter work should be consulted for an in depth look at the ITF's early FOC efforts in the ILO.

The seafarers claimed that ships were being transferred from traditional martime countries with high compensation and standards to other countries with lower compensation and inferior standards. In addition, the seafarers claimed that these transfers were taking place without any change in ownership. They asked the ILO to carry out an inquiry so that the ILO's work to improve the position of seafarers would not be jeopardized.

The shipowners objected that such transfers were beyond the ILO's proper sphere of activities. Although the Director of the Office suggested that the Office might investigate, first other duties and then World War II insured that the issue was not raised again until 1947.

In 1947, fourteen years after the issue was first raised by the ITF, the ILO report on transfers of vessels was presented to the 14th session of the JMC. Of the then current flag-of-convenience countries, only Panama drew special attention to this report. The seafarers' representatives on the commission took pains to point out that Panama had exhibited little previous interest in building a national fleet, that the director had concluded in 1933 that such transfers could undermine the ILO's efforts, and that Panama had not ratified a single ILO convention.[7] They further maintained that the transfers were detrimental to the conditions of work of seafarers in the traditional maritime countries.

The shipowners' representatives maintained that the transfers were for reasons such as taxes, and not aimed at lowering working conditions. The commission compromised on a resolution requesting the ILO "to urge governments . . . and seafarers' organizations to give due attention to . . . those cases of transfer of flags which may prove detrimental to the safety, conditions of employment and social protection of seafarers." [8]

Subsequently the ITF threatened an international boycott of Panamanian and Honduran ships. In December 1948, Panama requested that the ILO carry out an inquiry into its merchant marine. In March 1949, the ILO approved three members of a committee to carry out such an inquiry.

This committee met in four sessions in 1949. The committee consisted of A. Dagleish, a former union official from Britain, Hermann Vos, former minister of education of Belgium, and A.G.

---

[7] Argiroffo "Flags of Convenience and Substandard Vessels," p. 441. It should be noted that Panama has since ratified seventeen ILO Seafarer's Conventions, almost three times the number ratified by the United States.

[8] Argiroffo, p. 441.

Fenema, an employer representative from the Netherlands.[9] The committee heard the views of the ITF, the International Shipping Federation (an owners' group) and the government of Panama. The Panamanian representative stated that the government had come to terms with the ITF and that Panamanian laws and standards were "liberal and advanced." [10]

The committee not only summed up the available documentation about fleet size and condition, but selected thirty Panamanian ships at random for inspection. As might be expected for older ships in this period, labor conditions on many were found to be far from ideal. Articles of employment provided no overtime or holiday pay. In addition, accommodations and plumbing were found to be inadequate.

The committee's 1949 preliminary report concluded that the charges against Panama were in part justified. The age of the ships and the possibility that shipowners were avoiding safety and labor standards were of particular concern. The committee's report concluded, "Panama has virtually no laws or regulations regarding safety of life at sea . . . The legislation, of Panama concerning seafarers is inadequate . . . (and is) frequently unknown to masters." [11]

Twelve recommendations were made in the report:

1. Passage of a labor law.

2. Compilation of the law.

3. Specific guarantees of rights in event of sickness, injury, or termination of contract.

4. Adoption of regulations to give effect to load line and safety regulations.

5. Concentration in one authority of all matters dealing with Panamanian-registered ships.

6. Distribution of copies of the law to masters.

7. Strengthening of the consular service.

8. Arrangement for classification.

9. Requirement for ship inspection.

---

[9] Rodney Carlisle, *Sovereignty for Sale: The Origins and Evolution of the Panamanian and Liberian Flags of Convenience* (Annapolis: Naval Institute Press, 1981), p. 139.

[10] Argiroffo, p. 443.

[11] Carlisle, p. 140.

10. Verification of officers' certificates.

11. Establishment of a disputes procedure.

12. Adoption of a standard collective agreement.[12]

Although the report was no doubt embarassing to Panama and was greeted as a vindication of the ITF's position, it proved little more than a propaganda victory. Panama agreed to improve conditions, and its cooperation during the investigation insured that some measure of goodwill remained in the ILO.

In June 1950 the governing body of the ILO adopted a statement noting Panama's efforts to "improve conditions" and suggesting that Panama assist shipowners and seafarers in promoting negotiations for collective agreements.

At the eighteenth session of the JMC in 1955, a report by the ITF on the problems of FOCs was considered. The main change in the ITF position from 1949 was that additional flags, including Liberia's, were now under attack. The Commission agreed that the issue could be considered at the 1956 Preparatory Technical Maritime Conference and at the 1958 Maritime Session of the International Labour Conference.

A questionnaire on the FOC phenomenon was drawn up to send to the governments of thirty-two traditional maritime countries. The results of the questionnaire, along with an historical review of the problem and the comments of some FOC countries (Liberia and Panama had no comment), were incorporated into a report submitted to the Preparatory Technical Maritime Conference held in London in 1956.[13]

The report met with a simple reaffirmation of the shipowner's and seafarer's positions. The seafarers prepared a list of points that would have to be met in any solution which would satisfy them, as set forth in Table C-1.

The preparatory conference adopted a text which was submitted to the Maritime Session of the International Conference. After a brief discussion, the session adopted it as the Social Conditions and Safety (Seafarers) Recommendation Number 108. Its preamble referred to the United Nations Conference on the Law of the Sea, which stipulated the need for a "genuine link" [14]

---

[12] *Ibid.*, pp. 140-41.

[13] ILO, *Flag Transfer in Relation to Social Conditions and Safety,* document PTMC III/I Preparatory Technical Maritime Conference, London, Autumn 1956, cited in Argiroffo, p. 444.

[14] Argiroffo, p. 446.

between the ship and the state. This link was to consist of jurisdiction and effective administration.

The body of the recommendation strengthened the genuine link requirement regarding administration, regulation, inspection and

TABLE C-1
ITF Position—1956 Maritime Conference

---

(1) Notice should be taken of the declaration made by the International Law Commission of the United Nations on the subject of merchant ships having a broader link with the country of registration than merely the formality of registration.

(2) The country of registration should have greater and more intimate jurisdiction over ships flying its flag, possibly by requiring that—

(a) ships should be owned by companies having their principal place of business in the country of registration;

(b) each company shall have nationals of the registering country on its board of directors;

(c) meetings of the boards of directors shall be held within the territory of the registering country.

(3) The country of registration should make and adopt regulations designed to ensure that all ships flying its flag observe internationally accepted safety standards.

(4) It should establish and operate a government-controlled ship inspection service within its territory adequate to the requirements of the tonnage on its register and ensure that all ships flying its flag are regularly inspected within its territory to ensure conformity with regulations issued under (3) above.

(5) It should make regulations for the governance of the recruitment, engagement and discharge of seafarers serving in its ships according to internationally accepted standards and establish the requisite government-controlled agencies to give effect to such regulations.

(6) It should adopt regulations or legislation providing that not less than 25 per cent of seafarers in any one ship are nationals of the country of registration.

(7) It should make regulations or legislation, if not already provided in the country's general legislation, providing for the freedom of association of its seafarers.

(8) It should ensure by regulation that proper repatriation for its seafarers be provided.

(9) It should introduce provisions ensuring that seafarers will be covered by social security arrangements which in any case shall not be less than those provided for workers in other countries.

(10) It should ensure that proper and satisfactory arrangements are made within the country concerned for the examination of candidates for certificates of competency and for the issuing of such certificates.

Source: Enrico Argiroffo, "Flags of Convenience and Substandard Vessels." *International Labour Review*, Volume 110 (November 1974), p. 445.

control. Although as a recommendation this did not have the force of law, it must be regarded as a victory for the ITF representatives at the ILO.

At the twenty-first maritime session of the International Labor Conference in 1970, the workers' delegate from Finland (a major area for ITF anti-FOC activity) submitted a draft resolution on FOCs. The resolution requested member states to report on steps taken to implement recommendations 107 (which dealt with crews on foreign vessels) and 108. After debate, the resolution was passed with minimal changes. The survey requested in the resolution met with minimal response. By June 1972 only sixty-two countries had submitted reports. The only FOC countries to respond were Singapore and Cyprus.

When the twenty-first session of the JMC discussed the reports in 1972, the seafarers members again stressed that the FOC owners were trying to avoid safety and labor standards in order to make excessive profits. They further maintained that the FOC countries did not implement ILO Maritime Standards and Recommendations. In addition, they said the FOC vessels were likely to cause accidents and pollution. They recommended national agreements to apply to foreign as well as to national ships.

The shipowners said that they too were opposed to substandard ships, but not to all FOC ships, and that these issues could best be dealt with pursuing compliance with recommendations 107 and 108. A resolution to this effect was unanimously passed. Although the resolution did specifically mention FOC ships, it is apparent that it marks a shift in the emphasis of the ILO from FOC vessels per se to the question of substandard vessels regardless of flag.

The ITF and the shipowners continue to battle over FOCs within the ILO. At the twenty-third JMC (1980), forty-two seafarers including ITF Seafarers' Section Chariman K. Mols Sørensen, Vice Chairman S. Wall, and ITF Assistant General Secretary A. Selander were present as representatives or observers. At this meeting, the seafarers condemned Liberia for not supplying information to the ILO. They supported the use of ILO inspectors to conduct a physical survey of FOC ships. These demands produced a deadlock between the seafarers and shipowners. The seafarers requested that the ILO governing body put "phasing out of open registries" [15] on the agenda of the next ILO Preparatory Technical Maritime Conference.

---

[15] *ITF Newsletter*, No. 11 (November 1980), supplement, p. 2.

Much to the disappointment of the ITF, the next Maritime Session of the International Labour Conference will not meet until 1986. It can be expected that the ITF will attempt to see that the FOC issue is addressed at this conference. Because of the shipowners' successful strategy within the ILO of opposing both substandard ships and attacks upon FOCs, it can be presumed that, despite heavy expenditures of effort and manpower, the ITF may not find the ILO an effective forum for attacking the FOCs, except on publicity grounds.

The ITF seafarers have, however, found the ILO an effective forum for raising standards and for combatting sub-standard shipping. An example is ILO Convention 147, which may soon join the six maritime conventions which the U.S. has ratified.[16] This convention, entitled Minimum Standards for Seafarers, which has been in effect since November 1981, strengthens "Port State Control," [17] a potentially powerful tool for controlling substandard shipping. The ITF regards it as a "major, but limited, advance." [18]

Besides the conventions, ILO recommendations have proved of great value to the ITF. In particular the regular increase in the recommended minimum wage schedule for seafarers provides the ITF with an accepted set of criteria to judge whether wages on FOC ships are "substandard." As was noted in Chapter III, courts in various countries have tended to refer to these ILO recommendations when considering the legality of ITF boycotts. In addition, the regular increases in the ILO recommended minimum wage schedule are an important factor in reducing the spread between Western European and North American maritime wages and those paid to seafarers from underdeveloped countries. This is, of course, in line with ITF policy which is clearly designed to protect the jobs of seafarers from developed countries, in part by raising the wages of those from the Third World.

Other ITF Sections and the ITF

The seafarers have clearly been the most active ITF section working with the ILO, and have received substantial returns

---

[16] See Table A-11. The fact that six of these Conventions deal with seafarers, while the seventh deals with the articles of the ILO indicates how strong the seafarers' lobby is in the United States.

[17] Brian Groom, "Move to end flags of convenience," *Financial Times*, October 7, 1981, Shipping Survey, p. VII.

[18] *Ibid.*

for their great investment of time and resources. Other ITF sections have been active in the ILO as well, but with relatively less success, even though several of these sections actually revolve around the ILO. The original ILO international convention regulating the hours of work and rest periods in road transport, for example, was drawn up before 1940 with ITF participation. In October 1974, an ILO meeting of experts on the same subject met and recommended that a new ILO convention on road transport be drafted.[19]

From that time until 1979, the efforts of the Road Transport Section were concentrated on the formulation of this convention and an accompanying recommendation. The section's steering committee, composed of its Chairman Hans Ericson (Sweden), Vice Chairman Kurt Haussig (Germany), Peter Kung (Switzerland, and A. Kitson (United Kingdom) met twice between ITF congresses, both times to consider what policy should be in regard to the above mentioned convention and recommendation, and in 1979 the convention (Number 153) was enacted.

The Fishermen's Section's activities have centered mainly around the ILO's Tripartite Committee on Conditions. The success of this activity can be gauged from the fact that five ILO Conventions deal specifically with fishermen, more than any other section except seafarers.[20]

Representatives from the ITF's Dockers' Section were largely responsible for the drafting and adoption of the ILO Convention on Protection against Accidents which is the longest text adopted on safety and health since World War II.[21] The employers representatives to the ILO wanted a recommendation rather than a convention. Subjects as diverse as certification of lifting equipment, storage and handling of dangerous substances and goods, and fire-fighting equipment are covered in this convention, which was adopted in June 1979. The dockers follow the fishermen and seafarers in the number of ILO conventions covering their occupation.

The Inland Waterways and Railways Sections work with the Road Transport Section in the Inland Transportation Section to influence the ILO, but to date have not had any conventions

---

[19] ITF, *Report on Activities 1974-1975-1976*, p. 84.

[20] See Table I.

[21] ITF, *Report on Activities 1977-1979*, p. 69.

dealing specifically with their occupations to show for their efforts.

The Civil Aviation Section has also worked with the ILO, especially recently. Although to date it also has no conventions to show for its work, the section has been most sophisticated in its approach to the ILO. On December 5 and 6, 1977 the section conference was held in Geneva on the two days before the ILO Tripartite Technical Meeting for Civil Aviation. The section's main concerns to be brought before the ILO at this time included:

> a social convention for civil aviation workers; the establishment of permanent tripartite machinery within the ILO for civil aviation; the convening of a further meeting of the ILO on civil aviation as soon as possible to discuss the social repercussions of technological changes and the problems created by inter-airline mergers and cooperative efforts; and hijacking.[22]

The ITF's domination of the workers' group at the meeting is emphasized by the fact that the chairman and vice chairman of the workers group were Civil Aviation Section officers and the secretary to the workers' group was M.S. Hoda, an ITF section secretary.[23] According to the ITF the workers group had "significant success in getting most of its points accepted." [24]

At the ILO Meeting of Experts on Air Traffic Controllers in Geneva, May 8 to 16, 1979 the ITF was again represented by M.S. Hoda, who acted as secretary to the workers' group. This meeting adopted conclusions and recommendations on "industrial relations; social and labour aspects of ATC systems; hours of work; remuneration; retirement age and pensions; occupational safety; health and welfare; legal liabilities; manpower and career planning; training and retraining; and employment security." [25]

ILO-Conclusion

The ITF has found that the ILO is an excellent forum through which its program can be generated, publicized, and given credence and respectability. It has used the ILO more successfully

---

[22] ITF, *Report on Activities 1977-1979*, p. 107.

[23] *Ibid.*, p. 107.

[24] *Ibid.*, p. 107.

[25] *Ibid.*, p. 108.

in this regard than has any other international trade union secretariat, and probably more successfully than any other organization. Moreover, the forums of the ILO have provided the ITF with access to shipping companies and associations and to government officials which has been valuable in pursuing its various aims, particularly the control and eventual elimination of flag-of-convenience shipping.

Table C-2 lists the ILO conventions by the following categories: those relating to ITF sections, those relating to other (non-ITF) occupations or subjects, and those relating to general subjects. A measure of the ITF's performance at the ILO is that 42 of the 158 conventions—26 percent—relate to ITF sections; of these 42 conventions, 31 are concerned with seafarers and 4 with dockers (longshoremen).

TABLE C-2
International Labour Organisation Conventions

Title	Number	Year Enacted	In Force (* indicates convention in force)
I. Conventions Relating to Specific ITF Sections			
Dockers			
Protection Against Accidents (Dockers)	28	1929	*
Protection Against Accidents (Dockers) (Revised)	32	1932	*
Dock Work	137	1973	*
Occupational Safety and Health (Dock Work)	152	1979	*
Road Transport			
Hours of Work and Rest Periods (Road Transport)	67	1939	*
Hours of Work and Rest Periods (Road Transport)	153	1979	*
Fishermen			
Minimum Age (Fishermen)	112	1959	*
Medical Examination (Fishermen)	113	1959	*
Fishermen's Articles of Agreement	114	1959	*
Fisherman's Competency Certificates	125	1966	*
Accommodation of Crews (Fishermen)	126	1966	*

TABLE C-2—Continued

Title	Number	Year Enacted	In Force (* indicates convention in force)
Seafarers			
Minimum Age Seamen	7	1920	*
Unemployment Indemnity (Shipwreck)	8	1920	*
Placing of Seamen	9	1920	*
Medical Examination of Young Persons (Sea)	16	1921	*
Seamen's Articles of Agreement	22	1926	*
Repatriation of Seamen	23	1926	*
Officers' Competency Certificate	53 a	1936	*
Holidays with Pay (Sea)	54 a	1936	
Shipowners' Liability (Sick & Injured Seamen)	55 a	1936	*
Sickness Insurance (Sea)	56	1936	*
Hours of Work and Manning (Sea)	57 a	1936	
Minimum Age (Sea) (Revised)	58	1936	*
Food and Catering (Ships' Crews)	68	1946	*
Certification of Ships' Cooks	69	1946	*
Social Security (Seafarers)	70	1946	
Seafarers' Pensions	71	1946	
Paid Vacations (Seafarers)	72	1946	
Medical Examination (Seafarers)	73	1946	*
Certification of Able Seamen	74 a	1946	*
Accommodation of Crews	75	1946	
Wages, Hours of Work and Manning (Sea)	76	1946	
Paid Vacations (Seafarers) (Revised)	91	1949	*
Accommodation of Crews (Revised)	92	1949	*
Wages, Hours and Work and Manning (Sea) (Revised)	93	1949	
Seafarers' Identity Documents	108	1958	*
Wages, Hours of Work and Manning (Sea) (Revised)	109	1958	
Accommodation of Crews (Supplementary Provisions)	133	1970	
Prevention of Accidents (Seafarers)	134	1970	*
Continuity of Employment (Seafarers)	145	1976	*
Seafarers' Annual Leave with Pay	146	1976	*
Merchant Shipping (Minimum Standards)	147	1976	*

TABLE C-2—Continued

Title	Number	Year Enacted	In Force (* indicates convention in force)
II. Conventions on Other Specific (Non-ITF) Occupations or Subjects			
Women			
Maternity Protection	3	1919	*
Night Work (Women)	4	1919	*
Night Work (Women) (Revised)	41	1934	*
Underground Work (Women)	45	1935	*
Night Work (Women) (Revised)	89	1948	*
Minimum Age (Underground Work)	123	1965	*
Medical Examination of Young Persons (Underground Work)	124	1965	*
Agriculture			
Minimum Age (Agriculture)	10	1921	*
Right of Association (Agriculture)	11	1921	*
Workmen's Compensation (Agriculture)	12	1921	*
Sickness Insurance (Agriculture)	25	1927	*
Old-Age Insurance (Agriculture)	36	1933	*
Invalidity Insurance (Agriculture)	38	1933	*
Survivor's Insurance (Agriculture)	40	1933	*
Minimum Wage-Fixing Machinery (Agriculture)	99	1951	*
Holidays with Pay (Agriculture)	101	1952	*
Labour Inspection (Agriculture)	129	1969	*
Miscellaneous			
White Lead (Painting)	13	1921	*
Minimum Age (Trimmers & Stokers)	15	1921	*
Night Work (Bakeries)	20	1925	*
Marking of Weight (Packages Transported by Vessels)	27	1929	*
Sheet-Glass Works	43	1934	*
Reduction of Hours of Work (Glass-Bottle Works)	49	1935	*
Safety Provisions (Building)	62	1937	*
Plantations	110	1958	*
Rural Workers' Organisations	141	1975	*
Migrant Workers (Supplementary Provisions)	143	1975	*
Nursing Personnel	149	1977	*
Reduction of Hours of Work (Textiles)	61	1937	

TABLE C-2—Continued

Title	Number	Year Enacted	In Force (* indicates convention in force)
Commerce and Offices			
Hours of Work (Commerce and Offices)	30	1930	*
Weekly Rest (Commerce and Offices)	106	1957	*
Hygiene (Commerce and Offices)	120	1964	*
Coal Mines			
Hours of Work (Coal Mines)	31	1931	
Hours of Work (Coal Mines)	46	1935	
Indigenous Workers			
Recruiting of Indigenous Workers	50	1936	*
Contracts of Employment (Indigenous Workers)	64	1939	*
Penal Sanctions (Indigenous Workers)	65	1939	*
Contracts of Employment (Indigenous Workers)	86	1947	*
Abolition of Penal Sanctions (Indigenous Workers)	104	1955	*
Indigenous and Tribal Populations	107	1957	*
Non-Metropolitan Territories			
Social Policy (Non-Metropolitan Territories)	82	1947	*
Labour Standards (Non-Metropolitan Territories)	83	1947	*
Right of Association (Non-Metropolitan Territories)	84	1947	*
Labour Inspectorates (Non-Metropolitan Territories)	85	1947	*
Public Sector			
Labour Clauses (Public Contracts)	94	1949	*
Labour Relations (Public Service)	151	1978	*
Reduction of Hours of Work (Public Works)	51	1936	
Non-Industrial Occupations			
Minimum Age (Non-Industrial Employment)	33	1932	*
Minimum Age (Non-Industrial Employment) (Revised)	60	1937	*

TABLE C-2—Continued

Title	Number	Year Enacted	In Force (* indicates convention in force)
III. Conventions of General Subjects			
Unemployment	2	1919	*
Workmen's Compensation (Accidents)	17	1925	*
Workmen's Compensation (Occupational Diseases)	18	1925	*
Equality of Treatment (Accident Compensation)	19	1925	*
Inspection of Emigrants	21	1926	*
Minimum Wage-Fixing Machinery	26	1928	*
Forced Labour	29	1930	*
Fee Charging Employment Agencies	34	1933	*
Old-Age Insurance (Industry, Etc.)	35	1933	*
Invalidity Insurance (Industry, Etc.)	37	1933	*
Survivors' Insurance (Industry, Etc.)	39	1933	*
Unemployment Provision	44	1934	*
Forty-Hour Week Convention	47	1935	*
Maintenance of Migrants' Pension Rights	48	1935	*
Holidays with Pay	52	1936	*
Concerning Statistics of Wages and Hours of Work	63	1938	*
Migration for Employment	66	1939	
Final Articles Revision	80 a	1946	*
Labour Inspection	81	1947	*
Freedom of Association and Protection of the Right to Organise	87	1948	*
Employment Service	88	1948	*
Protection of Wages	95	1949	*
Fee-Charging Employment Agencies (Revised)	96	1949	*
Migration for Employment (Revised)	97	1949	*
Right to Organise and Collective Bargaining	98	1949	*
Equal Remuneration	100	1951	*
Social Security (Minimum Standards)	102	1952	*
Maternity Protection (Revised)	103	1952	*
Abolition of Forced Labour	105	1957	*
Discrimination (Employment and Occupation)	111	1958	*
Radiation Protection	115	1961	*
Final Articles Revision	116	1962	*

TABLE C-2—Continued

Title	Number	Year Enacted	In Force (* indicates convention in force)
Social Policy (Basic Aims and Standards)	117	1962	*
Equality of Treatment (Social Security)	118	1962	*
Guarding of Machinery	119	1963	*
Employment Injury Benefits	121	1964	*
Employment Policy	122	1964	*
Maximum Weight	127	1967	*
Invalidity, Old-Age and Survivors' Benefits	128	1967	*
Medical Care and Sickness Benefits	130	1969	*
Minimum Wage Fixing	131	1970	*
Holidays with Pay (Revised)	132	1970	*
Workers' Representatives	135	1971	*
Benzene	136	1971	*
Minimum Age	138	1973	*
Occupational Cancer	139	1974	*
Paid Educational Leave	140	1974	*
Human Resources Development	142	1975	*
Tripartite Consultation (International Labour Standards)	144	1976	*
Working Environment (Air Pollution, Noise and Vibration)	148	1977	*
Labour Administration	150	1978	*
Collective Bargaining	154	1981	
Occupational Safety and Health	155	1981	
Workers with Family Responsibilities	156	1981	
Maintenance of Social Security Rights	157	1982	
Termination of Employment at Initiation of Employer	158	1982	
Medical Examination of Young Persons (Non-Industrial Occupations)	78	1946	*
Night Work of Young Persons (Non-Industrial Occupations)	79	1946	*
Industry			
Hours of Work (Industry)	1	1919	*
Minimum Age (Industry)	5	1919	*
Night Work of Young Persons (Industry)	6	1919	*
Weekly Rest (Industry)	14	1921	*

TABLE C-2—Continued

Title	Number	Year Enacted	In Force (* indicates convention in force)
Sickness Insurance (Industry)	24	1927	*
Minimum Age (Industry) (Revised)	59	1937	*
Medical Examination of Young Persons (Industry)	77	1946	*
Night Work of Young Persons (Industry) (Revised)	90	1948	*

Convention Summary

Total Number of "ITF" Conventions	42
Total Number of "Other" Conventions	49
Total Number of "General" Conventions	56
Total Number of Conventions	147
Conventions Ratified by U.S.	6

Source: International Labour Office, *List of Ratifications of Conventions* (as of 31 December 1982), Report III (Part 5) (Geneva: International Labour Office, 1982); International Labour Organisation, *International Labour Conventions and Recommendations: 1919-1981* (Geneva: International Labour Office, 1982); International Labour Office, *Record of Proceedings, 68th Session* (Geneva: International Labour Office, 1982)

a Indicates U.S. ratified

INTERNATIONAL MARITIME ORGANIZATION

The Inter-Governmental Maritime Consultative Organization (IMCO), which changed its name to the International Maritime Organization (IMO) in 1982, has also been a major focus of the ITF. The IMO/IMCO was founded in 1948 as an organization of the United Nations. Its purposes are to "provide machinery for cooperation among governments on technical matters affecting international merchant shipping and . . . to insure that the highest possible standards of safety at sea and of efficient navigation are achieved; prevent pollution of the seas caused by ships and other craft operating in the marine environment; encourage removal of hindrances to international shipping services." [26] IMO/IMCO's duties include establishing standards concerning seafarer training, qualifications, and certification which are, of

---

[26] *Yearbook of International Organizations, 1978* (Brussels: Union of International Organizations, 1978), ref. no. A1117g.

course, areas most relevant to national seafarers' unions and the ITF.

International minimum standards on these matters for merchant shifts were formerly the sole responsibility of the ILO. This was preferred by the seafaring unions and the ITF because the ILO, unlike IMO/IMCO, is tripartite and a union (ITF) presence on ILO bodies was therefore assured. After the formation of a joint ILO-IMO/IMCO Committee on Training, and an IMO/IMLO Subcommittee on Standards of Training and Watchkeeping, the ITF was concerned that it would lose its key voice at intergovernmental levels on such matters because significant aspects of seafarer training, qualifications, and certification were transferred to IMO/IMCO jurisdiction. Fortunately for the ITF, shipowners were equally concerned about a loss of direct participation and control. At the third session of the Joint ILO-IMO/IMCO Committee on Training, held in July 1973, therefore, both seafarer and shipowner representatives came out in favor of complete coordination of the ILO and IMCO in "all aspects concerning seafarers' professional qualifications." [27] An agreement concerning ILO-IMO/IMCO coordination in these areas was announced at the fourth session of IMCO's Sub-Committee on Standards of Training and Watchkeeping.[28] Since that time there has been a Joint ILO-IMO/IMCO Committee on Training. This gives the ITF a stronger hand because of its strength in the ILO, where it has official status, as opposed to the IMO, where it does not. As a result the ITF officers reported: "IMCO [IMO] has continued to provide the ITF and its seafarer affiliate with a forum for airing their views on a variety of matters affecting or relating to maritime safety." [29]

The ITF has also participated in other IMCO subcommittees dealing with safety of life at sea, substandard ships, tanker safety, anti-pollution measures, search and rescue operations, lifesaving appliances, and radiocommunications. The twentieth anniversary of the original IMCO convention was celebrated by the ITF and other seafarer organizations on March 17, 1978, a day designated as World Maritime Day.[30] Currently Maritime Day is celebrated in September. In recent years IMO/IMCO

---

27 ITF, *Report on Activities 1974-1975-1976*, p. 113.

28 *Ibid.*, pp. 113-114.

29 ITF, *Report on Activities 1977-1978-1979*, p. 78.

30 *ITF Newsletter*, No. 3 (March 1978), p. 32.

conferences and council meetings on various subjects have found ITF representatives in attendance.[31] The ITF has thus been able to participate fully and effectively in IMO/IMCO activities and may be expected to continue to do so.

UNITED NATIONS COMMISSION ON TRADE AND DEVELOPMENT

The United Nations Commission on Trade and Development (UNCTAD) was founded in 1964. Its mission was to examine trends in international trade and to recommend policies and programs that would facilitate the development of Third World countries. In fact, by virtue of a radicalized secretariat and the support thereof of the Communist bloc and the Third World countries, UNCTAD has proposed a variety of measures designed to transfer wealth from developed to underdeveloped nations and to socialize the means of production. Such proposals can win support at UNCTAD meetings because consensus has been replaced by majority rule. Under these circumstances, the United States has refused to participate in some UNCTAD deliberations.[32]

Because UNCTAD is concerned with international trade, maritime issues have assumed a prominent place in its activities. By 1974, it developed a code that would divide up liner shipping between two countries on a 40-40-20 percent basis—that is 40 percent for each country and 20 percent for third parties. The proposed code has been ratified by nations representing more than 25 percent of the world merchant fleet and will become effective October 1, 1983. West Germany has ratified it and other European community countries have also pledged to do so. Most Third World countries have also ratified it. The code will become effective because of the rule stating that ratification by nations representing 25 percent of the world merchant fleet is the level necessary for the code to come into being. Meanwhile, European

---

[31] ITF, *Report on Activities 1977-1978-1979*, pp. 80, 95.

[32] See Stanley J. Michalak, Jr., *UNCTAD An Organization Betraying Its Mission* (Washington, D.C.: The Heritage Foundation, 1983). See also Art Pine, "Bombast and rhetoric at UNCTAD session likely to widen rift between rich, poor," *Wall Street Journal*, February 23, 1983, p. 31; Ian Middleton, "Attitudes are hardening," *Financial Times*, June 3, 1982, Shipping Survey, p. III; and "Protectionism Watch: Efforts to Divvy Sea Lanes Could Spell Trouble for Firms," *Business International*, Vol. 30, No. 13 (April 1, 1983) pp. 97-99.

Community nations have pledged to observe the code's provisions in their dealings with Third World countries, where apparently it does not vary substantially from current practice, but not in shipping relations with developed countries. The United States, however, remains opposed to it, regarding it as institutionalizing protectionism.[33]

As noted, the UNCTAD secretariat is considered highly politicized and anti-business. Moreover, by abandoning consensus in favor of majority rule, UNCTAD's makeup insures that developed countries—known as Group B—are in a minority. The underdeveloped countries—called the Group of 77—and the Communist bloc usually vote together to form the majority. Surprisingly (if one did not understand the issue), the ITF, which has supported the drive of developed world unions to suppress the competition of seafarers from the Third World, has consistently aligned itself with the Group of 77 within UNCTAD. The reason, of course, is that UNCTAD's codes would, if accepted, phase out FOC shipping by reviving the "genuine link" theory between country and shipowner. The developed countries oppose this and advocate following the more restrained policies of the ILO and the IMO on such matters.

UNCTAD and FOC Ships

UNCTAD meetings feature strong trade union representation. The ITF has official observer status with UNCTAD, works closely with its secretariat, and is represented on its key shipping committees.

Two major issues have dominated the maritime matter in UNCTAD activities, although it has appeared also to encroach upon the jurisdiction of the International Maritime Organization (IMO), as noted below. One is bulk cargo sharing agreements designed to insure that the exporting nation, particularly a Third World country, receive a major share of the shipping of its exports. The second is the elimination of FOC ships. It is the latter, of course for which the ITF lobbies.

The cooperation between the Group of 77 and the ITF at UNCTAD is clearly an alliance of convenience. If FOC shipping were phased out, the Group of 77 expect that shipping would go directly to their countries—the Third World coun-

---

[33] Brij Khindaria, "Liner conferences code ratified by 53 countries," *Financial Times*, June 18, 1982, p. 7; Bridget Hogan, "WG ratification of line code may fuel talks," *Lloyd's List*, April 8, 1983, p. 1.

tries. Nearly all open registry countries except Panama and Liberia have voted for the elimination of open registries, including presumably their own, on this doubtful assumption. The funds to acquire and support ships would presumably have to be donated by the developed countries under this extraordinary proposal. The UNCTAD proposal also ignores quality and cost of service, dealing only in numbers.

ITF's Third World union affiliates suport this proposal.[34] ITF's dominant group, and the real beneficiaries of its FOC campaign, are, however, its affiliates from the developed countries. They, and presumably the ITF hierarchy, obviously expect the traditional maritime nations to benefit if FOC vessels are outlawed. Thus, the ITF-Group of 77 alliance would appear to be possible only because UNCTAD's anti-FOC campaign has not been successful. A brief survey of UNCTAD's recent maritime activities demonstrates how the alliance works in practice.

At its May-June 1981 meeting, the third special session of UNCTAD's Committee on Shipping passed a resolution calling for the gradual tightening of registry conditions (and thus the end of open registries) and the creation of an Intergovernmental Preparatory Group (IPG) to decide how to accomplish this. The maintenance of standards and the welfare of crews were specifically mentioned in this resolution. The ITF claimed at least partial credit for the action: "There is little doubt that the presence of ITF seafarer union representatives at the Committee —some as advisors to their national delegations and some on the ITF's own observer delegation—made a substantial impact." [35]

The key role of the ITF was corroborated by the chairman of the Federation of American Controlled Shipping (FACS), the organization of FOC shipowners. He reported that in September 1982 the ITF "was permitted to have the last word at the two most recent UNCTAD meetings on open registries." [36]

---

[34] *A Brief Report on Attending the ITF Fair Practices Committee Meeting*, London, June 2-3, 1982, p. 8.

[35] ITF Press Release, June 8, 1981, p. 1; *ITF Panorama*, Vol. 3, No. 3 (September 1981), p. 1. See also James Brewer, "ITF attacks West for Geneva voting," *Lloyd's List*, June 11, 1981, p. 1.

[36] Eric Pace, "Uncertain crosswinds for 'flags of convenience'," *New York Times*, May 16, 1982, p. E3; Brij Khindaria, "No headway on flags of convenience," *Financial Times*, May 4, 1982, p. 5; *UN Report*, United States Council for International Business, Vol. 3, No. 4 (May 24, 1982), pp. 1-3; and UNCTAD, *Report of the Intergovernmental Preparatory Group on Condi-*

Late in 1981, the UNCTAD Trade and Development Board approved the resolution of the special session, and the IPG was established. The latter met in April 1982. It was boycotted by Liberia and Panama because of the prior action, and also by the United States because of the departure from the consensus principle. At this meeting the IPG passed a resolution calling for a 1983 UN Plenipotentiary Conference on Open Registry Shipping, but no final agreements resulted, even though drafts were circulated on conditions by which vessels would be accepted on national shipping registers.[37]

UNCTAD—Concluding Comments

UNCTAD has continued to expand its activities in shipping, moving into such areas as port congestion and surcharges, maritime fraud, transport of liquid carbons, international maritime legislation, and technical assistance and training.[38] These activities would seem to intrude upon those of the IMO and possibly the ILO in the same areas, which could give the ITF some doubts about UNCTAD. Again, this expansion of shipping activities by UNCTAD was done over the objections of the developed countries.

The ITF's support of the policies of the United Nations Conference on Trade and Development (UNCTAD) seems both shortsighted and perplexing. It is shortsighted because, if the open registries are eliminated, the ITF will have to deal with Third World national flags and crews. In the unlikely event that this comes to pass (unlikely because the capital is not available to such countries to acquire and control fleets), the ITF would be faced with wages and conditions on such vessels that surely would be below its minimum standards; yet, like the Soviet fleet, such vessels would not be FOC ships. What rationale the ITF would then use to attack such shipping without incurring reprisal against vessels manned by ITF affiliates has yet to be considered. The ITF insistence on equating FOC ships with substandard conditions has led it into this alliance of convenience.

---

tions for Registration of Ships at its First Session, April 13-30, Geneva, 1982; "UNCTAD at Sea," *FACS Forum*, September, 1982, p. 3.

37 "UNCTAD at Sea," *FACS Forum*, September 1982, p. 3.

38 *UN Report*, United States Council for International Business, Vol. 3, No. 6 (July 30, 1982), pp. 1-4.

The Third World country-ITF alliance within UNCTAD is also perplexing from the point of view of the countries which have fought the ITF on the issue. Liberia and Panama have opposed the UNCTAD anti-FOC ploy, but other countries have supported it in the hopes that they would gain a greater share of shipping for their countries. Yet the anamolies remain. Sri Lanka, for example, was one of the leaders of the UNCTAD proposed policy and voted to abolish FOCs; it then promptly announced that it was establishing an open register to become an FOC country. One must conclude that the Third World countries in UNCTAD, egged on by the Communist bloc, are looking for handouts by the Western world while maintaining what they have. Meanwhile, the ITF is an ally of the Third World labor in UNCTAD for the future handouts, an adversary over the present practice, and a potential adversary if the handouts do occur.

Appendix D

ITF ACTIVITIES IN AIR TRANSPORT

Although the ITF is the largest international union organization in air transport, and although it claims jurisdiction over all airline and ground service employees, it has played a minor role among two key groups, the pilots and the flight controllers, because both these groups have organizations devoted solely to their own interests. Most national pilot organizations are affiliated with the International Federation of Air Line Pilots' Associations (IFALPA), which considers itself more of a professional than a union group but which has elements of both. Air traffic controllers have been active in the ITF, but have an organization of their own, the International Federation of Air Traffic Controllers' Associations (IFATCA). Like the IFALPA, the IFATCA has swayed between professionalism and unionism. The balance between these two elements differs in IFALPA and IFATCA, however, as a result of the divergent policies of their United States affiliates, the Air Line Pilots' Association (US-ALPA), and the now defunct Professional Air Traffic Controllers' Organization (PATCO). A third organization, the International Federation of Air Traffic Safety Electronics Associations (IFATSEA), is a relatively recent organization, and a fourth, the Flight Engineers' International Association (FEIA) is a small United States union that acts within the structure of the ITF as an international secretariat for this declining craft.[1]

Despite its competition, the ITF has attempted on several occasions both to coordinate national union action and to meet with

---

[1] A discussion of IFALPA's multinational activities is found in Herbert R. Northrup and Richard L. Rowan, *Multinational Collective Bargaining Attempts*, Multinational Industrial Relations Series No. 6 (Philadelphia: Industrial Research Unit, The Wharton School, University of Pennsylvania, 1979), pp. 520-529, hereafter cited as *MCBA*. IFALPA and IFATCA policies are contrasted in an article prepared for the Summer 1983 issue of the *Columbia Journal of World Business*.

employers. As set forth below, such ITF attempts have been considerably less successful in air transport than in ocean transport.

ITF ATTEMPTS AT JOINT ACTION WITH IFALPA [2]

It is quite common for the various international employee organizations to attend one another's congresses as observers. At the 1977 ITF Congress in Dublin, the ITF suggested to the IFALPA observers that the ITF and the IFALPA adopt a joint statement on crew complements for the Boeing 757 and 767 (then being developed), a problem of great concern to pilots. Beyond simple policy statements, however, little joint action occurred. The executive secretary of the IFALPA noted that it would never ask the ITF for assistance nor would it become involved in ITF disputes.[3] Instead, the IFALPA has suggested that the ITF go through the local carrier or pilot group.

KSSU and ATLAS

One area in which the ITF would like to involve the IFALPA is the "pooling" of certain services by two European airline groups—ATLAS composed of Air France, Alitalia, Lufthansa, Sabena, and Iberia, and KSSU comprised of KLM (Dutch), Swissair, Scandinavian (SAS), and the French African line, (UTA). Under a formal agreement, each of these groups transfers and shares maintenance and other ground services among their members to obtain major cost savings. Thus, for example, one company will maintain all General Electric engines, and another all Pratt & Whitney engines, for all members of the group. Similarly, one will overhaul DC-10s, another Boeing 747s. Only day-to-day maintenance is carried out by the operating airlines, while overhauls, spare parts, etc., are exclusively the province of one of the member companies. The savings on inventories alone are enormous. Similarly, in each country, all reservation service is conducted by the host country, common training programs are developed, and interior aircraft design is coordinated.

The ITF sees such pooling agreements as diminishing employment and has been particularly active among unions in the KSSU group in an effort to offset such activities. A KSSU union group has been meeting for some years under ITF auspices and the

---

[2] Much of this discussion is taken from *MCBA*, pp. 515-520.

[3] Captain Laurie Taylor, Executive Secretary, IFALPA, interview in Egham, England, May 15, 1978.

ATLAS union group has attended such meetings.[4] The ITF now claims that the KSSU unions have agreed on a joint formulation of demands and on a common strategy. According to the ITF, "KSSU member unions will, within the limits placed on them by national legislation, offer practical support and solidarity to each other." [5] How solid this solidarity is may be indicated by the comment on the same page of the *ITF Panorama* that "we would respectfully point out to aviation affiliates in companies which at present operate quite independently that it may be their members tomorrow who face the problems that their European colleagues are struggling so manfully to overcome today." [6]

The ITF has also attempted to arrange a meeting with the KSSU companies but has been rebuffed, although it did have one meeting with a KSSU member, Scandinavian Airlines.[7] It then asked the Organization for Economic Cooperation and Development (OECD) to designate ATLAS and KSSU as "multinational corporations" and therefore subject to OECD guidelines.[8] The ITF's purpose in this submission was to charge these organizations with violating OECD guidelines by not consulting with it and its affiliates on their rationalization programs.

Although the IFALPA evidenced some concern about potential transfers of pilots from one airline to another, it has not been ready to give any specific aid to the ITF's efforts.[9] For one thing, the US-ALPA, whose membership comprises one-half the total affiliated membership of the IFALPA, does not see this as a major problem. In the United States, it is not uncommon for one airline to perform major maintenance or overhaul for another, for one airline to lease planes to another to handle seasonal traffic, or for pilots of one airline to take over and fly the planes of another to provide through service. The US-ALPA position, and therefore the major influence on the IFALPA, is that the key element is not who owns the equipment but whether the

---

[4] ITF, *Report on Activities 1974-1975-1976*, (1972), pp. 139-40, 144-47; ITF, *Report on Activities, 1977-1978-1979*, (1980), pp. 101-102.

[5] *ITF Panorama*, Vol. 1, No. 3 (1979), p. 1.

[6] *Ibid.*

[7] *Ibid.*; and ITF, *Report on Activities*, (1974-1975-1976), pp. 139-40.

[8] See, *MCBA*, Chapter XIX for an explanation and discussion of the OECD guidelines.

[9] Captain Taylor, interview, May 15, 1978.

US-ALPA labor agreement covering the operating pilots is applied. As long as that holds, the US-ALPA position is that ownership is irrelevant.

Nevertheless, Europilote, the IFALPA's semi-autonomous Western European pilot group, also requested meetings both with the individual European airlines and with KSSU and ATLAS to discuss plans to operate the new Boeing planes and those of Airbus Industries with two pilots instead of three (ITF wanted a flight engineer instead of a third pilot because of its flight engineer membership). The European airlines declined to discuss the matters either through their groupings or with Europilote. Moreover, neither Europilote nor the ITF received any support from the OECD. Its Committee on International Investment and Multinational Enterprises (CIIME) found that both KSSU and ATLAS were merely "instruments for cooperation . . . not constituted as legal entities and have neither management nor staff of their own." It further found that the locus of decision making remained with the national carriers, each of which had duly consulted with affected unions representing their employees. Accordingly, the ITF petition was not supported.

EC Level

At the European Community (EC) level, the ITF has also been seeking the cooperation of the IFALPA in forming an EC Joint Advisory Committee for Civil Aviation. As with previous efforts, the IFALPA has avoided any joint actions. Instead of working with the ITF, the IFALPA is consulted separately by the EC on questions concerning airline pilots. Because of the EC's regional nature, the IFALPA has moved to turn over this responsibility to Europilote, the IFALPA's European regional affiliate.[10]

Future relations between the ITF and the IFALPA will remain informal. As noted earlier, the main activities of the IFALPA are related to technical/safety problems and not to industrial actions, and the IFALPA especially does not desire involvement in industrial actions initiated by other organizations. This professional association posture will continue to keep the two groups separate.

------

[10] International Federation of Air Line Pilots' Associations, *Report of the Thirty-First Conference,* Acapulco, Mexico, March 31-April 6, 1976, Appendix G, pp. 2-3.

SOLIDARITY ACTIONS

When an airline is involved in a labor dispute, attempts have been made through ITSs to prevent the operation of their aircraft by refusing them fuel or service. Hence the planes are "captured." The ITF and at least one other secretariat have been involved in captures.

ICEF in Australia

In September 1977, flight attendants of Trans International Airlines (TIA), a United States charter carrier, struck. They were supported by TIA pilots and flight engineers until December 1977, when the attendants rejected a proposed settlement. Then the pilots returned to work, and TIA resumed operations with nonstriking employees.[11]

The TIA flight attendants were represented by the Teamsters union which, despite its preeminence in the motor trucking industry, then as now was not an affiliate of the ITF but rather was affiliated to the International Federation of Chemical, Energy and General Workers' Unions (ICEF).[12] The ICEF secretary general sent a letter to all affiliates on November 14, 1977, requesting a ban on TIA flights, and the ITF announced its support. Apparently unaware that such ICEF circulars generally receive little more than token support,[13] two Australian unions, apparently thinking that Latin American and European unions were already disrupting TIA service, placed a ban on TIA operations. The Australian Transport Workers Union refused to fuel and the Miscellaneous Workers Union refused to clean and otherwise service TIA planes, thus rendering them inoperative.

This "capture" continued for six weeks until TIA both introduced incontrovertible evidence that only in Australia was support being given to the ICEF request and began proceedings

---

[11] See Larry Kornhauser, "Two Aust unions get U.S. strikes backlash," *Financial Review* (Australia), January 9, 1978, p. 3, for a complete write-up of this case.

[12] The Teamsters disaffiliated from the ICEF in 1981.

[13] This Australian airline action described herein is one of the few successful interventions initiated by the ICEF. Despite extravagant claims, nearly all ICEF "interventions" have resulted in nothing more than letters, telegrams, or leaflets. See *MCBA*, chapters VI-XI for a detailed analysis of the discrepancies between the claims of the ICEF secretary general and the actual events.

under section 4D of the Australian Trade Practices Act for an injunction lifting the boycott. At about the same time, the TIA flight attendants reversed themselves and accepted the contract that they had earlier rejected. To our knowledge no ICEF request has since been accepted in such good faith by Australian unions as it was in the TIA case.

Malaysian Airlines System

A dispute beginning in December 1978 involving Malaysian Airlines brought the ITF in conflict with the government of that country as well. The strike took on serious dimensions when the government declared it illegal, and the ITF, whose assistant general secretary was visiting Malaysia, called on all affiliates to boycott Malaysian Airlines. He was expelled from the country, and the ITF's resident Asian representative and nineteen airline employees were arrested, thus exacerbating the matter.[14]

As a result of the ITF's efforts, a Malaysian DC-10 was "captured" for nine days in Sydney, Australia, and "rescued" only after the Australian government ordered the Royal Australian Air Force to provide for its return. Another DC-10 was delayed several hours to Frankfurt, Germany, because union adherents blocked its path and distributed leaflets to passengers protesting against the detentions resulting from the dispute. The protesting unionists maintained their blockade until the Frankfurt Airport police forced them to retire.

TWA and Pan Am in Europe

An incident involving French, Italian, and United States ITF affiliates, reveals the fragile nature of international labor solidarity in employment matters. In 1974, financial considerations forced the two largest U.S. international airline companies, Pan American World Airways Inc. (Pan Am) and Trans World Airlines Inc. (TWA) to review their respective situations worldwide, particularly in Europe where important routes were in

---

[14] See the Malaysian Employers Federation, "What Response From ASEAN to International Trade Union Action?" (Prepared for the First Conference and Seminar, ASEAN Confederation of Employers, Manila, May 12-14, 1979); "Malaysian Unionists Arrested," *AFL-CIO Free Trade Union News*, April 1979, p. 1; Barry Wainn, "Imprisonment of unionists, imposed salary settlement leave MAS future clouded," *Asian Wall Street Journal*, April 17, 1979, p. 1; K. Das, "Getting MAS off the ground," *Far Eastern Economic Review*, May 4, 1978, pp. 26-27; and "Concorde threat paid off for MAS DC-10s to London," *ibid.*, August 31, 1979, pp. 45, 48.

direct competition. As a result, Pan Am and TWA traded routes —with Pan Am flying exclusively the Frankfurt, Eastern Europe, and direct-to-Rome routes and TWA flying to Lisbon, Paris, and Madrid. TWA subsequently decided to close its Rome and Paris bases and to use only U.S. based flight attendants.

Italian and French unions whose members were affected by the decision, the Sindicato Nationale Assistenti di Volo e Complementari di Bordo (SNAVCO) and Syndicat National du Personnel Navigant Commercial (SNPNC), protested and the ITF requested a meeting with the U.S. Transport Workers' Union (TWU). At that meeting, a TWU spokesman explained that the airlines' financial difficulties were also causing employment problems in the United States. According to the ITF, TWU did offer to preserve the seniority of Italian and French cabin attendants should they decide to relocate in New York. SNAVCO and SNPNC reportedly refused the offer initially, preferring to continue negotiations with TWA. When it became apparent that the bases would indeed be forced to close for economic reasons, the French union, SNPNC, approached TWU regarding its former offer. In the meantime, TWU withdrew its offer stating that it had been made originally "in the spirit of international brotherhood . . . (but) would be impossible to repeat at this time." This was, in part, the result of the continuing adverse financial situation in the airlines and the fact that TWU was at that time "negotiating with the airlines for the absorption of the laid-off . . . cabin attendants." [15]

THE ITF AND AVIATION INTERGOVERNMENTAL ORGANIZATIONS

The ITF is active in aviation intergovernmental organizations, but here too its success is far less than in ocean transport.

The International Civil Aviation Organization (ICAO)

The ITF's Civil Aviation Section has pursued a number of matters with the aid of the International Civil Aviation Organization. The greatest concerns of the ITF have been incidents of hijacking and sabotage which have occurred during the last fifteen years. The ITF's continuing efforts in this area include appeals to the ICAO to "initiate inquiries in order to plug any

---

[15] ITF, *Report on Activities, 1974-1975-1976*, pp. 140-41,

loopholes in the security arrangements at various airports." [16]
As early as 1970, the Civil Aviation Section submitted detailed
recommendations to the ICAO on the prevention of hijacking and
sabotage. More recently, the ITF sponsored an International
Symposium on Hijacking and other Forms of Attack Against
Civil Aviation, in Bonn, Germany, on April 6 and 7, 1978. The
official ITF policy on this subject is that "affiliates—in cooperation with sympathetic states—should organize sanctions against
those states which continued to flout world opinion and the principles of the various international civil aviation conventions
(Tokyo, The Hague and Montreal) that had been evolved to deal
with this menace." [17]

Although the ITF is most interested in being heard by ICAO,
it is interesting to note that the ITF

> drew the attention of ICAO to the fact that the ITF was excluded
> from the list of interested organizations to be consulted on security
> matters and that the Federation had been overlooked when the
> Air Navigation Commission appointed a Study Group to assist
> the Secretariat in reviewing [an annex] . . .[18]

Other Intergovernmental Bodies

At the ILO, as described in Appendix C, the ITF has worked
in the civil aviation sector, but it has been unable to push through
any aviation conventions. The ITF has more hope for UNCTAD.
At the September 1981 meeting of the UNCTAD Trade and Development Board, a report entitled "The Effects of Discriminatory
and Unfair Civil Aviation Practices on the Growth of Air Transport in Developing Countries" was submitted. If UNCTAD does
become heavily involved in this field, it will be interesting to see
what positions and/or relationships are developed by the ITF.

---

[16] *Ibid.*, p. 150.

[17] *ITF Newsletter*, No. 4 (April 1978), p. 52.

[18] ITF, *Report on Activities, 1977-1978-1979*, p. 108.

Index